Sexuality
God's Gift

"This book has three huge strengths: The authors write from their own experience rather than from 'theories' or 'theologies' about sex and sexual morality. Sexuality is seen as a fundamental and pervasive human reality, not reducible to sex acts or moral dilemmas. The book provides up-to-date data about sex, marriage, and relationships in the U.S. *Sexuality: God's Gift* will make a wonderful tool for adult and youth study groups, ministerial education, and for any Christian trying to discern teachings about sex, marriage, and celibacy."
—*Lisa Sowle Cahill, professor of theology, Boston College*

"The church must address sexuality if we believe God cares about our bodies as well as our souls. This substantially revised edition of *Sexuality: God's Gift* continues and deepens conversation about our sexual selves. Such talk can lead toward more honest, thoughtful Christian living in a time when many take cues uncritically from dominant cultural attitudes toward sexuality. Second-time readers as well as new ones can benefit from this thoughtful revision."
—*Gayle Gerber Koontz, professor of theology and ethics, Associated Mennonite Biblical Seminary*

Sexuality
God's Gift

Second edition

Edited by Anne Krabill Hershberger

Herald Press
Scottdale, Pennsylvania
Waterloo, Ontario

FAITH MENNONITE CHURCH
MINNEAPOLIS, MINN.

Library of Congress Cataloging-in-Publication Data
Sexuality : God's gift / edited by Anne Krabill Hershberger.—2nd ed.
   p. cm.
Includes bibliographical references.
ISBN 978-0-8361-9514-9 (pbk. : alk. paper)
   1. Sex instruction—Religious aspects—Mennonites. 2. Sex—Religious
aspects—Mennonites. I. Hershberger, Anne Krabill, 1936-
HQ31.S515655 2010
261.8'357—dc22
                                                            2010015288

Unless otherwise noted, Scripture is from the *Holy Bible, New International Version* ®, copyright © 1973, 1978, 1984 Biblica. Used by permission of Zondervan. All rights reserved. Texts marked NRSV are from the *New Revised Standard Version Bible*, copyright 1989, by the Division of Christian Education of the National Council of Churches of Christ in the USA, and are used by permission. Texts marked TLB are from *The Living Bible* © 1971, owned by assignment by Illinois Regional Bank N.A. (as trustee), used by permission of Tyndale Publishing House Publishsers, Inc., Wheaton, IL 60189, all rights reserved. KJV from *King James Version*.

SEXUALITY: GOD'S GIFT
Copyright © 1999, 2010 by Herald Press, Scottdale, PA 15683
   Released simultaneously in Canada by Herald Press,
   Waterloo, Ont. N2L 6H7. All rights reserved
Library of Congress Control Number: 2010015288
International Standard Book Number: 978-0-8361-9514-9
Printed in the United States of America
Cover by Gwen Stamm

15 14 13 12 11 10   10 9 8 7 6 5 4 3 2 1

To order or request information please call 1-800-245-7894 or visit www.heraldpress.com.

Dedicated to the memory of Willard S. Krabill (1926-2009)
sexuality educator extraordinaire

He did not go where the path led.
He went where there was no path and left a trail.

Contents

Foreword

Those who believe in a creating God must acknowledge that a bodily existence—our sexuality—and our spiritual essence—our souls—are both part of God's creative action in bringing forth into existence human beings. James Weldon Johnson, in his poetic sermon "The Creation," voices the truth in this way:

> Till [God] thought, "I'll make me a man!" . . .
> And there that great God Almighty . . .
> Kneeled down in the dust
> Toiling over a lump of clay
> Till He shaped it in his own image;
> Then into it he breathed the breath of life,
> And man became a living soul.

We are human because we are embodied souls. Jesus was incarnated, becoming an embodied spirit, and, thereby, fully human.

Our sexuality and spirituality are both gifts from God integrated in our being; they cannot exist in us as separate entities. But this is not what the church has emphasized historically. Its teaching has encouraged the idea that somehow our bodily and spiritual existences are separate, that the one is superior in worth and value over the other, the spirit over the body. Hence our sexuality has not been emphasized in our teaching and preaching. So a void of silence has been created in which a number of negative societal issues have emerged and been allowed to flourish unaddressed and unchallenged by the church.

This need not be. To our detriment, we neglect to wrestle in Christian communities with what it means to be gifted with both soul and body, inseparably integrated, as we live as disciples of Jesus Christ and believers in our creating God. The silence must be broken and the dialogue opened up. *Sexuality: God's Gift* is a doorway through which those who fear the conversation or who do not know where to begin or who even deny the need for it can enter the struggle and begin the dialogue.

I used the first edition of *Sexuality: God's Gift* in my classes at Wesley Theological Seminary in Washington, D.C., where I teach "Sexual Issues in Parish Ministry" each year. Although it is an elective course, my students are diverse in their understanding of and willingness to accept and acknowledge a variety of sexuality issues. They are also diverse in their theological orientations. It is important for every student to have readings that honor their spiritual journeys, challenge them in their beliefs and understandings, and inform them of where others are in their beliefs and journeys. This book is an important contribution in helping Christians connect their spirituality and their sexuality. May the dialogue break forth among all Christians!

If you are hoping to open the door in a conservative setting, this book is ideal. If you are seeking to widen the conversation in a progressive setting, this book will assist you in that endeavor. It is appropriate for a variety of learning and exploring opportunities: classes and individual study for both lay and clergy alike.

—Youtha C. Hardman-Cromwell, Assistant Dean
Wesley Theological Seminary

Preface

When the original edition of this book was published in 1999, we asked, Can there be anything more to write about human sexuality than what has already appeared in existing literature? Each year new textbooks are published with updated content. Popular bookstores devote increasing amounts of shelf space to books related to sexuality. Information on sexuality is found through the Internet and creative audiovisual media. Pornography, a distortion of sexuality, continues each year as a multibillion-dollar industry. Research reports in many fields of study show how sexuality issues are related to the concerns of those disciplines. More and more people with faith and religious perspectives have shared their thinking and study regarding sexuality. Literature on sexuality has been written for all age groups.

As all of this continues, new venues dealing with sexuality have opened during the past decade. So again we ask, "What special purpose does this second edition of *Sexuality: God's Gift* attempt to fulfill?"

The book's mission is to perpetuate into the twenty-first century an updated and expanded version of its initial conception. The idea for such a book began in the 1980s when Delores Histand Friesen approached Willard S. Krabill about collaborating on a sexuality volume written from a Christian perspective. Such a book would complement excellent secular texts used by students in the sexuality classes Delores was teaching at Mennonite Brethren Biblical Seminary (Fresno, California) and Willard at Goshen (Indiana) College.

As years passed, Delores and Willard continued to believe in the importance of this project, but neither found time to give leadership to it. Willard was writing and speaking throughout the Mennonite church about living whole lives and respecting God's good gift of sexuality. In 1991 he retired from teaching the sexuality course he had originated at Goshen College in 1973. It was always a popular course. He had developed extensive resources, class and speech notes, and publications that seemed appropriate to adapt for the envisioned book.

After Willard's retirement from teaching, I, as Willard's sister and an associate professor of nursing at Goshen College, began to team-teach the sexuality course, first with Thomas J. Meyers, professor of sociology, and later with Keith Graber Miller, associate professor of Bible, religion, and philosophy. It became clear to me that a book such as Delores and Willard had discussed would be quite useful in the course.

In 1996 I was granted a sabbatical leave for one year and met with Willard and Delores to discuss the future for this book. A decision was made to move forward with the project. My sabbatical schedule made it possible for me to begin editing and writing. I combined and edited some of the good work already prepared and enhanced it by adding new material and additional authors.

This second edition builds on the original book. The chapters written by Willard, who died in 2009, have been left intact except for some updating. New authors and several new chapters have been added. We now look at sexuality across the lifespan, from childhood through aging. We, unfortunately, felt the need to enlarge the chapter "The Gift Misused": the sections on pornography and sexually transmitted infections were expanded and new material on sexual addiction and sexual abuse of children was added. New chapters on sexuality and adolescents, singleness, grief, and celibacy were added as well.

This book is not intended to be an exhaustive treatise nor the last word on the topic of sexuality. To help us understand the field, many textbooks present thorough and research-based findings, charts, illustrations, and descriptive narratives. This volume, instead, is an attempt to put in accessible form some topics on sexuality that have special meaning for Christians and to interpret them from a Christian, Anabaptist, biblical perspective. This is the current thinking of several persons who have spent many years studying these issues, who want to further the discussion, and who care deeply about reflecting Christian values in life.

Sexuality: God's Gift is meant to provide help for both individuals and groups. We hope it will be useful as a complement to secular textbooks in sexuality classes on Christian campuses. It may also serve as a resource for parents, pastors, teachers, youth leaders, small discussion groups and Sunday school classes in congregational settings.

To fulfill these purposes, the book has been organized by headings keyed to the metaphor of sexuality as a gift from God. Each chapter offers questions to help stimulate group discussion. Chapter 17 lists resources for further study. The references at the end provide the documentation for each chapter.

The authors desire that each reader will perceive healthy sexuality as vital to human wholeness, intimacy, joy, and caring relationships, and as a reflection of God's creative love.

The chapter contributors are Christian educators who also have professional roles as physician, nurse, theologian, pastor, counselor, dramatist, and musician. We believe it has been worthwhile to bring all these perspectives together for further educating readers about sexuality as God's good gift. We trust the readers will agree.

—Anne Krabill Hershberger, Editor
Associate Professor of Nursing Emerita
Goshen College

Acknowledgments

The success of any work of this kind depends on the cooperation and goodwill of the collaborators. The wisdom and insights of my brother, Willard Krabill, the primary contributor to this book, are only in memory because of his recent death, but they very much continued to permeate the development of this second edition of the book.

The other contributors—Delores Histand Friesen, Keith Graber Miller, Lauren Friesen, Sue L. Conrad, Barbara J. Meyer, James H. Ritchie Jr., Rachel Nafziger Hartzler, and Julie Nash—brought their unique and significant interpretations and experiences to expand and facilitate better understanding of sexuality from a Christian perspective. Their good counsel along the way was very helpful.

The staff at Herald Press constructively contributed to the final shaping of the book. Amy Gingerich, editorial director, believed in this project and was very supportive in helping bring it to fruition.

My level of computer ability called for assistance from several people at various times. My neighbor Kendal Sommers patiently walked me through a number of steps. Staff at the Goshen College Good Library Reference Desk (Mary Beth Schlabach and Lisa Guedea Carreno) and the Information Technology Service Computer Help Desk (Pamela Kistler Osborne) gave helpful assistance.

Many friends as well as my family were supportive of this project in so many ways. My husband, Abner, was great at listening and reacting to ideas. He had good suggestions for many "crises" and made many meals during this book's development. When someone asked him whether he read this book, he replied, "Have I read it? I was home-schooled with it!" Our daughters, Kay and Sue; Kay's husband, Brian Burnett; and Sue's husband, Jon Yoder, made encouraging comments at just the right times.

To all of these persons, I say a deep-felt thank-you.

—Anne Krabill Hershberger

1

The Gift

Anne Krabill Hershberger and Willard S. Krabill

What is it about a gift that is so appealing? The very fact that someone has given me a gift is a gift in itself. Someone thought enough of me to prepare a gift. Surely the presentation is part of the appeal. Gifts come in a variety of forms, of course. Often bright-colored paper and ribbons show that something special is being presented. Sometimes there is just a word, picture, or brown butcher paper in the presentation.

Often there is mystery—what could it be? We enthusiastically and literally tear into a package or gently handle the gift so we will not damage any part of it. Then we discover what a person who cares for us thought would bring us pleasure.

True gifts are pleasurable. The gift may be something in line with our interests, with a good fit, or with a pleasing color. It may be an item, event, resource, or word that is so helpful or delightful, and yet we never might have thought to buy it or to be able to get it for ourselves. It may be a humor-packed something that keeps us laughing every time we think of it. The gift might be a thoughtful gesture that can come only from someone who really knows what we are dealing with in our lives. A gift brings pleasure in so many ways.

So why is our sexuality being named a gift from God? If we compare it with the characteristics of gifts mentioned above, we think about the fact that God chose to make us sexual, both alike as people and different in gender, but each of us as a sexual being. Sexuality has been given to us. It is here, with us, a gift. It is key in making us who we are.

This gift also is inherent in our presentation. From the earliest moments of conception and embryological development, while God was knitting each of us together in our mother's womb (Ps 139:13), our sexuality was established, determining our gender. When presented to our parents, we were a newborn baby girl or boy and all that those labels represent. No bright paper or bows accompanied our presentation. Yet there certainly was an excitement and expectation that there was a new life in either male or female form. Each of us was a new person with potential to make a difference in the world in a unique way.

The mystery of our sexuality is present throughout life. Infants touch and explore their own body parts. They thrive only when older human beings touch, cuddle, coo, gaze upon, rock, carry, and sing and talk to them. During preschool years, children solve the mystery of whether they are girls or boys. No amount of teasing or arguing will talk them out of their determination.

As a child enters the school-age years, many developmental tasks require attention, but permeating everything else is the mystery of sexuality: "Why am I like I am?" "Where did I come from?" "Am I normal?" "What is right for me to be doing as a girl or as a boy?" This interest in and exploration of the mystery of sexuality is right there, all the time.

When people enter puberty, they "tear into the package" or, in fear and trembling, respond to the bombardment of sexual thoughts, images, and feelings coming from within and without. For many people, trying to understand the mystery of sexuality at this time of life almost becomes a preoccupation.

As we move into adulthood and throughout our middle and older years, we have the potential to gain greater insights into the mystery and to experience the mature richness of our sexuality. We realize that sexuality refers to all those parts of the human personality and body that collectively identify us as male or female. Sexuality is not just genital sex or sexual intercourse. Always, from birth to death, we all are sexual beings.

The gift of sexuality, like other gifts, is meant to be a source of pleasure. This pleasure is expressed poetically by Solomon's Song of Songs in the Bible: "How much more pleasing is your love than wine, and the fragrance of your perfume than any spice!" (4:10). The marriage at Cana was a cause for celebration as well as the occasion for Jesus' first recorded miracle, turning water into wine (John 2:1-11). Throughout, the Bible gives a clear message that love should permeate relationships of all kinds and bring the greatest of pleasures. Of course, all of these relationships are formed by sexual people.

As Christian adults, we do not believe that things "just happen." We believe in a God who has created the world orderly and predictable, and we are a part of that creation. It is predictable that if we transgress God's design for our lives, we will have to pay a price. Our right decisions about our sexuality today can bless our future days tremendously. Our wrong decisions about our uses of and purposes in sex today can blight our tomorrows in many ways. Later in this book, we will discuss these right and wrong decisions related to sexuality.

To build our gift of sexuality into an optimally healthy sexuality, we must carefully lay a proper foundation. To do so, we identify and discuss specific foundation stones needed for this important grounding.

Theology of the Body

The first foundation stone for a healthy sexuality is a proper theology of the body, a proper system of belief about our bodies. Over the centuries a false belief has crept into our thinking, suggesting that the body is evil and the spirit is good. Somehow we have grown up thinking that it is wrong to enjoy and feel good about our bodies—really about ourselves, for in our bodies we are ourselves.

We say we believe in the wholeness of persons; that we are body, mind, and spirit; and that preaching, teaching, and healing are all valid ministries. We talk about holistic health concepts. Yet in our churches we seem to recognize only the spirit. Too often in our colleges, we recognize only the intellect and regard a good academic record as far more important than a proper heart rate, a needed weight loss, or a fitness score.

A circle, not a triangle, is a better presentation of this concept of the human organism. We are integrated and continuous whole beings, not isolated sides held together. By separating our physical selves from our minds and spirits, we too easily go right on overeating, overworking, overdrinking, overdriving our cars, and overspending time in sitting around and spectating. Nowhere is our failure to have a proper attitude toward our bodies more damaging to us than in relation to our sexuality.

Sexually speaking, if my body is evil and not really "me," I cannot be held responsible for the wrong things my body does. I may try to excuse myself: "I just couldn't help it. I had this overwhelming passion." James B. Nelson said in his classic book, *Embodiment* (20–21), that when my body ceases to be fully personal, my relationships to other body-selves are diminished. If my body is not good and fully me, then neither is your body anything I need to hold sacred. I can more easily use your body or abuse mine. Subtle thoughts and inferences can run in that direction.

Our false thinking about the body also keeps us from speaking openly and honestly about our sexual bodies. We are often reluctant and even ashamed to talk about them. It is amazing how many married couples have slept together for years and even have raised a family, yet not once have they been able to talk with each other about their bodies. Not once have these couples spoken about pleasuring their bodies, about their sexual lives, or about their sexual feelings and preferences.

Having a proper theology of the body would lead us to feel exuberant about the way our bodies allow us to express ourselves, enjoy a wide variety of sensations, reach out to others in fostering relationships, experience this good creation, and reflect the image of God. This is surely a gift.

Sexual Theology

The second foundation stone, a proper sexual theology, follows closely and naturally. Do we really believe and understand that sex is good and that our sexuality is a good gift from God? We could have been designed to reproduce in another way, but this is the way we are. How does the church view the meaning of sex?

The church should have a truly Christian attitude in educating about sexuality, in our witness to the world, and in our practice. Of all people, we as believers ought to have the most positive attitude toward our bodies and toward our sexuality. We are the ones who know the God who made them. We who know God best should best reflect the true nature of human sexuality.

How then does it happen that today we allow those who do not know the Creator of our sexuality to define sexuality, to determine what is true or untrue, and to set our sexual standards? We have permitted some harmful misconceptions and false attitudes to creep into our thinking about sexuality. As a result, we do not have a good track record in dealing with those who are hurting in this area of their lives.

We Christians need to put our sexual stance, message, and practice in tune with the Creator of human sexuality, and then spread that true word and become visible in the debate. Let the message become loud and clear that our sexuality is a source of true joy, healing, love, caring, and unselfishness. It is not the source of misery, hurt, and pain so often caused by people misusing sexuality.

Let us read the Bible, expecting to find a positive message about human sexuality. It is there. We have read everything else; so here we might observe, "When all else fails, read the directions." In the Bible we will find an affirmation of gender differences, a blessing from God when we allow love to permeate our relationships, and a sense that each individual is valuable as a sexual person.

Respect for Males and Females

A third foundation stone in building healthy sexuality is a proper understanding of respect for males and females. In spite of all our scientific knowledge, we do not fully understand how alike males and females are—biologically, developmentally, and physiologically. Where we are not alike, we are either equal or complementary. There should be no room for a double standard in Christian circles.

Nevertheless, we have a long way to go in understanding proper male-female roles, responsibilities, and expectations. African-American leaders tell us that America is never so racially segregated as it is on Sunday morning. It is likely also true that America is never so sexist as it is on Sunday morning. Paternalistic attitudes are frequently apparent in some church settings. If we really believe that God has created us sexual, male and female, and that each is of equal value and unable to exist without the other, we will have difficulty giving hierarchical value to the genders.

We are all exposed to less-than-ideal views of the other gender. This apparently starts early in life. A classroom teacher asked the children to write anything they pleased about people. A little pigtailed girl wrote, "People are composed of two kinds, boys and girls. Boys are no good at all until they grow up and get married. Boys are an awful bother. They want everything but soap. A woman is a grown-up girl with children. My dad is such a nice man that I am sure he must have been a little girl when he was a boy." This little girl's last comment reveals a truth that many adults would do well to note: ideally, male and female attributes are found in all of us.

It is apparent that respect in male-female relationships is lacking when one notes a "scoring," aggressor-conquest mentality. This communicates an attitude of overpowering others instead of mutual respect. Such an attitude or a male-infallibility complex tends to block marital communication and marital counseling efforts. In effect, the man says, "Problem? I've got no problem. She's the one who has the problem." Too many men cannot understand how any sexual problem in a marriage could be the male's fault.

Young people sometimes experience a double standard when exposed to the attitudes of those who excuse inappropriate male sexual behavior by saying, "Boys will be boys." Females in this same situation are often referred to as "loose," "sluts," or worse. Such responses do not demonstrate respect.

If we have true respect for each other as males and females, that can help us to be comfortable in each other's presence, share common interests and concerns on many levels, and develop a genuine concern for others. We can bring out the best in each other's behavior, consciously recognize the fundamental way in which we are part of each other, and find joy in our relationships. Individuals thrive best in community, not in isolation. Our own sexuality is enhanced by honoring and respecting the sexuality of others. Promoting this kind of respect is worthy of great effort on the part of each of us.

Integration of Sex and Life

The fourth foundation stone for healthy sexuality is the understanding that our sexuality is an integral part of who we are. It reaches through our whole life. As mentioned earlier, we—all of the time—are sexual beings. All of the time we communicate as sexual beings. Our sexuality is that pervasive essence of our personality that forever defines us first as humans and second as males or females.

We always relate to others as sexual persons, but that does not mean we necessarily have genital sex in mind. Genital sexual intercourse is only one part of sexuality. A person can be a whole, healthy, fulfilled, and vibrantly sexual being without ever experiencing genital intercourse. Our sexuality is who we are, not what we do. Sex is not a compartment of our lives and beings that we can treat separately. "Sexuality is . . . about our full body-selves, about love and connection and attachment and friendship, about relating in its many forms" (Graber Miller: 24).

Let us compare the different styles of integrating and compartmentalizing our lives, as is sometimes seen in the marital sexual relationship. A successful sexual experience begins when the married couple gets up in the morning. The attitudes, the caring, the tenderness, and the messages communicated all day—whether about finances, the children's lessons, the in-laws, the cold soup, or the soggy pie crust—are all the prelude to yet another message, a message of "love."

In another scenario, two people may fight, nag, scold, argue, put down, or ignore all day and all evening—and then expect great things to happen in bed at night. Such inconsistency does not make sense.

Marriage counselors estimate that when couples present themselves for help with sexual problems, 80 percent of the time the problem is not sexual. It may be about finances, a clothing allowance, in-laws, tension and dissension over disciplining the children, personal hygiene, or other conflicts. Because of these stresses in the marriage, the sexual relationship suffers and often gets the blame.

Our bodies should say the same thing the remainder of our being is saying; otherwise we live a lie. If I say "I'm yours" with my body when it is not true in reality, that is dishonest, destructive, and inexcusable.

Affirming the Sexuality of All People

The fifth foundation stone is the affirmation of the sexuality of all people. Many people show that this stone is missing by denying the sexuality of their parents. This denial may run like this: "Sex is dirty; my parents are nice people; therefore my parents are not sexual." Our presence in the world is effective testimony that this denial is ill-founded.

We cannot and should not deny the sexuality of anyone—whether male or female, young or old, parents or children, ill or well, disabled or those without visible disabilities, mentally brilliant or dull, married or single.

In his excellent book *The Sexual Celibate*, Donald Goergen promotes a valid concept, strange as it may seem:

> A celibate person is not asexual. He or she has a full sexual life which needs to be understood in order to have a richer understanding of Christian sexuality itself as well as in order to assist people in living a celibate life. . . . The sexual life of a celibate person is going to manifest itself primarily in the affective bonds of permanent and steadfast human friendships which are exemplifications of God's way of loving. Through a rediscovery of friendship within the Christian tradition and through an integration of community, friendship, ministry, and prayer, the present discussion of celibacy can lead to a revival of a truly Christian value, the value of friendship, which is a service for the entire Christian community. (Goergen: 224–25)

When we affirm the sexuality of all people, we include older people. We tend to desexualize seniors. It is false to assume that they have no sexual feelings, no sexual needs, and no need for affection. A passage from the book *Sexuality and the Sacred*, edited by James B. Nelson and Sandra P. Longfellow, comments pertinently on "Older Adults":

> Faithfulness to the gracious God who has created us for wholeness requires that we affirm . . . the possibility of securing sexual justice for older adults, of transforming relationships, of reclaiming God's gift of eros for persons of all ages. As sexual beings, we require and reach out for the physical and spiritual embrace of oth-

ers. As Christians, we seek to make such embrace possible for all persons by securing right relatedness and the concrete well-being of individuals and communities. (Nelson and Longfellow: 301–2)

The general population often denies or ignores the sexuality of another large group of people, the disabled. What able-bodied people's attitudes have done to the disabled is unconscionable. Christians cannot permit it to continue. "To desex someone is profoundly to dehumanize that person" (Nelson 1978: 212). People with all types of disabilities continue to have interest in sexuality and sexual expression. They may have non-progressive physical disabilities such as blindness, amputation, or spinal cord injury; progressive physical disabilities such as cystic fibrosis or multiple sclerosis; or a serious illness or mental retardation. "Regardless of the degree of physical incapacitation, if there is consciousness there is still self-awareness of one's masculinity and femininity, one's body image, one's desire and need for intimate human relatedness" (Nelson 1978: 217). The development of creative and satisfying means of sexual expression has brought pleasure and true intimacy to many disabled people and to those with whom they relate.

When persons are mentally retarded, special individualized approaches to sex education must be devised to communicate in meaningful ways. Concerns regarding contraception, sterilization, marriage, and parenting must be faced realistically. Many mentally disabled people are sexually abused. They need special protection because they may not be able to recognize when they are particularly vulnerable to this kind of relationship. Whatever the special needs of the mentally disabled, "they share with the rest of us the basic human interests in closeness, affection, physical contact, and simply being in on things" (Nelson 1978: 228).

The disabled need advocates who can help to raise consciousness and to legitimize their sexuality and need for close human contacts and sexual expression.

Sound Sex Education

The sixth stone necessary to build a foundation for healthy sexuality is sound sex education. Our understandings about human sexuality and our sexual attitudes are learned. They need to be communicated by the best teachers available. Sound sex education is imperative for a happy, safe, and positive sexual destiny.

Loving, affectionate, and communicative parents are basic necessities in a sound sex education program. Parents must be able to talk about their sexuality with ease and candor. Children are helped most when their parents' sexual lifestyle reflects Christian values.

A second element is a caring and loving faith community. The church that ignores or does not speak about the subject of sexuality indirectly communicates that sexuality does not warrant a place on the Christian education agenda. The church group is (at least theoretically) best equipped to educate children, young people, and adults alike about sexuality. Church members know the Creator of our sexuality. We presume to have a growing knowledge and understanding of the Bible, the primary textbook on how to live abundantly and as whole people. We care about modeling the spiritual values upheld in the Bible.

Our young people are receiving sex education every day. Nevertheless, we wonder, "What kind?"

Ideally, sex education begins in the home with loving parents, and sexual modeling certainly takes place there. Many parents, however, are still embarrassed or insecure with their own sexual feelings and their ability to talk about sexuality. This makes it hard for them to open up the subject with their children.

Schools can provide some knowledge and counseling, but children need more emphasis on spiritual values related to sexuality than many schools are permitted or able to provide. Children need a foundation in sexuality with spiritual values before they experience the onslaught of hedonistic mass media influences or are passionately involved themselves.

The church is ideally suited to model, interpret, and promote a spiritual frame of reference for sexuality. Whatever the setting for spiritually sound sex education, the messages communicated must be accurate, clearly defined, developmentally and culturally appropriate, and pertinent to the students. The basic message is that our sexuality is a good gift from God and is given for our pleasure. We must also include the message that in growing up sexually, each person needs to establish her or his identity before becoming physically intimate with another person. On all sides, we see tragic results when young people have experienced sexual intercourse before they have found their own identity.

Another important message is that sexuality is far more than anatomy, physiology, and the sexual response system. It is most of all a matter of communication, relationship, and commitment.

Whatever else can be said about sexual intercourse, it is never casual, even though some would treat it so. Our popular culture proclaims that so-called casual sex is nothing but fun, nothing but freedom, nothing but this or that—no big deal. Yet Willard's experience as a physician with many patients and college students revealed that it is a big deal. Some consider it as casual as sharing a Coke or holding hands, but their sexual behavior exhibits a monstrous denial of their basic humanity. Their behavior is crude and animalistic and does not show human sexuality—not in its character and not in its potential.

Sex is not individualistic, not a "do your own thing" kind of activity. Some have the notion that the decisions a young couple makes about sexual lifestyle are of no concern to anyone else. That is not true. In a *New Republic* article, Henry Fairlie put this into perspective:

> There is no more pat shibboleth of our time than the idea that what consenting adults do in private is solely their own business. That is false. What we do in private has repercussions on ourselves; and what we are

and believe has repercussions on others. What we do in our own homes will inevitably affect, not only our own behavior outside them, but also what we expect and tolerate in the behavior of others. A change in manners or discipline in the family will not leave unchanged the manners and discipline in the wider society. When we recognize how deeply our sexual feelings are registers of our whole beings, it is mere trifling to say that our societies ought not to be constantly alert to the manner in which we employ them. (Fairlie: 20)

Sound sex education promotes a broader understanding of the term *good-looking* than the usual definition. In our media, *good-looking* and *sexy* tend to get intertwined with each other. Hence, to be "good-looking" usually means to be "sexy" or at least sexually appealing, never mind one's character, thoughtfulness, loyalty, generosity, values—all of which enhance one's attractiveness. Striving for what the world considers "good looks" can become an obsession when "good looks" are defined in terms of handsome faces, shapely legs, thigh proportion, hairy chests, or bust measurements. Such ratings ignore the personal worth of many people.

Our culture has prescribed for women an image of female beauty that does not fit healthy physiology. It is contrary to what normally happens as women mature. Thus the majority are automatically consigned to the ranks of the "not good-looking." The desire for thinness and unrealistic body image is one of the pernicious factors that has made eating disorders, such as anorexia and bulimia, major problems with young North American women today. The false value assigned to physical good looks is one of the prime characteristics of our culture.

Celebration of Sex

The last foundation stone for a healthy sexuality is that sexuality is to be celebrated. How does God recommend that we celebrate our sexuality? The first and greatest commandment given sets the tone for all the other recommendations: "'Love the Lord your God with all your heart and with all your soul and with all your mind.' . . . And the second is like it: 'Love your neighbor as yourself'" (Matt 22:37, 39). Adherence to these two commandments could remove the need for any other recommendations. If we truly loved God and loved our neighbors as ourselves, we would treat others as we would like to be treated.

"While the Bible does not spell out a detailed theory of sex, it does . . . open up for us a perspective on life as a whole, including our sexuality," said Neil Clark Warren. Our beliefs regarding human wholeness and personhood are derived from biblical truth, and the Bible has a high and celebrative view of sexuality.

The following descriptions show what living a celebrative life as sexual people at each stage of life could be like:

• As *infants and children*, we are loved, protected, and nourished. We are stimulated to learn and develop. We are humored but also have appropriate limits set for us. We do not need to be warned about or experience inappropriate touching or sexual behavior by family members, relatives, neighbors, friends, or strangers. We can safely explore the wonderful world of nature, science, and art, inside or outside.

• As *preadolescents and adolescents*, we continue to experience the security of an intact, loving family. Such a family has the good sense to know when to reach out and when to allow privacy, and is always there to help interpret life and our concerns about growing up. Our life experiences include school programs, teachers, and classmates that stimulate us to become the best we can be. We go to schools that make learning fun in a safe environment and that augment positive sexual learning at home. We are part of a church and community that cares about spiritual development and creates many wholesome, fun activities where we can be with our peers, try out our social skills, and experience the satisfaction of doing things together that are helpful to other people. We are not mercilessly teased as we experience the stirrings of sexual attractions.

• As *young adults*, the disciplines and patterns of living and thinking established earlier serve us well as we continue our education and explore options in living arrangements, work, and friends. We gain a clear sense of who we are becoming and like what we see. Our choices regarding lifestyle, singleness, marriage, and geographical location give us feelings of satisfaction and fulfillment. As women or men, we can feel accepted and appreciated for who we are. We are seen as people of character rather than as sexual objects. We live where no man or woman dreads going to work because of coworkers' use of verbal and body language laden with sexual innuendoes, and where going for a walk morning, noon, or night feels safe. We know that a date means a fun opportunity to learn to know another person better—not an invitation to sleep together. We want a world where it is not necessary for any of us to figure out how to tell the person we hope to marry about a sexually transmitted infection that will always be with us. We want to be free of the need to discuss sexual partners in the past, a child born out of wedlock, or an abortion. We want to be free of the need to explain that we were sexually abused and raped and therefore will need a lot of sensitive understanding before it will be possible for us to feel comfortable with sexual intercourse.

• As *adults*, we find that the choices we have made contribute to a sense of great personal satisfaction as well as the knowledge that we make a positive difference in the lives of others. We who remain single find significant social interaction and support from caring friends of both genders, opportunities for both receiving and contributing in important ways in church and community settings, and freedom from sexual harassment. We who marry experience open and clear communication and can learn with our spouses what is pleasurable to each in our sexual relationship without feeling we are being compared with previous partners. Children are viewed as gifts from God, for whom we joyfully assume responsibility. We who want children can have them. We offer hospitality in our homes to many others. Learning and spiritual development are a continuing process, and service is a way of everyday life.

• As *older adults*, we enjoy the results of a life that is and has been well lived and filled with wise choices and adventure. We experience companionship with family and friends from all age ranges as well as acceptance, tender care, and desired touching. We are offered spiritual resources to help us cope with the growing number of losses older people inevitably experience. We continue to focus on people and events beyond ourselves and contribute to improving the lives of others as is possible. A life lived according to God's design fosters contentment and a peaceful conclusion to our earthly life.

Do these descriptions of life at every stage sound like heaven? They are a bit of heaven. After all, Christ indicated that he came to earth that we might have life, and have it to the fullest (John 10:10). The whole biblical story is about relationships—human beings' relationships to God, to each other, to themselves, to family members, to brothers and sisters in Christ, to orphans and widows, to "the least of these," and to enemies. In all of these relationships, the people interacting are doing so as sexual beings. They cannot do otherwise, since to be human is to be sexual.

We also know that these interactions are occurring in imperfect societies made up of people with flaws. God knows this, of course, and has provided principles and guidelines in the Bible to help us to deal with what is less than ideal in the human experience, to recognize the temptations that fight against living life abundantly as God would have us do, and to pattern our lives in the way God would have us live.

For people in biblical times, God prescribed principles on

which to base attitudes and behavior. Our culture is quite different from that of biblical societies. Yet the same principles are just as appropriate for us today. Living as sexual beings while following God's way truly does lead to the most rewarding, satisfying, healthy, uncomplicated, freeing, nurturing, and intimate life possible. Even in an imperfect world, God's recommendations for human interaction can help to prevent the pain, grief, destruction, and unfulfilled dreams that so often occur when people yield to selfish, undisciplined, and unloving attitudes in their sexual interactions.

Sexuality is for rejoicing; sexuality can be a source of happiness; sexuality should mean fulfillment. How beautiful that sexuality was created as a dimension of God's highest creation.

We realize a sense of peace and true sexual freedom when we are part of a community that honors our sexuality and our uniqueness, that frees us from compulsive genital expression and preoccupation, and that shows us how to trust each other. We can only imagine what would happen if the male half of the human race and the female half of the human race could achieve true peace with each other, living together in harmony, equality, love, mutual respect, and honor. Both individual peace and world peace would be remarkably enhanced.

Someone has said that those who are mentally and emotionally healthy are those who have learned to say three things: when to say yes, when to say no, and when to say whoopee! Our sexuality can be one of the whoopees of our lives—a very special gift from God.

Discussion Questions

1. What are some examples of false thinking about the body that keep us from speaking openly and honestly about our sexual bodies? From reaching out to others to foster relationships?
2. Are my attitudes about sexuality the same as or different from how I perceive my parents' or guardians' attitudes? Why?

3. How might Christian attitudes and understandings of sexuality be made more visible in our society?

4. If we truly believe that God created us sexual, male and female, and that each is of equal value and unable to exist without the other, what changes might we observe in our congregations, institutions, families, and interpersonal relationships?

5. Identify and explain how you might develop male attributes you as a female would like to possess to a greater extent, or female attributes you as a male would like to possess to a greater extent.

6. If you were to design an ideal sex-education program in your congregation, what would it be?

2

Guidelines from the Gift-Giver: Sexuality and Scripture

Keith Graber Miller

In sexuality, as in all areas of life, our ethical discernment and understandings are rooted in multiple sources, including but not limited to the biblical text. In a church I once attended, one Sunday school class was studying the matter of women in church leadership. The teacher began by saying he wanted everyone, on entering the room, to leave their "baggage" at the door. He wanted them to set aside their preconceptions about the issue, their social locations, their gender, their experiences, their education, ideas from their culture, and all other notions that had shaped them. With that baggage discarded, the teacher said, they would simply look at the Bible and see what the unadulterated Scripture had to say to them on the issue.

When I learned of that approach, I thought, "What a horrendous deception! It's impossible to leave all these things at the door." Instead, when I teach, I want people to bring their baggage with them. Together we can place the baggage on the floor in front of us and open it. It will take time to sort through the luggage, unpacking, laundering, repacking, and shifting. We will throw out some of the muck and maybe the hyper-tight jeans from earlier days. We will try to make everything fit a little better. But we will not get anywhere with any integrity if we do not see how much we are shaped by all of these other factors, and if we do not begin to accept the impact of those other formative influences.

In our understandings of sexuality, most of us, implicitly or explicitly, draw on our own experiences and those of our parents, siblings, friends, work associates, and church family. We consider the sciences; we ask what contemporary social and natural scientists are saying about genetics, biological predispositions, and social construction of our sexual desires, inclinations, and perspectives. We examine what seems "natural" or "unnatural," based on the way God has apparently ordered the world. For some Christians, these other sources function as independent authorities alongside the Bible. For others, they are interpretive lenses through which we look at the biblical text.

We also ask how the church—the larger church or our own denomination—has weighed in on a given issue over the centuries. In doing so, we need to acknowledge that the living tradition has developed and changed over the ages. In addition, we should recognize how our views of the Bible itself have been shaped by the church's tradition in ways we often overlook.

Saint Augustine of Hippo (354–430), one of the most influential early-church theologians, had a profound impact on the church's views of sex and sexuality. Before he committed himself to Christian faith, he'd had a rather active youth. He fathered a child outside of marriage, lived with a woman, and constantly struggled with his sexual impulses. After his conversion and as he processed his personal experience, Augustine and some of his peers decided that it was coitus, and more specifically the male erection, that showed the will's inability to maintain control over the passions. Such uncontrollability was a major issue for those concerned that one's "spiritual nature" should control one's "physical nature."

Augustine also linked the act of sexual intercourse with the transmission of original sin. Since such sin was handed on from generation to generation and since future generations were created through coitus, genital-genital intercourse became inextricably linked with sin.

In subsequent centuries, then, the Christian tradition developed into what some critics disparagingly call a "sex-negative" one. I would like to believe that is not true. But even if, by some measures, the Christian tradition is a sex-negative one, the Bible itself is not.

Hebrew Scriptures

From the beginning of the Hebrew Scriptures (Old Testament), sex and sexuality are considered good. In the creation stories in Genesis 1 and 2, human beings, including their sexual identities and means of relating sexually, are considered good. The implication is that sexual relating is edifying, in part because it is a means for reproduction, necessary for the survival of humans. It is also good because sexuality contributes to holistic human relationships and provides sensual and affectional enrichment.

Humans are not created to be solitary individuals; they are meant to be in relationship with others. The animals, says the text, were not sufficient companions for the original human. Eve became the most appropriate companion for Adam, as well as the fitting helper and lover. Men and women are to leave their parents and cling to their spouses, becoming one flesh (Gen 2:24).

From those opening passages on, we find an extraordinary amount of material about sex and sexuality in the biblical text, including both healthy relationships and damaging, destructive ones. While sex and sexuality are not intended to be the Bible's major theme, in the Hebrew Scriptures we find many stories about or references to sexual behaviors.

- Genesis 26:8 speaks about marital foreplay, with Isaac fondling his wife Rebekah.
- We read about adulterous affairs, not just between outliers, but also between some of God's chosen ones.
- We are told of King David's attraction to the bathing Bathsheba, his subsequent seduction of her, her preg-

nancy, and his plot to have her husband killed in battle so he could not discover David's wickedness (2 Sam 11:1-27).

- There are rapes, both heterosexual and homosexual, including gang rapes of women, and reference to homosexual rapes of heterosexual men (Gen 19:1-10; Judg 19:1-30; 2 Sam 13:1-20).

- Many Hebrew men had polygamous marriages. Jacob took two wives (Rachel and Leah). Solomon had seven hundred wives and three hundred concubines (1 Kings 11:1-4).

- Ruth, the godly woman who had a book named after her, was instructed to sneak in at night, crawl under the covers with Boaz, and lie near his loins. Most English translations say near his "feet," but in Hebrew the reference is considerably further up the legs. The story speaks of Ruth doing so, and then of her eventual marriage to Boaz (Ruth 3:1-15).

- Song of Songs describes a female lover's breasts as fawns; her body as a mountain of myrrh and a hill of frankincense. A male lover's legs are described as alabaster columns and his body as ivory work encrusted with sapphires.

- There are instructions about coitus interruptus, particularly in the case of Onan and Tamar, where it broke covenant responsibility to Onan's brother (Gen 38:9-11). According to Hebrew understandings, Onan was to "go in to" his brother's widow and then have children with her so his deceased brother would have heirs. Knowing that any offspring would not legally be considered his, Onan took advantage of the sexual encounter but then "spilled his semen on the ground whenever he went in to his brother's wife" (NRSV).

- Leviticus 18–20 gives guidelines for not having sex during menstruation, not having sex with animals, and not showing one's nakedness. It also comments on a wide range of other sexual behaviors.

- Song of Songs 8:3 gives implicit recommendations for foreplay with a woman, including where to place your left arm and what to fondle with your right.
- There was sacred temple sex, the religious practice of some who did not follow Yahweh. They had intercourse with a priest or priestess at the temple for the sake of worship, fertile lands, and financial support of the religious cult (1 Sam 2:22; 1 Kings 14:23-24).

The Hebrew Scriptures are loaded with such references to sexual issues. Yet it is also clear that the Hebrews sought to distinguish themselves from their fertility-cult neighbors, whose sexuality was inextricably intertwined with their gods and goddesses. For the most part, the Hebrew people perceived God not as a sexual being, but as one who stands behind and beyond sexuality. Certainly we find gendered references to God in the Hebrew Scriptures, and most of these are male ones, but we also find female images. These male and female images from life tell us some things about God, but God is not fully captured by any of them. Sexuality is a created reality, created by God for the good of humanity.

According to the Old Testament, sex and sexuality—even though not a part of the divine being—are to be celebrated. The most dramatic affirmation of sexuality is in Song of Songs, where we find pictures of erotic joy between the sexes portrayed as good. The book consists of two lovers, a bride and bridegroom, speaking back and forth to each other. Sometimes the book has been understood to be about the relationship between Yahweh and Israel.

There are examples in the Hebrew Scriptures of a human sexual relationship describing the relationship between God and humans. Notably, Hosea talks about his marriage to Gomer, a "harlot." This relationship is used as an allegory for God's relationship with Israel: Israel had so often left God behind to worship other gods, but God continues reaching out to Israel and accepting her back. God's faithfulness, fidelity, and forgiveness are shown even in Israel's periods of failure and infidelity.

While this spiritualizing is sometimes appropriate, in the Song of Songs such an interpretation seems to be a misreading of what was intended to be a celebration of love and courtship: "I am my beloved's, and his desire is for me. Come, my beloved, let us go forth into the fields, and lodge in the villages. . . . There I will give you my love" (7:10-12 NRSV).

Proverbs 5:18-19 evokes a similar passion: "Let your fountain be blessed, and rejoice in the wife of your youth, a lovely deer, a graceful doe. May her breasts satisfy you at all times; may you be intoxicated always by her love" (NRSV).

Any faith tradition that includes such poetry among its sacred writings has an appreciation and respect for sex and sexuality. Certainly heterosexual intercourse is intended partly for procreation, as the Hebrew Scriptures make clear. But as we see in such passages, sexual relating is also to be enjoyed as a good gift of God, as powerfully passionate and unifying.

Perhaps because of this unifying power, the Hebrew Scriptures also make it clear that sexual relating should take place within particular contexts. It is a special human expression appropriate in some settings and not in others. In Leviticus and Deuteronomy, we find a range of counsel regarding the sexual aspects of marriage, sexual intercourse, adultery, incest, rape, prostitution, male-male sex, and sex with slaves and animals. While we should carefully analyze and critique passages such as those in the Holiness Code (Lev 17–26), just as we do other injunctions in these sections of Scripture, we should note the text's concern about appropriate relationships.

The Hebrew Scriptures also make clear that sexual relating carries with it certain responsibilities and obligations. In some ways, intercourse functions as the marriage bond. In the polygynous (a man having more than one wife) and patriarchal culture of the Hebrews, a man who had intercourse with a virgin was obligated to take her as his spouse. Sexual relating had tremendous moral significance. In such sexual uniting, one was making a binding commitment to care for the good of the other.

A Word About Self-Pleasuring

While *self*-pleasuring is one of the most common sexual activities in all cultures, there is tremendous variation in attitude about this behavior. The ancient Egyptians included an act of masturbation in their creation story. According to their tradition, the universe began with the god Atum ejaculating into his hand, and from his semen all life evolved. In some Mesoamerican religious myths, the god Quetzalcoatl masturbates on the bones of previous civilizations, and from that act a new people is created.

The Judeo-Christian tradition includes no such stories, but neither does it condemn or speak directly about self-pleasuring. Historically, several Hebrew or Christian texts have been seen as having apparent concerns that may be loosely related to masturbation. The moral codes embedded in Leviticus associate uncleanness with the emission of any kind of bodily fluid (including urine and feces). There is specific reference to the emission of semen in Leviticus 15:16-17, with instructions for a man to bathe if he has an emission or for both a man and a woman to bathe if they have been lying together when this occurs.

For many centuries, self-pleasuring was mistakenly associated with the sin of Onan (Gen 38:9-10), whose actual sin—as noted earlier—was using coitus interruptus as a means of avoiding his covenantal responsibilities. In medieval Judaism, masturbation was condemned on the basis of Onan's unrelated sin, and men were even forbidden to hold their penis while urinating.

In Christian Scriptures the primary passages historically

associated with self-pleasuring had to do with lusting (for example, Matt 5:28), although masturbation is not explicitly mentioned in those injunctions.

Later, among the early-church fathers, Augustine viewed masturbation as unnatural since it could not lead to procreation. In spite of the fact that procreative behaviors such as fornication and prostitution can be detrimental to the development of right relationships, Augustine preferred these behaviors over self-pleasuring. Thomas Aquinas, in the thirteenth century, similarly—and equally strangely—believed that prostitution was necessary because it drained off the lust that might otherwise lead to masturbation.

This became increasingly important during the Renaissance, when anti-masturbation attitudes were furthered by the mistaken biological belief that all the elements of human life are present in semen and that women serve only as incubators for this human (male) seed. In that framework, masturbation would be akin to an early form of abortion, eliminating a potential life. Our biological understandings about both bodily needs and procreation have increased dramatically since that time.

Christian Scriptures

As was true in Hebrew Scriptures, Christian Scriptures at their best see goodness, power, and significance in sexuality and shared sexual relationships. Between the time the Hebrew Scriptures were recorded and the time the Christian Scriptures were written, Greek philosophy had made a sharp division between the body and the spirit. Although Augustine fought this notion in the fourth and fifth centuries, he could not fully escape such a dualism in his own theological reflections.

In Greek dualism, which has pervasively influenced the West for the past two millennia, the body is evil, and that makes bodily functions and practices likewise evil. Such a perspective also tends to denigrate women, who are historically more associated with the body, partly because of childbearing and breastfeeding. The spirit, on the other hand, is perceived as the part of us created in God's image. Dualistic perspectives suggest that somehow the spirit needs to be kept separate from the body, this cage which temporarily traps us. The body is perceived as a prison that keeps the more godlike spirit or soul from reaching its goal of union with the divine.

The Hebrew Scriptures had no concept of this division, nor did Jesus, as he is depicted in the New Testament: the person is unified, body and spirit. We are embodied beings, not dismembered ones. The Christian Scriptures more generally fight against this dualism, though the body-spirit split no doubt influenced some of the New Testament writers. However, the fundamental tenet of Christian faith—that God became flesh in the incarnation of Jesus Christ—militates against such dualism.

As in the Hebrew Scriptures, sex and sexuality were not the primary concerns of Jesus or other New Testament figures or writers. Perhaps under the influence of various early-church theologians, too often the church has linked sin primarily with sexuality. Certainly destructive forms of sexual relating can be sinful. According to the biblical record, though, Jesus was far more concerned about the dangers and sins of wealth and the injustices of inequality.

When the rich young man went to Jesus and asked him what he needed to do to inherit eternal life, Jesus told him to keep the commandments, including injunctions about adultery, truth-telling, respect, killing, and theft. Then Jesus said the young man lacked one thing: "Go, sell your possessions, and give the money to the poor, and you will have treasure in heaven; then come, follow me" (Matt 19:21 NRSV).

In Jesus' words, Paul's writings, and elsewhere in the New Testament, when sexual abuses are listed as sins, they are placed alongside equally condemned acts and dispositions such as envy, idolatry, theft, slander, pride, deceit, foolishness, anger, selfishness, murder, and enmity (for example, Mark 7:21-22; Gal 5:19-21).

According to the Gospels, the sexual issues Jesus did address are marriage, fornication, adultery, lust, divorce, and remarriage (Matt 5:27-32; 15:19; 19:3-12; Mark 7:21; 10:2-12; Luke 16:18). In these passages Jesus expanded the notion of adultery and constricted the justification for divorce. Behind such words are the principles of respect, commitment, and care, particularly for women, who could rather easily be used and discarded in Jesus' culture. While Jesus' primary emphasis was not on (narrowly defined) sex and sexuality, he was committed to the formation of deep, meaningful, and intimate relationships.

Many of Jesus' stories—even ones that deal with money or with enemies or with the reign of God—have to do with developing relationships of trust and faithfulness. Jesus himself found it essential to surround himself with a group of friends, whom we now call disciples. According to the biblical text, these relationships with men and with women were a fundamental part of who Jesus was.

If we accept the basic Christian understanding that Jesus was fully human as well as fully divine, we also must recognize that he was subject to the same temptations other humans experience. Unlike painters before them, Renaissance artists frequently depicted the baby Jesus with his genitalia exposed, and occasionally depicted the loincloth-covered adult Jesus in a state of sexual arousal. The apparent point was that Jesus' chastity was real, and his struggles were similar to ours: it would be no great virtue to be chaste if one were not a vigorous sexual being.

It is not unreasonable to speculate that Jesus wondered what a sexual encounter would be like, even though he consciously chose celibacy as a vocation. Novelist Nikos Kazantzakis's movie *The Last Temptation of Christ* created an enormous stir in Christian circles. The "last temptation," which Jesus ultimately resisted, was for him to abandon his godly mission and settle down with Mary Magdalene, his friend and follower. The film was based largely on Kazantzakis's imagination, but it was not as far-fetched or heretical as some Christians believed. If Jesus was a human being, which the Christian church has affirmed, he no doubt knew what it was like to experience human emotions and passions.

According to the Gospel record, Jesus also did not make marriage the supreme goal for his followers, the place where God's good will could be best realized. Jesus was most concerned that people would have passion for the reign of God, a passion that would overrule all other desires. He called the disciples to give themselves fully to God's reign. Jesus said, "No one who has left home or wife or brothers or parents or children for the sake of the kingdom of God will fail to receive many times as much in this age and, in the age to come, eternal life" (Luke 18:29-30; see also parallels). Spiritual commitment and maturation may happen in the family, but marriage is not essential to such development. The primary social relationship is the disciple group, not the family.

At the same time, Jesus honored marriage and considered it blessed by God. He celebrated with friends at their wedding in Cana, making water into wine as the "first of his miraculous signs" (John 2:1-11). In Matthew 19:4-6 (see also Mark 10:8-9), Jesus described marriage with the Genesis term "one flesh." He said, "What God has joined together, let no one separate" or "put asunder" (Matt 19:6 NRSV; KJV), language we still hear in some wedding ceremonies.

More so than for some of his contemporaries, Jesus viewed marriage as a permanent covenant built on fidelity and nurtured by loyalty, commitment, respect, and love. Such commitment and respect meant guarding oneself against entertaining lustful looks at a person not one's spouse and thereby being unchaste in heart and thought (Matt 5:28).

Regarding Paul

The apostle Paul spoke most extensively about sexual relationships in 1 Corinthians 5–7. Even more explicitly than Jesus, he counseled single people to remain so, just as he was. Most scholars believe Paul was widowed, so he knew what it was like to be both married and single. In Corinthians, his counsel was based, in part, on his eschatological expectations. He believed that the end of time was near, the world was passing away, and therefore marriage would be a distraction. Marriage would simply make followers of Jesus anxious about the affairs of the world, and Paul wanted them to be concerned about the affairs of the Lord.

Thus Paul affirmed singleness, just as Jesus did by his teaching and example, as a good and right way of living, allowing for more undivided devotion to God. We might want to temper Paul's words with the recognition that his apparent sense of Jesus' imminent return was mistaken. We should note, also, that he made concessions for those who do not have the gift of singleness. Those who cannot practice "self-control" should marry rather than be "aflame with passion" (1 Cor 7:7-9 NRSV).

Nevertheless, we should recognize a distinctive contribution of early Christianity in idealizing permanent vocational celibacy (see Matt 19:12; 1 Cor 7:7, 32-35). Such a vocation allowed for full commitment to the faith community and a way of breaking out of state-controlled family functions, including the duty to procreate. Intentional virginity especially allowed Christian women direct access to a "higher calling" in the church, eroding the subordination of women to men.

In this same Corinthian passage, which was prompted by accounts Paul had heard about a believer living with his father's wife (1 Cor 5:1), Paul gave wide-ranging counsel about sexuality. He spoke against incest, sexual perversions, and adultery. He reminded his hearers that "the body is not meant for sexual immorality, but for the Lord, and the Lord for the body" (1 Cor 6:13).

Because in the act of sexual intercourse, "the two will become one flesh," Paul condemns joining oneself with a prostitute. He indicates that sexual sins are sins against one's own body, which is also a temple of the Holy Spirit. Paul further encourages believers to honor God with their bodies (1 Cor 6:15-20). In marriage, he urges a mutual self-giving of bodies, unless the couple voluntarily chooses to abstain for a time so they can be more devoted to prayer (7:3-6).

On Same-Sex Sexuality

Paul addresses male same-sex sexual acts on several occasions. In the Corinthian passage where he lists those who will not inherit the kingdom of God, he uses the Greek terms *malakoi* and *arsenokoitai*, sometimes collectively translated as "sexual perverts" (1 Cor 6:9). Scholars disagree on the specific meanings of the terms, which may carry some reference to same-sex sexual behavior—perhaps pederasty (adult men having sex with young boys) or male prostitution. A similar list identifies some for whom the law is laid down: perverts, adulterers, the unholy and irreligious, slave traders, liars, perjurers, and other ungodly and sinful persons (1 Tim 1:8-11).

In Romans 1:26-27 and its context, we find Paul's clearest condemnation of same-sex sexual acts as he understood them. It is also the only biblical passage that appears to deal with sexual relating between women. Paul sees such sexual behavior as "unnatural," saying that "God gave them up in the lusts of their hearts to impurity" (1:24 NRSV). Men who "committed indecent acts with other men," said Paul, "received in themselves the due penalty for their perversion" (1:27).

Space does not permit a full exploration of biblical perspectives on this issue here. (Physician Willard Krabill more thoroughly addresses homosexuality later in chapter 8 of this book.) We should note, however, that several passages in the Hebrew Scriptures also address same-sex sexual acts. The possibility of homosexual rape is mentioned in Genesis 19 and Judges 19, though it is not the focus of those stories. Instead, the "sins of Sodom" are listed elsewhere in the Old Testament as pride, thoughtless ease, abuse of the poor, adultery, lies, and haughtiness (Jer 23:14; Isa 13:19; Ezek 16:49-50). We also must acknowledge the often-overlooked horror of the rape and murder of women implicit or explicit in these passages.

The other biblical places where male same-sex sexual acts are condemned are in Leviticus 18:22 and 20:13. This is part of the Holiness Code (Lev 17–26), which is concerned with ritual purity and being holy to the Lord and separate from the abominations of the Canaanite nations (18:30; 20:26). This code condemns a range of other behaviors such as nakedness, adultery, prostitution, incest, child sacrifice, bearing grudges, wearing "clothing woven of two kinds of material," lying, stealing, and eating sacrifices more than three days old.

The biblical writers had no sense of homosexuality as a psychosexual orientation, a concept that emerged in the late nineteenth century. Those who study the texts should consider the impact of modern notions of sexual orientation—that the basic sexual attraction of some men or women may be to those of the same sex.

In the highly patriarchal Hebrew society, one major concern was that a man might lie with another man "as with a woman." The danger was that male dignity might be offended. From such a perspective, when a man acted sexually like a woman (that is, becoming a receptor for a man's penis), he degraded himself and lost status—for himself as well as for other males. This says more about cultural misogyny (the hatred of women) than it does about same-sex sexuality. In several biblical passages where male-male sexual acts are addressed, they appear to be between unequal partners (adult and child) or in abusive contexts (the Sodom story) rather than in relationships of mutuality, respect, and commitment. Such observations are relevant for interpreting biblical perspectives on same-sex sexual behavior.

Toward Equality

One more word should be said about biblical perspectives on sexuality. Jesus and Paul both sought to break down many of the cultural and religious barriers between men and women.

Jesus related to the women around him in a remarkable way. Women were among those who followed him from village to village as he preached and taught, and they were financial supporters of his ministry. He spoke with women openly in public, whether they were potential believers who had come to hear his message, the Samaritan woman at Jacob's well, an unclean (menstruating) woman who touched the hem of his garment, or a woman caught in adultery.

These were not typical male responses in first-century Palestine. Jesus endangered his own standing by relating to such women. He knowingly challenged some of the prescriptions of his religion and culture, and elevated women's status by risking his own.

Too often the Christian tradition has focused on an unequal partnership between women and men, based partly on misunderstandings of biblical texts or on cultural prescriptions. Genesis offers two accounts of God's creation of humans. In the first, we are told that God created humans (generic, not just *man* in the original Hebrew) in God's own image: "So God created humanity in God's own image; . . . male and female God created them" (Gen 1:27, author's paraphrase).

In the second creation account, which begins in Genesis 2:4, there is first one human (male), and then the woman is created out of the rib of the man (2:22). The woman is created for companionship, so the male human is not alone. She is also created as a "helper suitable for him" (2:18). Sometimes this "helper" status has been interpreted to mean a subordinate role. However, in Hebrew the word for "help" is used elsewhere for the way God cares for people. God is the people's "help" (or "helper" or "helpmate"). Together male and female do God's work, just as God is the helper for God's people.

Inequality in the male-female relationship does not occur until after the fall (Gen 3). Such inequality, with the male ruling over the female (3:16), is evidence of fallenness, a movement away from God's original intentions. In the biblical story, it is not to be celebrated but lamented.

In the Christian Scriptures, in the writings of Paul and others, we find several passages that address a hierarchical ordering of relationships. Children are to be subject to their parents; slaves must obey their masters; and wives must be subject to their husbands (Eph 5:21–6:9; Col 3:18–4:1; 1 Pet 2:13–3:7).

In these passages Paul and other writers did not set up an ideal from scratch but drew on a pre-Christian, culturally prescribed institution (often called *Haustafeln*, "household precepts"). Other-than-Christian writers of the time similarly enjoined women to subordinate themselves to their husbands. Biblical writers who drew on these ethical instructions then modified them with their own Christian teachings.

Paul did not instruct women to do anything differently, but he did suggest a new pattern for men: "Husbands, love your wives, just as Christ loved the church" (Eph 5:25). Men loving their wives—not wives submitting to their husbands—was the new Christian teaching in a culture where love was not part of the cultural expectation for the household.

Paul backed up those words elsewhere with the hope that for those who have put on Christ, "there is neither Jew nor Greek, slave nor free, male nor female, for you are all one in Christ Jesus" (Gal 3:28). Such words were revolutionary in Paul's day. Radical egalitarianism is the trajectory toward which Paul and Jesus point us regarding relationships between and respect for men and women.

A Closing Word

From the biblical perspective, sexuality is an integral part of our created being, whether we are male or female. It is a dimension of human existence that we honor and celebrate, and share in the context of covenantal relationships. On the biblical line of development, the *quality* of such relationships becomes increasingly important. At their biblical best, genital sexual encounters come within the context of permanent, committed, community-affirmed, monogamous, loving, mutually edifying relationships.

In a broader sense, love, intimacy, and deep personal relationships rooted in Christ are near the heart of the gospel. People can embrace such emotions and commitments whether they are single or married. Christians are embodied beings who accept with joy the goodness of their God-given bodies and who respond to such sexual goodness with responsibility, sensitivity, and care.

Discussion Questions

1. Do you think the Christian church has made progress in moving from what some critics call a "sex-negative" attitude in recent years?

2. Are gender-free references to God important to you? Why or why not?

3. Can you think of examples of how the Greek concept of a division between body and spirit continues to affect us today?

4. Why do many Christians seem to think sexual sins are more important than sins of greed and wealth?

5. How does Jesus' attitude toward women impact us today? How should it?

6. How do you respond to the idea that a true understanding of the biblical text does not support a hierarchical relationship between males and females?

3

The Gift and Intimacy

Willard S. Krabill

When we think about intimacy, we often reflect society's corruption of the term and society's preoccupation with sexual matters. We equate "being intimate" with sexual intercourse, and in so doing, we empty *intimacy* of its deepest meaning. They are not synonymous. We must recognize that the common societal use of *intimate* and *intimacy* is a counterfeit of what we, especially Christians, should mean by true intimacy. Sexual intercourse is only one small, nonessential part of true intimacy in a world that acts as if it is the only thing.

Intimacy and love are not the same. Intimacy is a dimension of love. I can love the people of my neighborhood, but I am not intimate with all the people in my neighborhood. I need personal relationships to meet my human needs. Humans of all ages need to be loved, to be understood, to be accepted, and to be cared about. We need to be taken seriously, to have our thoughts and feelings respected and held in confidence, and to be trusted.

These statements describe our human need for loving, intimate relationships, not the need for sexual intercourse. We are made for relationships: relationships with God through Jesus Christ, relationships with each other, and relationships with ourselves. The most energizing relationships are intimate relationships. Intimacy is not only desirable; it is also a real need for everyone at every age.

As a physician, I have shared in the deepest moments of people's lives, the good and the bad: birth, first illness, accidents, marriages, addictions, rejections, reunions, and deaths. Never have I seen anyone die from the lack of sexual intercourse. I have, however, seen many people die premature deaths because they felt rejected and lonely, and they lacked intimacy. They did not know that they were cared about and prized by another person and that they mattered to another person. To achieve the worthwhile goal of becoming intimate with those we love, we need to know what it is and is not, what creates it, and the barriers and aids to developing intimacy.

What Is Intimacy?

Webster's says intimacy is sharing what is intrinsic and essential. Other sources define it as familiarity, friendship, or privacy. A church leader, Harold Bauman, defined intimacy as "the experience of a close sustained familiarity with another's inner life; it is to know another person from the inside."

Rod Cooper wrote in an article in *New Man*, "The word *intimacy* literally means into-me-see. Intimacy is the ability to experience an open, supportive, compassionate relationship with another person without fear of condemnation or loss of one's identity. It is knowing another person deeply and appreciating them anyway."

Once, while assisting a heart surgeon with an open-heart operation, I was asked to put my finger inside the beating heart to break up a calcified heart valve. The surgeon said, "That's getting pretty intimate with a person, isn't it?" In a physical sense, he was right. But that intimacy is nothing compared to the experience of communicating on a deep level with a person who is awake, sharing, and communicating in a setting where I, like that heart patient, am vulnerable and also taking risks.

Some years ago, wide attention was focused on intimacy because of a poll taken by Ann Landers among readers of her newspaper column. She asked women to respond to this question: "Would you be content to be held close and be treated tenderly and forget about the 'act,' sexual intercourse? Answer

yes or no and give your age." Over 100,000 readers responded, and 72 percent replied yes: I would be content to be held
close and be treated tenderly and forget about the act. Forty
percent of the respondents were under forty years of age. Here
are some of the replies:

- From Columbus, Ohio: "I am under forty and would
  be delighted to settle for tender words and warm caresses. The rest of it is a bore and can be exhausting. I am
  sure the sex act was designed strictly for the pleasure of
  males."
- From Anchorage: "I am twenty-six years old, to be exact.
  I want three children, so obviously I need more than conversation. After I have my family, I would happily settle
  for separate rooms. Sex doesn't do a thing for me."
- From Kansas City: "I am fifty-five and vote yes. The
  best part is the cuddling and caressing and the tender
  words that come with caring. My first husband used
  to rape me about five times a week. If a stranger had
  treated me like that, I would have had him arrested."
- From Texarkana, Texas: "Yes, without the tender embrace,
  the act is animalistic. For years I hated sex and felt used.
  I was relieved when my husband died. My present mate
  is on heart pills that have made him impotent. It is like
  heaven just to be held and cuddled."

Obviously, there were many "no" answers as well (28
percent), but the nature and tremendous numbers of the
"yes" answers give evidence of a serious problem in male-
female communication in our society. The Associated Press
quoted Landers on the poll: "The importance of the sex act is
overrated. Women want affection. They want to feel valued.
Apparently having sex alone (in and of itself) doesn't give
them the feeling they are valued."

"As for men," she added, "too many are using sex as a

physical release, and it has no more emotional significance than a sneeze. There is a tremendous lack of communication. It is troublesome" (Landers: 1985).

When Landers later asked her male readers the same question, the overwhelming response was no: I would not settle for being held tenderly and forget about the act. Only 8 percent said yes, and almost all of those men were over sixty years old.

The following response from New York represents the essence of many: "After a year of marriage, my wife said, 'Let's just cuddle.' The following day, I suggested that we go to her favorite restaurant. When we got there, I told her we weren't going to be seated. Instead, we would just stand by the kitchen and smell the food. (We are both forty.)"

And from Brisbane, Australia: "Anyone who would settle for being held tenderly is looking for nothing but companionship. I suggest he buy a dog" (Landers: 1995).

Clearly, differences in male and female biology, psychology, and conditioning help explain the differences in the above responses. However, sexual apathy is common in North America among both genders, especially among women. During the sexual revolution, a kind of "sexual anorexia" developed in our society.

With increased promiscuity and emphasis on sexual technique, commitment became almost irrelevant for many. The chief aim was to try every kind of sexual expression possible and not be uptight in doing so. Instead of this being a utopian experience, however, a certain anxiety developed. People were asking questions such as, "How am I performing?" and "Why am I sleeping with this person I hardly know and don't even like that well?" In spite of much sexual activity, people felt empty. They sought counseling and wondered why all their "lovemaking" was so unsatisfying. In that situation, a kind of "sexual anorexia" set in. In my medical practice, the most common sexual complaint I have heard over the years, by far, is from the woman who has lost her sexual interest (which she had initially). She says, "He just uses me. I feel like a thing." I have heard it over and over again. These persons need intimacy. We all need intimacy, a relationship closer than the physical.

I think that usually my female patients were lacking intimacy in their marriages because it was never there in the first place. Common North American cultural dating practices do not foster the development of genuine intimacy. The absence of intimacy is not surprising when the dating scene is characterized by such terms as "making out" and "scoring," with friends asking, "How far did you go?" In many relationships between unmarried people today, the question is not whether intercourse will be a part of it, but when. Making sexual intercourse the objective is destructive to true intimacy.

Dating in North America takes place in a milieu that encourages experiencing physical intimacy before developing the other dimensions of intimacy. Emotional, aesthetic, spiritual, and intellectual intimacy should precede physical intimacy. It is emotionally disastrous for a person to attempt physical intimacy before her or his personal identity is even established (as in the case of a teenager).

Intimacy is the unending marvel of understanding and being understood by another person. If people want true intimacy, their relationships must include certain characteristics.

What Creates Intimacy?

The first ingredient and step in building an intimate relationship is *friendship*. Are you drawn to the person—not the person's body, but the person? Do you really like her or him? Can you imagine spending hours with that person, talking about things that are really important to you? Can you imagine going to that person's home and spending time together in the context of his or her family? Can you imagine being that person's close friend and not letting "that sex thing" get in the way of your friendship? Some of the greatest intimacies in the world are between people who for one reason or another are not dating, engaged, or married, nor do they intend to be married. Friendship is the first ingredient of intimacy.

Another part of intimacy is *acceptance*. Do you accept the person for who he or she is as a person, not as a body or sex partner? Or do you think you may need to fine-tune the other person a bit, make a few changes here and there, or manipulate her or his personality to fit better? In an intimate relationship, both people need to be accepted. If we are assured of acceptance, we do not need to defend our failures. We know we are not on trial with an intimate friend. An intimate friend sends a clear and unconditional message: "You are okay, worthwhile, and valuable." Those who experience the unconditional love of God are best able to love and accept other people unconditionally.

Communication is absolutely essential for developing an intimate relationship. This must be open, honest communication—no deceit or pretending, no lies, and no hidden agenda. Intimacy requires open people who are willing to bare their souls. Closed people cannot achieve it.

Openness is frequently a problem for males. Deep sharing involves vulnerability, and vulnerability does not fit the usual stereotype of the macho image that some men try to portray. But we must share deeply if we are to become intimate with the ones we love.

Lillian Rubin, in *Intimate Strangers*, suggests that in our society, conditioned as men are, they are often denied effective emotional expression. For some young men, sexual intercourse becomes the main way emotional content can be expressed. This explains why genital expression is such an urgent matter for so many men. However, it is conditioned learning and thus can be unlearned.

Some women do not honestly communicate their feelings and their values, and continue compromising their demands for intimacy. As a result, they will make poor choices—poor choices of friends, men who do not understand intimacy, men who fake intimacy to get their way, or men who are so badly conditioned regarding male-female relationships that they simply do not know how to be tender, sensitive, honest, and vulnerable.

Equality is another important ingredient of intimacy. To dominate another person destroys intimacy. The worth of both partners in a relationship has to be equal. There can be no coercion, no power play, no manipulation, and no using the other for selfish purposes. Equal! Whether the intimate friends are of the same sex or not, both must express and experience total equality. I must feel just as important to you as you are to me. Today male dominance and the double standard are not acceptable and should be over. In an intimate relationship, both persons must come from an equal power base.

Trust is an ingredient of intimacy that is an overlooked essential in many relationships. To become intimate with someone is risky. There are many emotional risks in deeply sharing and caring, and that is scary. Why? Because we are afraid we might be rejected. Few if any experiences are as devastating as being rejected. Developing trust is so important and critical. If we do not send honest messages, if we pretend to be trustworthy, a painful outcome is inevitable. If we want to become intimate, we have to become very vulnerable.

Dependability, loyalty, and honesty all build the trust that we need before we are willing to risk sharing our deepest feelings. Deceit and dishonesty are quite prevalent in our society. Trust is in short supply, as revealed in the world of soap operas and the 50-percent divorce rate. Before we can risk disclosing ourselves, we need to be able to trust. Trust allows us to put our fears and our deepest feelings in our friend's hands, knowing that they will be treated carefully. No reasonable person communicates what is deeply personal in an environment infected with doubt, uncertainty, failed expectations, social betrayals, slighted feelings, or confidential sharing exposed. Few things bind us to each other like a promise kept. Nothing divides us like a promise broken.

The greatest intimacy is possible between people who have *shared values*—those who share the same lifestyle and life goals. True intimacy is unlikely to develop if two people are on a different life quest, a different road or journey, and have a different worldview. In an intimate relationship, shared values make all the ingredients of intimacy more attainable. When people have a shared faith in Jesus Christ and a shared faith community, these add a dimension to an intimate relationship that our secular society does not comprehend.

Jesus illustrated God's intention for each of us to experience intimacy. He was renewed by his visits to Bethany. John tells about Jesus' visit to the safe house of Mary, Martha, and Lazarus, where he went to enjoy deep friendship, to rest, and to be renewed and encouraged in his prophetic mission (12:1-3).

Affection is an ingredient of intimacy. Do you have feelings of affection for the other person? Does your face light up when his or her name is mentioned? Do you really care when the other person is hurting? Do you desire to be close to each other, and do you feel encouraged in each other's presence?

Touch is another important ingredient of intimacy—affirming touch and not exploiting touch. Intimate touching makes us feel better, not guilty. If the touching makes us feel important and not used, then it is an affirming touch. Until and unless we know the difference between affirming touch and the exploiting touch for inappropriate sexual arousal, we cannot trust. If we cannot trust, we cannot achieve intimacy.

True intimacy means being with another person in a way that is closer than the contact of two bodies (that, incidentally, is no big accomplishment). It is the interaction of those persons in a relationship of knowing and trusting that is closer than just the physical. When physical intimacy is divorced from true intimacy, it is hollow and meaningless. It leaves one frustrated and often breaks up the relationship. Sexual intercourse never creates intimacy. Sexual intercourse can energize and cap the relationship only when all the other components are already present.

To develop true intimacy takes lots of *time*. It is a process, a dynamic, growing experience. There is no instant, easy way to experience true intimacy, despite what soap operas, movies, and songs may tell us. It takes time to develop true intimacy and to be fully available to other persons, to share their joys and hear their suffering. True intimacy cannot be fallen into and out of in rapid succession. Two people need long stretches of time for them to develop all the characteristics of true intimacy.

It is not realistic to talk about developing intimate relationships with many people. We have time for only a few really intimate relationships. We should select them well and build them strongly and solidly.

Commitment is the final ingredient and step. We make a decision to really be there for the other person. This is the promise we intend to keep. True intimacy is more than friendship, equality, or communication. It requires commitment, the kind of loving commitment that keeps us present for and involved with the friend, partner, or whomever, and keeps us caring and loving over time. Such intimacy keeps two people together, not just when the road is smooth and maybe sensuous, but also when the road is rough and difficult.

Many non-genital friendships are far more intimate than many marriages. The commitment might be between two dating partners who commit themselves to saving the genital relationship for marriage, and that too is a commitment that builds intimacy.

To become the genital partner of another human being is to become very vulnerable. The trust that should be present for sexual intercourse to take place can hardly occur outside commitment. Sexual intercourse is the most self-giving, self-exposing exchange two people can make. It is precisely because it is so self-giving and self-exposing that the act of rape is so devastating, violent, and inexcusable.

Two old lines have fooled many people: "Prove your love" and "You would if you loved me." The real proof of love is the demonstration that our commitment and intimacy are so strong, so solid, and so faithful that we can remain with each other and be true and faithful to each other without getting involved in genital intercourse until marriage. That is true love—proof that I want you and not just your body. Without true intimacy, genital activity is often distancing and not uniting.

Today the mechanical stimulation of genital nerve endings often passes for getting intimate, but that does not satisfy our need for intimacy. Some truly intimate friendships do lead into marriage and a fulfilling sexual relationship. When they do, that is great, but only after the other dimensions of intimacy are achieved. The marriage of two people who have already experienced true intimacy is one most likely to endure. Their physical intimacy is most celebrative because the other ingredients of true intimacy are present.

Unfortunately, I have had to work with many married couples who have never experienced real intimacy in their lives, some who are hardly friends. They just got entangled in physical infatuation and were never intimate.

Love, though, is bigger than intimacy. If we think in New Testament terms, it is much bigger. As we understand and experience intimacy, we can begin to understand love. When we are able to say "I love you" to someone with whom we are intimate, love takes on its true meaning—not the meaning expressed in popular songs, television, and movies, but the deep Jesus-difference meaning. When people who are intimate say, "I love you," they are saying, "For you, I would give all of myself."

Barriers to Developing True Intimacy

The barriers to developing intimate relationships are the opposite of the ingredients or requisites of intimacy. If trust is a requisite, lack of trust is a barrier. There are, however, some particular barriers that deserve special mention. Two barriers to intimacy will be discussed here.

First, many people use sexual intercourse to shield themselves from the scariness of true intimacy: the exposure, the unmasking, and the vulnerability. Many individuals use sexual promiscuity to avoid real intimacy. Others use sexual athletics to bolster self-esteem, to combat anxiety, or to avoid genuine communication. Constantly searching for sexual thrills without truly sharing each other's personal worlds tears the physical aspect of sex from its integrated place in the whole person. A meaningful and fulfilling relationship needs more than sexual intercourse to sustain it.

Coitus, we must recognize, is the only aspect of intimacy that some people experience. When this is true, even this dimension ends in disillusionment. We may overburden intercourse with our real need for emotional, verbal, and spiritual intimacy; for the expression of all kinds of feelings; for overcoming loneliness; for finding fulfillment in life; and for feeling needed and wanted. If we do so, we ask far more of intercourse than it can possibly deliver.

A second barrier is rigidly held traditional masculine and feminine roles, and socialization to maintain stereotypes. The more readily people accept and live out traditional male and female roles, the less likely it is for them to develop intimate relationships.

To promote the development of intimacy, we must help our children and help each other achieve the goal of being fully human, not just of being a typical man or typical woman. Children can be reared to combine the so-called feminine attributes of gentleness and sensitivity with the so-called masculine attributes of strength, independence, and confidence. In the process, they recognize that they are all human attributes and of equal value.

It is high time we learned what Carol Gilligan has taught us in her book *In a Different Voice*. She says that women perceive the moral problem as one of relationships, care, and responsibility. Their perception is just as needed and valid as men's perception of the moral problem as one of rights, rules, and justice. The ethic of justice proceeds from a premise of equality, that everyone should be treated the same. The ethic of care rests on the premise of nonviolence, that no one should be hurt. The typical moral premises of men and women are equally needed if we are really to understand human relationships in any setting.

We have noted what intimacy is and what it is not, what creates intimacy, and the barriers to developing intimate relationships. We have known for a long time that the most important and protective factor against emotional and physical illness is the presence of an intimate and confiding relationship, one of trust, in which feelings can be shared whether or not sexual intimacy occurs.

As we consider the strength and power of intimacy, we need to heal the most pervasive and damaging rupture in the human family, the rupture between the sexes. The foundation for more intimate relations between men and women is being laid today in many places and in many ways. Progress is being made, and there is much hope. The borders of the shared worlds of men and women are being enlarged, but there is a long way to go.

Aids to Developing True Intimacy

Sex education is a part of that growth toward true intimacy. But sex education needs to be *sexuality* education. It needs to be *intimacy* education. Too much sex education still deals largely with how babies are made, diseases to be avoided, or how to produce orgasms. Acquiring loving habits and attitudes and acquiring the capacity for true intimacy requires more than a study of the technology of arousal. It requires, first and foremost, the understanding that genital relationships are not even required for the experience of intimacy. Single celibate people can fulfill all the criteria for experiencing true intimacy.

For many of us, a Christian worldview is an essential, enabling, and invigorating aspect, providing promise for the future. This Christian worldview values the renewal of Christian family life, the development of true human intimacy, and the nurturing of mature faith in a church community. Such a worldview can help us resist the pressures of our consumer society and focus on what matters most in life: love for God and for each other.

We all need to experience intimacy at all stages of our lives. In the discovery of true intimacy, we have the possibility for a new era in male-female relationships, in family relationships, in all human relationships, and in the possibility for world peace. Developing truly intimate relationships is a worthwhile goal for all people.

Discussion Questions

1. Can the ability to be tender, sensitive, honest, and vulnerable be taught and learned? How?
2. How does having shared values make all the ingredients of intimacy more attainable?
3. What convinces us that it is safe to risk disclosing our innermost thoughts and selves to another person?
4. A couple is married thirty-plus years, and the husband declares he is no longer committed to this relationship. What is wrong with this picture? How would you counsel the couple?
5. What steps might be taken to heal the rupture between the sexes?
6. Some men have difficulty expressing their emotions. Can they be helped to do this better? How?

4

The Gift and Its Youngest Recipients

James H. Ritchie Jr.

"In the beginning when God created the heavens and the earth." With these words of introduction, the ancient storyteller deftly crafts a mental image of that which existed before all that exists ever existed. No modest task for one limited to a post-creation perspective! Taking advantage of the artistic medium at hand, God fashions creation from limitless supplies of *chaos*—the "formless void," "darkness," and "the deep"—as only God can, making all things from nothing.

Chaos Tamed, Diversity Introduced

As the Spirit-wind of God blows across the surface of this swirling, churning, lifeless, disordered sameness, chaos tingles with anticipation at the touch of God's own life-giving breath. A single word breaks the primordial silence and simultaneously births diversity. "Light!" says the Creator to what had heretofore been exclusively dark. Day and night take form, and God then envisions a great dome called "sky." Above this dome collect waters that will become the rain. Below collect waters that form rivers and oceans—the domestication of chaos! Light and dark, waters above and below: diversity expands dramatically.

The division of land and sea brings even more variation with the first yield of vegetation—food for wildlife yet to come. The sun, moon, and stars mark the days, months, and years, establishing a rhythm for waking and sleeping. With these crucial elements in place, animals are introduced into the ecology, filling seas, skies, and then the dry land. Diversity explodes!

With all now ready, the Creator fashions one more being—one marked with the creative genius that serves to distinguish it from all other beings, the creative genius that identifies it with its source. In Genesis 2 a second story describes how the individual components of this magnificently diverse creation each deserve a name to acknowledge and celebrate their uniqueness and their God-pronounced goodness. Using the gift of godly imagination, the human one creates those names and, with the naming, accepts the role of steward and the responsibility for the well-being of creation.

Children: Closest to Creation

The newness of children positions them closest to this grand, creative enterprise. Not long ago, *they* were the formless void that occupied the darkness and deep waters of the womb over which the Spirit-wind moved and called forth life. That life, at first, paralleled all other life. Crocodile and crustacean, mammoth and mole, hyacinth and human—in their beginning, each life form resembles all others as a female and a male cell unite and initiate the reproductive process.

With each division of that merger of cells, both category and contrast emerge to reveal their unique genetic essence. The seemingly chaotic, formless cluster of cells takes on distinctive form. Soon the gills and tails that link us to the rest of God's creation disappear, and a human shape emerges. Before long we are called into the light, given a name, and begin the movement toward the possibility that we ourselves might become life-initiators and name-givers.

While animals are limited to questions such as *What is this? Haven't I seen, heard, smelled, or tasted this before?* and *How do I get it?* humans can offer an unending string of inquiries. *What do you call this? How are babies made? Why do I look different from other people? Why do I look different than I did six months ago? How did I get here? Why do I exist? What is the deal with all this hair in places that never had hair before?*

As they ponder, question, and explore, each child has both the need and the right to know two interrelated truths regarding the gift of his or her birth. The first is the awesome miracle of his or her being and the second is his or her singular contribution to the diversity of the human race and of God's creation. Each of us is the product of the paring of two specific reproductive cells—one out of hundreds of thousands of ova stored inside the ovaries and one out of billions of sperm generated inside the testicles. Had another ovum released from our mother's ovary been the one fertilized, or had any other sperm managed to win the race and make it all the way inside the ovum, the DNA of the new life conceived could have been completely different.

Going back to the miracle of our being, so many conditions had to be right for the union of sperm and ovum to take place. When the union *does* happen, more often than not the ensuing rapid division of cells fails to result in a sustainable pregnancy, and even then there are no guarantees that the pregnancy will lead to parenthood. Timing is everything in the great reproductive drama. Every entrance and every exit is both tenuous and crucial.

That we made it into the world at all and that we are who we are needs to be celebrated. Telling children how special they are has become clichéd and, in their ears, either patronizing or an indication of some kind of privilege. Telling children that they are who they are because of a specific divine plan can backfire in any number of situations. Who wants to hear that a loving and/or omnipotent God has a purpose and would intentionally design a significantly flawed body or brain? Tell them the details of how human life comes to be and of the odds against their being. Tell them of the odds against their being who they are and then assure them that God was fully prepared to love them no matter which sperm and which ovum merged to mark their beginning, and to welcome them into the community of faith.

When and Why?

Just as crucial as the timing that brought us into the world is the timing of our families and our communities of faith as they take up the task of teaching about this miracle and about how male and female bodies mature so that they might also have a chance at bringing new lives into the world, nurturing them into lives of faith, and faithfully transforming the world in the process.

In the absence or delay of such teaching, our culture rushes in to fill the resulting vacuum. Without the broader and more godly perspective, individualism seeps in and threatens us with a return to the formless void/chaos/sameness. When life is all about "me" and not about "we," each person becomes a law unto herself or himself. Without the broader, more godly perspective, culture steps in to offer a substitute mode of organization: stereotypes. Stereotypes set up categories that narrowly define who "we" are or who "they" are, putting forth the lie that to know *one* thing about a person is to know *everything* and to know exactly what to expect from that person in the future.

Today we hear more often the word *profiling*, typically used with respect to race, ethnicity, or national origin—a "you've seen one, you've seen them all" mentality. This is precisely how stereotypes operate to reduce the uniqueness that is you and the uniqueness that is me—a uniqueness with which the Creator gifted us and celebrated as "good," long before the culture suggested that diversity is to be avoided rather than embraced.

Sexual stereotyping suggests that all males are the same and all females are the same. Each gender has its characteristic "package" or "profile" as to appearance, abilities, and preferences. Deviation from the "norm" leads to ostracism and harassment. "The opposite sex," a seemingly innocent designation by one gender of the other, serves to reinforce the stereotype, focusing on the differences between the sexes rather than on the commonalities, and setting them in *opposition* to one another. Males and females are not the same, but the genders are more alike than they are different.

Focusing on shared characteristics is not, however, good business. Placing boundaries on what constitutes masculinity or femininity—what makes a male "all boy" or a "real man," or a female "all woman" or a "real girly girl" expands the potential market for almost all goods and services—especially when we begin to establish those boundaries in the minds of children at an early age. Those same boundaries place our children at risk and make them vulnerable. When the "ideal" is drawn so narrowly that few have any hope of ever matching it, we place our children at risk. They strive for the unattainable and feel a sense of failure and even self-loathing when they do not match the stereotype, or they become prey to abusers who pick up on low self-esteem and position themselves to offer a manipulative affirmation that provides abusers with sexual access to these children.

Early in my two decades of teaching preteens about human sexuality, I believed that I was seeing signs suggesting that stereotyping was in decline. In more recent years I have come to realize that our cultural stereotypes are alive and well. Why should they not be when they are fed on such a regular basis? Product manufacturers and advertisers must create a market for their products. Unable to isolate a real need, they fabricate one. Can people live well without the newest, the fastest, the largest, the sexiest, the easiest, or the most enjoyable? Of course they can. So persons with a new product to market must convince others that what is true—our ability to live full, complete, successful, meaningful, enjoyable, godly lives *without* their product—is actually a lie.

Sex is central to marketing strategy. Marketers have to take control of the public understanding of who represents the embodiment of sexuality or sensuality—what the artificially defined "we" ought to all strive to be. The more people who are left out of that representation or who are distanced from that masculine or feminine ideal, the greater the market and the greater potential for sales. What are *real* men and *real* women wearing? What scent identifies a person with masculinity or femininity? Where do sexy persons vacation? What communication devices are they using? What games do they play? Where are they working? What movies or television shows do they see? What music do they listen to? What or where do they eat? Where do they live? How do they talk? What appliances do they purchase? Where do they get their educations? Marketers' task is made so much easier when they can market to feminine and masculine stereotypes rather than to individual persons.

Competing for Children's Hearts and Minds

This is the cultural context into which our children are born. If we do not assist them in filtering the messages with which they are going to be inundated from a very early age, we surrender to that culture. Simply put, we are competing for our children's hearts and minds, and doing so with a significant handicap. We grow weary at the thought of competing with the bombardment of fast-paced, multisensory promises of instant gratification. At the same time, we grow dissatisfied when the church fails to support us in presenting an engaging alternative to what the culture offers. While the church debates what to say and what to do about sexuality, the cultural message—with all its proverbial ducks in a row—grows louder and ever more seductive.

Like many jokes, the oft-repeated witticism "Sex is dirty, save it for the one you love" evokes a self-knowing kind of laughter—a recognition of the kind of double message of which our culture and church are guilty. Consider other mixed messages children receive on a regular basis.

- You are God's good creation, but please do not ask about how you were created.
- It is okay to listen to or tell jokes about sex—using all the accompanying slang terminology—but do not try to have a serious conversation using those seldom-used, unfamiliar, uncomfortable, and embarrassing proper terms. (And note which vocabulary is rated by our culture as "adult.")
- Be yourself but do it by looking like everyone else of your gender, dressed in what the current trendsetters establish as being the most attractive "you" or the most masculine or feminine "you."
- On one hand, being "adult" means embracing responsibility, thinking rationally, caring for others, observing moral boundaries, and embracing a mature faith. On the other hand, being "adult" means reading graphic literature, seeing movies and television shows and playing video games that glorify both violence and sex, wearing provocative fashions, drinking alcoholic beverages, using tobacco products, engaging in sexual behaviors, and often making the decision to abandon the faith of one's childhood. This behavior is what our culture has labeled "adult."

Where do young people learn to manage this paradox? They learn from their parents—those who have been gifted with the privilege of naming them. This education takes place with or without intentional guidance. Despite embarrassment, guilt, discomfort, and feelings of inadequacy, parents do not have the luxury of opting out of their role as the primary sex educators for their sons and daughters. Regardless of their skill or comfort level, parents will inevitably teach their children about appropriate and inappropriate attitudes toward sexuality simply by either accepting or avoiding this parental responsibility.

Even when parents are silent, they are under the scrutiny

of their children. Sons and daughters observe how parents relate to one another based on gender and how parents relate to other persons of their own and of the other gender. They listen to conversations and pick out references that are overtly sexual or have sexual overtones. They are aware of parents' attitudes toward and care for their own bodies. They observe the dating behaviors of widowed, formerly married, or never-married parents. They watch how parents react to sexual comments, behavior, and innuendo in movies and on television, and to blatantly sexual marketing ploys.

In the absence of conversation that intentionally responds to what has been heard, read, or seen, sexuality becomes part of the null curriculum—what we teach by omission. Silence teaches that *sex* falls into the category of uncomfortable, inappropriate, and outside the bounds of family conversation. The *culture* can speak of it; the church and the family cannot.

When the Silence Is Broken

The silence around the gift of our sexuality can be broken in many ways. Sometimes young persons' curiosity or anxiety gets the best of them, and they recklessly speak the unspeakable or dare to ask the unaskable. When not reduced to a cautionary tale, a teen pregnancy can serve as an effective, if not desirable, discussion starter. The onset of menstruation can force the conversation because it cannot in good conscience be overlooked. Horror stories told by older adult women, who, in the absence of information, interpreted their first menses as a symptom of imminent death, are evidence of what that silence can do. The sexual victimization of a child means that silence is no longer an option.

Nocturnal emissions *can* prompt a talk between parents and sons but far too often they are simply ignored, leaving puzzled and/or mortified sons to assume that (a) they are losing control over their bodies, (b) they are the only ones ever to have experienced this phenomenon, or (c) parents are too uninformed to realize what is happening or too squeamish to address evidence of their sons' sexual maturation. Those uninformed or squeamish parents are content to play along with their sons' assumptions, since wet dreams, unlike the onset of a menstrual period, seldom happen during seventh-grade geography class.

The revelation of homosexual orientation or activity on the part of a neighbor, Sunday school teacher, middle school guidance counselor, or scout leader can stir things up and prompt conversation. Parental infidelity has the same potential. That very uncomfortable moment when a child walks in on parents engaged in sexual intercourse or when parents walk in on a child engaged in masturbation or in sexual activity with a friend can occasion an invitation to talk—once heads have cleared and reason has been restored. Being teased about the presence (or absence) of preteen pubic hair or early breast development is yet another opportunity for unanticipated circumstances to break the silence.

Or we can approach the subject of sexuality in a more intentional fashion. We even can be *proactive* if we time things right. What is the right timing? In a perfect world, conversations begin *before* becoming parents, if parenthood is in one's future. Even if one's life course is not aimed toward becoming a parent, he or she is still a sexual and social being who will need to learn to deal with personal sexual issues and possibly be the kind of person to whom young people turn when they cannot bring themselves to talk with their parents. Healthy attitudes about ourselves as male or female can facilitate conversation. Even if we are not all on the "parent track," the world will benefit from adults who are comfortable with themselves and with their sexuality and therefore less susceptible to sexual marketing ploys.

Intentionally breaking the silence begins with the recognition that sexuality, without exception, is a key component of the identity of every human being. As James Nelson states, "Sexuality is a sign, a symbol, and a means of our call to communication and communion. . . . The mystery of our sexuality is the mystery of our need to reach out to embrace others both physically and spiritually" (Nelson: 18). We cannot attain spiritual maturity—loving God with all our heart, soul, strength, and mind and loving our neighbor as though he or she was close enough to *be* us, while ignoring our sexuality.

Unless we value ourselves as God's good creation, our sexuality as God's good gift, and our individual uniqueness as a precious response to God's passion for diversity, we will find ourselves seriously limited as we attempt to convey these values to our children.

In the Beginning

Parents are curious—and often anxious—about how much information and what information their children need to have and about the age at which they need to have it. In most cases, parents see the instruction regarding sexuality they themselves received as limited and their preparation for passing it on inadequate. They generally want to do a better job with their children but are unclear as to how to begin.

1. Know and grow. It begins with a knowledge upgrade. Parents who are confident with their basic understanding of the male and female reproductive systems, puberty, reproduction, and relationships are going to be better equipped to respond to questions raised by their children. In addition to having answers, their ease in responding will communicate that family is a natural setting for conversations about sex and sexuality. A question that a parent is unable to answer speaks to the awesome complexity of human sexuality and presents an opportunity to instruct children as to where they can go for answers. "That is a really good question. I do not know the answer, but I am wondering about that too. How about if we find the answer together? Where do you think we should start?" is an excellent parent response when stumped.

Deborah W. Haffner has three superb books published by Newmarket Press that I highly recommend: *Beyond the Big*

Talk: Every Parent's Guide to Raising Sexually Healthy Teens—From Middle School to High School and Beyond (2002); *From Diapers to Dating: A Parent's Guide to Raising Sexually Healthy Children—From Infancy to Middle School* (2004); and *What Every 21st-Century Parent Needs to Know: Facing Today's Challenges with Wisdom and Heart* (2008). She speaks with great openness and with the sensitivity of one who is both a parent and a pastor as well as being a nationally recognized voice for sexual health and justice.

Justin Richardson and Mark A. Schuster, a pair of pediatricians, have written *Everything You Never Wanted Your Children to Know About Sex (But Were Afraid They'd Ask)*, which is another excellent resource (Three Rivers Press, 2003). These books are ones that should keep parents several steps ahead of their sons' and daughters' questions.

Among the books I recommend for parents and children to be reading together are those written by Lynda Madaras, also published by Newmarket Press: *On Your Mark, Get Set, Grow: A "What's Happening to My Body?" Book for Younger Boys* (2008); *Ready, Set, Grow: A "What's Happening to My Body?" Book for Younger Girls* (2003); *The What's Happening to My Body Book for Boys: A Growing Up Guide for Parents and Sons* (2007); and *The What's Happening to My Body Book for Girls: A Growing Up Guide for Parents and Daughters* (2007). Specifically targeting the preteen/parent audience and doing so from a faith perspective is *Created by God: Tweens, Faith, and Human Sexuality*, a book I have written and revised for Abingdon Press (2009).

The Internet can provide very helpful resources, but be cautious and verify the source of information. For persons of faith, investigate what your denomination is publishing on the subject. Where offered, family participation in educational events in the church is especially helpful in the opening of lines of communication and in grounding the subject of human sexuality in Scripture and faith tradition. The aforementioned *Created by*

God is one such resource with a student book, parent booklet, and leader resources for conducting a six-session study in the church for preteens and their parents. After taking more than two thousand young persons and their parents through the program, I can personally attest to the effectiveness of this kind of guided experience for families.

The mystery of human sexuality can engage us for many, many years. There will always be more to know, more to understand. With the constant multiplication of challenges to a faithful approach to sexuality, committing ourselves to continual growth is a wise choice.

2. The diaper test. For those with more acute olfactory senses, this will be more difficult than for those with a less-developed sense of smell, but treating babies during a diaper change as though they are the primary source of the world's toxic waste is bound to have an effect on their self-esteem. *It's dirty, I produced it, therefore it stands to reason that I must be dirty and my body must be bad.* If one parent is more tolerant than the other, the child will believe that she or he has done something to displease the less tolerant one. General discomfort with the changing process will leave the child with the impression that he or she has done something wrong. Since exposure of the genitals is part of the changing process, there must be something wrong with the genitals. Treating changing time as something normal and something being done out of care for the baby teaches self-acceptance. Bowel movements happen, thank goodness, and we deal with them.

3. Watch your language. I spend a lot of time as I teach defending the use of proper terms for body parts and functions. Parents are overwhelmed by words they have never themselves become comfortable using and kids often consider those terms "gross." I suspect that this is because they are unfamiliar with all the vocabulary, intimidated by the volume of words, and victimized by a culture that promotes the provocative and evades the educational.

Young persons ask me how they can get more comfortable with the language of sexuality, and I always respond by encouraging them to practice using the words. Most of us are challenged by learning a second language, especially when we are expected to speak it aloud. Comfort comes only through repeated use of that language. So it is with proper sexual terminology.

The use of childish euphemisms means that terms must eventually be unlearned and replaced—generally at the point when "pee-pees" and "hoo-hoos" start getting larger, more sensitive, and sprout hair. Exchanging one set of euphemisms for another (replacing childish designations for genitals with slang terminology) seems to many an easier course than shifting to proper terms. Using the proper terms from the beginning eliminates the awkward and difficult leap later. Grandma and the next door neighbor will just have to deal with hearing the words *vulva* and *penis* coming from a four-year-old.

4. Talk with children repeatedly about sexuality. Having one big talk might be better than nothing, but not much better. Open, ongoing conversation with parents has the greatest influence on young persons' avoidance of at-risk behaviors, including sexual activity. Children *want* to hear from their parents, even when their attitudes, body language, and words suggest otherwise. Peer pressure and cultural pressure may be loud and powerful, but children are attuned to their parents' voices and are more vulnerable when those voices are silent.

Unfortunately, many parents assume that it is a lost cause and give up too soon. As a parent, I have been astounded at the messages our three sons both heard and retained at times I was convinced they were not listening. So we need to keep talking even when we do not get immediate responses.

Recognize that memories can be tender. What our children are going through as their sexuality emerges prior to and during adolescence can very easily touch on sensitive recollections of our own experiences—some that we might be reluctant to revisit. We recoil at flashbacks to scenes of our ignorance exposed, of parents' fumbling attempts to talk with us or total avoidance of communication on sexual matters, of being the victim of sexual abuse, or perhaps of sexual activities when we were young or prior to marriage that we look back on with regret. Painful as they may be, those memories can build bridges to our children. Our willingness to remember the challenges associated with "coming of age" and to expose our vulnerability may give them the opening they need to do likewise.

Clearly communicate your values and beliefs regarding sexuality. Do not assume that children are aware of your views on such issues as dating, attire, language, sexual activity, contraception, sexual orientation, and pornography. Be specific. Do not make them guess what you are trying to say. However, do not see yourself as a guest lecturer. You want your children to have a clear picture of who you are and to whom they are relating, but the objective is to keep the lines of communication open.

Know that children have questions about sexuality. You might not have heard them, but the questions are there. When children are given the opportunity to ask and feel that it is safe to do so—meaning that they will not be laughed at or judged for their questions—they *will* ask their questions. Assume that they come with some information—regardless of how accurate it might be. Establish a starting point with leading questions such as, *What have you heard about . . . ? What do you think about . . . ? What have you read about . . . ?* They need to know that you respect what they bring to the conversation.

5. Focus on intimacy as something they can say yes to at any age. While there are many who think that "just say no" says it all, it is a very negative approach to something that God has declared positive and good. God's desire is that we live in an intimate relationship with God and with one another. Remember the Spirit/breath of God moving across the face of the deep? God is all about closeness, all about intimacy. Our sexuality, as it draws us into and helps to shape our relationships, serves as a clear indication of God's intent.

Unfortunately, our culture inaccurately uses the word *intimacy* as a euphemism or substitute for "sexual intercourse." Coming from the Latin *intimus* meaning "closest," the word *intimacy* refers to a close friendship that is founded on and nurtures qualities such as trust, honesty, openness, listening, caring, compassion, commitment, sensitivity, communication, confidentiality, patience, and respect. These qualities are ones that we might see evidence of and work to develop in any of our relationships. Intimate friends are comfortable with one another. The expression of emotions is safe in that context. Intimacy cultivates a sense of selflessness where we learn to put another's needs before our own.

Intimacy takes time. In a culture with an increasing demand for immediate gratification, sexual activity seems a much easier sell. So how do we get our children to see the blessing and buy into the wisdom of intimacy? They must get a taste of it. They must experience it for themselves. Where? In the home and in the church. When intimacy is modeled in these two arenas, children are better equipped to nurture it elsewhere.

Sexual activity, when paired with intimacy and commitment, is a gift. However, sexual activity is a poor substitute for intimacy. When sexual activity becomes the focus in a relationship, intimacy struggles to survive.

When we guide our children in the direction of intimacy, we guide them toward God. Children who are part of intimate circles at home, in the church, and with their friends have access to the kind of support that they will need when hormones begin raging, reason is clouded, and chaos stands ready to reassert itself.

Discussion Questions

1. What do you remember as being the best and the worst parts of growing up—especially into and through adolescence?

2. What are your earliest memories of being aware of sexuality?
3. What was the first sex-related question that you can remember asking, and what response did you get?
4. As you were growing up, were there adults other than your parents to whom you could turn when you had a sex-related question?
5. How might the church most effectively support families in the process of cultivating healthy sexual attitudes?

The Gift and Nurturing Adolescents

Barbara J. Meyer

Having examined the scriptural and human contexts of sexuality and intimacy as integral to God's good gift to us, God's beloved children, we are ready to discuss more fully how we pass on our understandings of this beautiful but sometimes consternating gift to the young folks among us. How can we talk about this gift with those whose care is entrusted to us in the church?

As a community-based family practice physician and a lover of God, I come to this question with a sense that the Christian church in most of our denominations has largely failed up until now. Both my experience and my observation are that much of our sexuality education, whether in churches or in homes, has been fear-based and has consisted mostly of vague and threatening prohibitions. As Keith Graber Miller sometimes tells his students in a human sexuality class at Goshen College, "The convoluted message we often send as parents and church leaders is, 'Sexuality is a dirty, disgusting thing, so you should save it for someone you love.'"

This is unfortunate for several reasons. First, it has not prevented what we sought to prevent: unwanted pregnancies, unnecessary broken hearts and wounded spirits, abortions, and sexually transmitted infections among young people. Second, it has not communicated what we want to communicate: what we really believe about sexuality, which has been so beautifully described in the foregoing chapters of this book.

The adolescents we love often are confused and frustrated

by what we say and even more poorly served by our over-whelming silence. They are hearing lots about their sexuality elsewhere—and much of it is unhelpful and potentially damaging. The goal of this chapter is to encourage pastors, parents, and youth leaders to engage young people in conversation about sexuality. If we believe that the church has something to say about the role of intimacy in our lives and the ways our sexuality is lived, we need to be willing to take some risks in real conversations. What we say will not always be perfect—and we will not like everything we hear back.

The gift of sexuality is not neat and tidy. Our feelings and ideas about our sexuality are often hard to identify and express. But if we fail to listen and share from our experiences, we will have lost a time-limited opportunity with each of our young people, since the church will seem irrelevant to this (and other) important parts of their lives.

Fortunately, young people are amazingly forgiving and flexible with us when we try to be honest and helpful about something we all agree is important. They are ready for con-versation and want to get better at talking about these issues too. By talking about sexuality in the context of the church, we demonstrate to adolescents and to ourselves our belief that our bodies and minds and spirits are meant to be integrated—that they were lovingly created this way. Integrative work in this area is part of the redeeming work of the body of Christ.

The topics that need to be addressed with young people in the church include many of the topics addressed in the other chapters of this book, particularly those involving understand-ings around intimacy and healthy human relationships. We will not take space here to reiterate what is written elsewhere. But those of us who want to be discussing these ideas with young people need to take time to become comfortable and familiar with these ideas, so that we can talk about them in an infor-mal, straight-forward way that will speak to our audience. The intent of this chapter is to set a positive tone, to present some ideas of how we most helpfully can share these with the young people among us, and to name some specific issues of particular interest to adolescents in their developmental stage.

Ideally, as many people as possible in the congregation will be involved in talking with young people about sexuality, because all have important perspectives and stories to share. But it may make more sense to start the conversation with those who are most comfortable with these subjects either by virtue of personality, vocation, or experience in life. My professional background in anatomy and human development, as well as having lots of experience talking with people about various aspects of their sexuality, has been helpful; so I may be able to help get discussions started in a no-nonsense way. Clearly, however, the conversation must not begin and end with the professionals in the congregation.

Here are some helpful ground rules to keep in mind when engaging young people in conversations about sexuality:

- *Always tell the truth*. Young people have especially sensitive "feelers" for hypocrisy and fakeness. If you do not know something, say so. This does not call for over-disclosure, but it is very powerful to speak honestly from personal experience, whether it is exciting or not. Our message is compromised if we prattle platitudes or rules we do not really believe ourselves. ˙
- *Do not talk down*. We may be surprised with what young people know and understand. Ask open-ended questions and listen. Invite them to write anonymous questions and responses. Their openness is amazing when they believe they are being heard and believe they will not be jumped on for asking the questions they actually have. Be matter-of-fact and straightforward. It is all right to be surprised, but being shocked about someone's sharing is usually not helpful.
- *Have an agenda*. Be open, transparent, and unapologetic about it. At the same time, listen carefully to where our

agenda differs from that of our conversation partners. What they value and want to talk about matters too.
* *Base the conversations on these criteria:*
    1. Accurate information
    2. A call to wholeness and integrated sexuality
    3. A message of grace

The bottom line is that adolescents are sexual beings; living in denial about this has not worked. If we would be willing to actively engage with people from childhood to maturity around issues of sexuality lived responsibly and joyfully, we could have a more complete message of healing and hope to offer the world.

Understanding True Intimacy

All of us need and hunger for intimacy: to be known for who we are and to be loved as that person. For most young people, those who know and love them best are probably their families and close friends. These are people with whom they have non-romantic relationships. This is as it should be, and we hope that we will all have nonromantic, intimate relationships throughout our lives.

Physical Intimacy in a Romantic Relationship

Our culture tends toward shortcuts, especially to important, desirable things like intimacy. But healthy bodies and spirits revolt if we try to cut corners. If we push too fast in a relationship, we will experience a self-protective pulling back. All of us probably have felt this happen in some situation and know the truth of this for ourselves. It is not only in romantic relationships that we may share something of a more personal nature than the intimacy level of the relationship justifies, or we are the recipients of that kind of sharing. The gap between the intimacy of the disclosure and what the relationship can bear can lead to hurt feelings, misunderstandings, or unhealthy patterns of relating.

In a healthy relationship, the physical relationship will be a manifestation of the intimacy level of the other elements of the relationship—the emotional, intellectual, and spiritual aspects. Our bodies are how we express externally what is happening inside. As adults, we want more than simply keeping young people from having sex inappropriately. What we really want is healthy relationships for them. We all know people who are involved in physical relationships that go far beyond the true intimacy level of the relationship. But I would argue that when the church encourages couples not to allow their physical relationship to develop in conjunction with the intimacy level of their emotional relationship, this also is a problem and represents a misunderstanding of the role of healthy sexuality.

As a young person, I was told of a single, older woman in a Mennonite community who was marrying a similarly aged widower. The woman had never been married and was heard to note at the time of her wedding service that she had never so much as kissed a man in her life. She meant this, I believe, as a statement of her sexual purity and was proud of the fact. But it horrified me to hear it. The idea that anyone in the church would condone the practice of developing an intimate, emotional relationship to the point of marriage, without encouraging the appropriate growth of a physical relationship, seemed out of kilter to me. I never heard how this couple fared after their wedding, but I can imagine many less-than-helpful ramifications of the unnatural stilting of their intimacy walk during courtship. I was particularly bothered by the woman's decision in light of the unevenness of the couple's levels of previous sexual experience: the man had been married for years. The best I can hope is that they were willing to go very slowly with the development of their physical relationship after their marriage since, apparently, they had not allowed themselves a normal courtship beforehand. We can laugh at this extreme example, since it is unlikely to be a problem for most of us.

A much more common phenomenon in the church occurs

when young people are told year after year, or at least are led to understand without words, that sexual relating is "bad, dirty, wrong." All through courtship, they may be warned in more or less subtle terms about the evils of sex. Then suddenly after the wedding they get a different message: "Sex is a gift from God. Enjoy!" Most of us cannot go suddenly from *forbidden* to *blessed* without some transition time. Do we really want to burden new marriages with this kind of agenda? If, instead, we treat physical sexual relating appropriately as a growing outward expression of the true intimacy of the relationship, we can improve the health of our bodies, spirits, and relationships all through our lives.

It may be interesting for young people to consider that married people also would do well to ask themselves, "What might it mean for our covenant relationship if we continued to consider our sexual relationship as an outgrowth of the ongoing intimacy in other aspects of our relationship?" While marital intimacy will not be a primary focus of our conversation with young people, fostering a sense of the intergenerational nature of many of the truths we are discussing enriches the conversation for everyone and helps us all remember that expressing our sexuality well is a lifelong journey.

The Intimacy Walk Continuum

In talking with young people about sexuality, it is helpful to place specific behaviors on a continuum. By placing something on a continuum, we adults are not saying that behaviors have to come in the order they are placed or that we are recommending any of them to adolescents. We just need a place to start if we are going to have practical conversation, and this is a possible spectrum.

So we could start with a spectrum of behaviors that looks like this:

holding hands → kissing → sensual touch → lying together → intentional orgasm → genital intercourse

As relationships move from left to right, this is a spectrum of increasing vulnerability and, therefore, increasing risk to both people involved in several ways. In general, as a couple moves along this continuum there is an increasing inner desire for relationship security (meaning that the partner will still be there tomorrow) and exclusivity (meaning that the partner is not engaging in these same behaviors with other people at the same time).

Several other things happen in moving to the right on the continuum: in general, partners have more body contact (in terms of surface area) and fewer clothes between them (and fewer other people around).

Many more behaviors could be added here, including normal, healthy "pre-romantic" activities. In earlier times there was "walk-a-mile," square dancing, and back rubs at young people's retreats. Today young people would identify high-school dances or sitting piled together on a couch at youth meetings. The idea is simply to notice that there are many important, enjoyable, and developmentally appropriate points along an intimacy spectrum.

We could also point out that "sensual touch," which is given a point on the spectrum, encompasses a range of behaviors. I chose this term in place of "petting" or "feeling up"—terms from my youth that sound objectifying, devoid of emotional and relational warmth. The term "sensual touch" is here to represent more general touching of each other's bodies, but while both members are clothed and not intending to bring their partner to climax.

Putting a few behaviors on a spectrum opens interesting opportunities for conversation. For example, it becomes clear that in order to move along this spectrum in a healthy way, both members of the couple need to be able to talk about what they are experiencing and how they are feeling—and to listen to the other person's experience and feelings with respect. Leaders can point out that if this is not possible, this probably indicates that the couple is at an inappropriate place on the physical spectrum for their relationship.

Here are a few other points worth making in a discussion about behaviors on the spectrum with young people:

1. *Building intimacy takes time.* Respect and enjoy each stage fully rather than rush blindly to whatever is next. Something important is being built here. How one treats one's self and one's partner matters tremendously. Remember, there is a lot to master in the early points on the spectrum, and a lot to savor. Let us not let excellence in handholding become obsolete!

2. *Recognize the power of hormones.* Make decisions in thoughtful moments of conversation and contemplation, not in the passionate heat of the moment. Age matters, and young people have powerful hormones. Do not underestimate that. What this means practically is that it makes the most sense to "draw the line" earlier rather than later, until it is possible to stop comfortably where desired.

3. *Needs and dangers may be very different for each partner.* There is a tremendous range of "normal" drive in both males and females. There is no good reason to push the boundaries. A situation that is comfortable, not pushing boundaries too much, for one person may be experienced quite differently by the partner. These differences will be known only by talking about them together. Also, it probably is not helpful to push things as far as one can, so that stopping becomes a recurring tension in the relationship. The physical aspect of the relationship should not dominate and distract from the growth of other aspects.

4. *Distrust urgency.* (This one is a corollary of several others). It is easy to feel as though a certain situation creates a "now or never" scenario. That should be a red flag. If one partner is feeling pressured, this suggests that her or his best interests are not being valued by the other partner at the moment. A growing relationship

will continue to grow. One does not need to worry that a particular behavior has to happen now. While different choices can be made the next time, one cannot undo something he or she wishes had not been done.

5. *Talk to God about the relationship.* The level of comfort experienced as this is done and the response one "hears" can be another good check and balance on decisions.

6. *Whether part of a couple or not, make it a practice to hang out in larger groups.* Healthy relationships happen in a community setting—a community of helpful and loving friends and family gives us support and feedback on how we seem in relationships. This is especially true in a dating relationship. Trusted adults to turn to for good relationship advice can be a big help with the intensity of the feelings and impulses of romance. We also get helpful information when we see how our partner treats others and us in a group setting.

God Knows Us and Is Gracious

After presenting the above information to a group of young people, a young woman expressed concern that I spent so much time talking about the ideals of healthy sexual relating that she hardly could connect with what I was describing. What she saw being lived out all around her at school and in the world seemed to have little or nothing in common with what I was saying. She thought listening to this talk felt alienating. All the unhealthy sexual stereotypes and outright abusive situations and power imbalances that she was aware of made this vision seem far away and impossible.

As adults, we need to be aware of this possible dynamic with young people (and adults) when we have conversations about sexuality in church settings. We need to be very clear that our God is in the business of meeting us right where we are. God loves us as we are and desires our healing and our increasing wholeness over time. We do not come to God pristine and perfect. Life is messy and not fair—and God knows that. The point of presenting ideals and guiding principles is to help us steer, not to give us another weapon to use against ourselves or each other.

Back to the Intimacy Walk

Where does this leave adolescents on the continuum, as dating young people? Using the thought process we have developed so far, this will vary depending on several factors, including the maturity of the partners and the commitment level of the relationship. But it is important for us to be specific in discussing reasons to have "stopping points" at various places along the spectrum.

One example that has received far too little attention in our conversations about sexuality in the church has to do with the great vulnerability increase that happens on the physical behaviors spectrum before intentional orgasm. A description that may be useful to young people is that coming to orgasm with a partner is allowing one's self to be *emotionally* naked with her or him. It is not to any of our advantage to learn to do this lightly, because much of the value and intensity of sexual relating is lost if it is detached from emotional vulnerability. In other words, once one learns to separate physical intimacy from emotional intimacy, it is not easy to relink them—and this seriously hampers full enjoyment of sexual relating for males and females alike.

We can also point out that there is a way in which people add value to certain experiences by being very selective about how and when they are experienced. We do not wear tuxes and prom dresses every day—thank goodness! Neither do we eat Thanksgiving dinner every week. Special things are special partly because we are selective about how we choose to experience them. Intentional orgasm in a relationship requires a high level of security and exclusivity.

Of course, the more commonly discussed stopping point is the one before genital intercourse. I was frustrated as an adolescent that most church-related commentary on sexual relating implied there was only one decision to make in a physical relationship: "sex" or "no sex." However, as I have spent more time thinking about these questions, I have come to appreciate several reasons, both practical and emotional, why this stopping point gets so much attention. For one, sexual intercourse involves risk of pregnancy. No contraception is perfect. Pregnancy is a huge issue in a relationship, not to mention in the life of the child and the families and communities involved. I used to think of this cut-off as mostly a practical consideration—how to avoid becoming pregnant.

But when it came time for me to decide about intercourse for myself, I realized that taking the chance of pregnancy, even if we used "good" birth control, would change the emotional tone in my relationship with my partner. I did not want us to experience this until we were married.

It is also true that intercourse brings with it more risk of numerous serious infections than we get with almost any other form of physical relating. This is not a risk to be taken lightly. Most of these infections are treatable, but not all are curable; some can put future fertility at risk for women. Young people are very interested in discussing these concerns.

The point in mentioning risk to adolescents is not to be threatening but to talk about consequences rather than damnation. Our God is a God of second chances. We never have to say, "I have blown it now. That seals it for me!" Such an attitude does not reflect how God views or treats us. If we are unhappy with the choices we make once, we get to try again. If any of us experience unwed pregnancy or infections in our relationships, we will try again with extra baggage, and that baggage must be taken seriously. But we need to be clear with young people that it is not too late to do something differently from here on and that nothing we do or think shocks God. At the same time, we are responsible to keep growing and choosing and learning to live honest, healthy sexual lives. Our world desperately needs a message of grace when it comes to sexuality. We in the church need to extend it to ourselves and to others.

When we refer to specific behaviors on the spectrum, the main point to emphasize is that healthy romantic relationships grow with a balance of emotional, intellectual, spiritual, and physical closeness. God prizes relationships above all else: our relationship with God and our relationships with each other. Our physical expressions in general and our sexual expressions in particular are intended to express appropriately the real intimacy and commitment level of the relationship that truly exists in these other realms.

This is not to avoid designating specific stopping points; rather it is to give us a framework that helps us to make good decisions about relationships. If we can place specific questions in the context of the overall health of the relationship, we are in a much better place than if we just go with what seems right at the moment "as long as we do not do X." The ironic part, of course, is that this way of thinking and deciding will probably stop many people earlier on the spectrum than a black-and-white "never do *that*" way of thinking would.

It is important to remind young people that intensity of feeling does *not* replace commitment. Sometimes I am asked, "How do I know if this person is the one?" I have come to realize that part of what prompts this question is this: "If my partner is the one I am going to marry, it is probably all right for us to move through the spectrum faster, right?" Not so! *Especially* when dating one's long-term partner-to-be, there is all the time in the world. It is worth walking the intimacy walk with care and attention. One cannot hurry real intimacy with intensity. Intimacy and intensity dare not be confused.

Oral and Anal Sex as "Safe" Sex?

Missing from this behavioral spectrum are oral and anal sex. Certainly many married adult couples stroll happily along their physical intimacy walk without ever experiencing either. But another reason for their absence is my indecision over where to put them. Oral intercourse, while not carrying the risk of pregnancy, can otherwise surpass the emotional vulnerability of genital intercourse, although it carries a relatively low risk of transmitting infections. Anal intercourse also seems quite vulnerable. It carries a higher risk of transmitting sexual infections than other sexual behaviors, because it tends to cause rectal micro-tears. These attributes do not make either of these behaviors "wrong," but the emotional and physical vulnerability involved with them should be taken very seriously. One should not consider them to be "safe" sex just because they do not cause pregnancy.

Questions from patients and other young people about oral sex are actually part of what prompted me to get involved with sexuality education for young people in the church. The old "no sex until marriage, period" did not give people adequate information about how to care for themselves emotionally or physically around specific issues such as oral intercourse.

As a physician, I see increasing numbers of young women with herpes and human papilloma virus infections (genital warts, abnormal pap smear results, and so on). These can be contracted from oral intercourse and non-intercourse contact. Many affected young people assume they are practicing "safe" sex, because no one has ever talked with them about either the emotional or the physical aspects of various sexual behaviors.

Why Do Adolescents Need to Hear All This?

My goal is to challenge adolescents to become strong, responsible people with healthy relationships rather than simply give them rules to memorize or someone (and something) to push against.

The intimacy needs of most teenagers are actually best met by their families and their close, nonromantic friends, people who know them and love them for who they are. Many never experience true intimacy in a dating relationship, which is very normal developmentally. This is because the purpose of dating for young people in our culture is to have fun and to get to know themselves and each other. Most high-school students in this country will date without thinking seriously about the long-term possibilities of a specific relationship. This is as it should be, as long as they remember what that means for the commitment and intimacy level of the relationship and where it therefore falls on the spectrum of behaviors.

It would be preferable for most teens to experience purely social dating for quite a while before they embark on an intimate dating relationship. Nonetheless, young people are, in fact, making choices about intimacy and sexual behaviors all along the spectrum. And it is clear from both written and spoken responses that they have many questions and concerns that are not being addressed. Adolescents are not too young to be given truthful and detailed information, and they are eager and ready to think about and discuss how this spectrum looks when responsibly lived.

What to Do with "Leftover" Sexual Energy

Let us assume that young people are building healthy, respectful, balanced relationships. They are living healthy sexual lives as singles or, having a partner, they have talked with him or her about the limits they want to respect. What can we recommend to adolescents as healthy outlets for the excess sexual energy that many will have? Here are some points to discuss with adolescents:

1. *Recognize the normalcy of sex drives and the range of what is normal.* Both males and females have a wide range of normal sex drives. Being at either end of the range does not make one perverted or frigid. The important thing is to know one's "normal" and to learn to talk about this with the person with whom physical intimacy is contemplated. Respect the partner enough to believe what she or he says about the experience of sexual drive,

even if it is very different. For example, any person's history of sexual abuse has a profound impact here. Sexual abuse is very common and can interrupt healthy sexual development significantly and long after the abuse is over. Counseling of various types can be very helpful to those with this kind of experience. If abuse has been part of the experience of one of the partners in a relationship, know that it can be too big a burden to try to deal with in the relationship without outside help.

2. *Do not underestimate the power of sexual drives.* I have acquaintances who were living in different states during college. They were dating seriously and were not planning to have intercourse. During a particularly powerful visit, however, they did, and she became pregnant. They married and had the child, and they now have a lovely family. Unplanned intercourse or pregnancy is not necessarily a tragedy. I think this couple made good choices in a difficult situation. But it is not the story they would have chosen. The pregnancy altered both the order and the timeline of the steps they had hoped to take. This can happen to anyone.

3. *If the relationship with a partner is too sexually charged, get out in public.* Talk in a coffee shop instead of in a car or at home. Hang out with other people for a while.

4. *Get physically active, together or separately.* Go for walks or runs, play basketball or soccer. Physical exercise is good for burning all kinds of energy, including sexual energy, and exercise is a lot more pleasant than a cold shower.

5. *Masturbate.* This can be a safe and helpful way of managing leftover sexual energy.

Masturbation/Self-Pleasuring

Guys have to hold their penises to wash them and to urinate from the first day they are learning to use a toilet. This literal "hands-on" stimulation leads quickly and naturally to knowing what feels good to a penis. Besides this, their bodies produce involuntary ejaculations at night (wet dreams), often in response to pleasant erotic dreams. This, too, makes natural connections for guys.

The situation is vastly different for girls. Occasionally a girl may unintentionally notice the pleasantness of physical stimulation of her vulva, but this is much less frequent. A girl may almost never have direct stimulation of her clitoris unless she actually checks it out for herself, which many girls do not do. It is a testimony to girls' sexual interest that many do discover these areas and what feels good to them.

Let me be clear: there is nothing wrong with a person to whom this sounds weird or uninteresting. But also, there is nothing wrong with a person to whom this is interesting, or even helpful. Young people in our groups will be all across this spectrum.

For a variety of reasons, there are very strong feelings against masturbation in many churches. One of these reasons is a concern that masturbation necessarily involves lust. But just as there is a difference between normal hunger and gluttony, there is a difference between healthy sexual interest and lust. Sex and sexuality are God's idea. Our bodies have been called "very good" by our Creator. When we are determining the distinctions between healthy and unhealthy masturbation, we should use the criteria of what is good for building and supporting healthy people and relationships, as we do with other decisions regarding sexual behavior.

If masturbation seems to be taking over someone's interest in place of relationships with other people, this is a problem and needs to be addressed. I do not personally know anyone for whom this has been the case, but it can happen, and we want to be aware of this.

Another concern is that for many people masturbating is accompanied by fantasies and images. This is normal and can be good. People can learn things about themselves by noticing their fantasies. Imaging themselves in healthy relationships is not a bad thing for young people, but we can talk with them about giving some attention to which fantasies they will indulge. A good rule to pass along is to avoid fantasizing about people we know who are not our real partner. It is also important to notice and choose not to dwell on fantasies involving sexual violence or coercion. The rule of what is helpful to real-life healthy relationships is probably a good way to set boundaries in fantasies.

This is where the connection with pornography comes in. And this is a very good reason many people are uncomfortable with masturbation. Many people assume that masturbation will involve the use of pornography.

Pornography, as described very well in chapters 13 and 15, consists of images of people, usually women and sometimes children, used as sexual objects. This means these individuals are robbed of their natural personalities, emotions, and intellects, and used only as images to excite. Adolescents reportedly represent a large portion of those viewing pornography, especially on the Internet. It behooves us as educators of young people to familiarize ourselves with these concerns and address this as part of our sexuality curriculum.

We need to be clear with young people that no one needs pornography to masturbate. We all have better imaginations than that. Healthy masturbation allows imaging of healthy relationships and situations. It can help us learn to know our sexual selves in a safe and private way. This, in turn, can enhance our relationships with others.

Most males *and* most females masturbate at one time or another. It is good for young people to know that masturbation can be a helpful gift in every life phase, right through healthy marriages. People travel away from their spouses. Most couples are not perfectly matched in terms of sexual interest at all times.

Some people marry late in life. Some people's spouses die young. There are many situations when masturbation may be helpful to people. And as suggested in the above list, I believe that feeling free to care for themselves sexually in this way can increase the patience young people have in choosing sexual behaviors wisely.

One last thing about masturbation: I am not aware of any physical dangers from normal masturbation. Use of some foreign objects can change this, and any use of choking or near choking is very dangerous and even fatal.

Sexual Differences Between Women and Men

Another area of conversation that is of interest to adolescents is that of female and male sexual differences. Our maleness or femaleness is intrinsic to who we are, and our hormonal environment has helped to shape our development and our self-understanding from our very first moments of existence. We do not have bodies that are separate from our souls and our minds. So our sexuality, including our gender, is connected to every other part of ourselves, and understanding some common differences can be helpful in our relationships.

Sandra L. Bem, a professor at Cornell University, has been doing research in the social construction of gender and sexuality since the early 1970s. This graph, derived by Bem in the 1970s, shows that there is more to any individual person than stereotypically "feminine" and "masculine" personality or physical characteristics.

Adolescents can identify examples of "manly" men and "feminine" women from popular culture (movies, television, music, and sports) and list their names or some of their characteristics at the appropriate places on the graph. It is easiest to start with these two categories because they are so stereotypical. As we move away from stereotypes and start thinking about ourselves or people we actually know, it becomes apparent that some individual men and women may have a noticeable blend of typically masculine or feminine personality

Masculinity Score

		Below Median	Above Median
	Below Median	Undifferentiated (low-low)	Masculine (low fem.- high masc.)
Femininity Score	**Above Median**	Feminine (high fem.- low masc)	Androgynous (high-high)

Used with permission of the publisher, www.mindgarden.com, from the *Bem Sex Role Inventory*, by Sandra Bem. Copyright © 1978, 1981.

characteristics, while some may have more personality characteristics that are not strongly associated with either gender. This helps us reflect on the variety of people who exist in the world and the amazing combinations of personality traits they each have.

According to Bem, masculinity and femininity are not opposite ends of a single continuum but rather represent two separate continua—shown here as the two axes on the graph. This separates individuals, men and women, into the four quadrants of people shown. An individual person, then, could have mostly high levels of typically feminine-type characteristics (such as nurture and relational connectivity), high levels of mostly typically masculine-type characteristics (such as competitiveness and initiative taking), high levels of a blend of these, or low levels of both "gendered" types of characteristics.

The terms *feminine, masculine, androgynous,* and *undifferentiated* are Bem's terms for each of the four quadrants. People of all ages tend to be interested in thinking about these shades of difference and the added variety this represents in ourselves and the people we know. Starting with this exercise, or another like it, helps adolescents to be more subtle and productive as they think about typical male/female differences.

Although much more could be included about many types

of female/male differences, the differences having to do with sexuality and sexual response will be the focus here. As in the case of personality traits, however, we need to remember that specific males and females may vary somewhat, or quite a lot, from these generalizations.

When we think of the evolution of our species, males and females bear very different burdens when it comes to passing on genes. Human males *make* sperm constantly from their pre-pubertal to senior years. To some degree, the more they use, the more they make. It is obvious that the evolutionary pressure involved is to get those sperm out there. The more sperm get spread, the more likely a few may survive. Female humans, on the other hand, are *born* with all the eggs they ever will have already present in their ovaries. They usually release one egg a month starting in puberty. Therefore, in evolutionary terms, it is of paramount importance for this one egg to be fertilized by the best male specimen around and for that male to help raise the resulting offspring to give this youngling the best chance of survival.

The contrast is clear, although it is overdrawn here to make the point. This biological background, however, allows us to recognize the basis for some of our primitive differences. It is very easy to criticize each other's tendencies without recognizing that we all have some primitive impulses with which to deal. We are more likely to deal with them better if we can recognize and talk about them in a respectful and informed way.

In addition to differences in how we pass on our genes, males and females also differ in what is called *sexual activation*. Men tend to respond viscerally and quickly to visual stimulation. Most women are aroused much more by touch and emotional closeness.

Both genders certainly enjoy sexual relating much more in a setting of emotional closeness and slow buildup, although many men can climax very easily with only visual and physical stimuli. This tends to be especially true for young men. Many women, on the other hand, will not get close to climax—or even feel interested—if they are not feeling safe and comfortable, and also experiencing a certain amount of romantic buildup. A sense of being treated with respect and feeling emotionally close may be as big a turn-on to many women as any particular word or touch.

Same-Sex Orientation

Same-sex orientation (as understood for the general population) is presented in chapter 8, so concerns specifically related to adolescents will be the focus here.

Studies have shown that it is not unusual for young people to engage in some same-sex behavior. This is important for all adolescents to know. We also need to be clear that same-sex attractions or behaviors do not necessarily mean that adolescents are gay or lesbian. They may simply mean that young people are in the process of evolving their sexual identity, which takes time (Savin-Williams and Lenhart: 6).

It is difficult to imagine a situation where unconditional love and support is more needed than in the lives of adolescents who are struggling with their sexual identity. If lesbian and gay youth have to negotiate this process on their own or do not know of positive role models and ways to live integrated and productive lives, the coping behaviors and attitudes they develop in adolescence may serve them poorly now and as adults. If they separate their sexual and social identities, they are at increased risk for serious physical and emotional problems, including substance abuse, depression, and HIV/AIDS (Ryan and Futterman: 7). Particularly worrisome is an increased suicide rate. "Based on available research, reported suicide attempts among lesbian and gay youth range from 20 to 42 percent, compared with estimated rates of 8 to 13 percent among high school students in general" (Hershberger and D'Augelli: 13).

For all these reasons, it is important to specifically address issues of same-sex orientation with adolescents. In the church, we need to demonstrate God's love as we strive to find ways to reach adolescents who may be struggling with their sexual orientation and to seek their wholeness and well-being. Their peers also need some education to be able to be good friends to them.

Because the question of sexual orientation is so visceral and so fraught with divisiveness in our culture and also in the church, adults need to take great care in leading conversations on this topic. Asking young people to suggest ways to be good friends to people who might wonder whether they are lesbian or gay can engage them without asking them to be more self-revealing than they want to be. Discussing situations at school or in popular culture may also allow youth to engage with questions of sexual orientation, identity formation, and social stigma without needing to reveal more than they feel comfortable doing. Asking both adolescents and adults in the group to submit anonymous questions and comments after this portion of the presentation will allow leaders to give responses to specific issues about which the group may benefit from hearing, but no one wanted to say out loud.

A Word of Encouragement to Youth Leaders

It is a great privilege and joy to present God's glorious idea of sexual fulfillment and of two people coming together in profound intimacy to young people in the church. If we can open ourselves to have real conversations and to listen with respect to their questions and concerns, we will experience new levels of growth and community that will serve young people and our wider congregational communities well.

Discussion Questions

1. What do you think is the most important message we have for young people about their sexuality?
2. What do you find to be the greatest obstacles to good sexuality education in our churches? What about in your congregation?

3. What do you think of the idea that the physical aspects of a romantic relationship should reflect the intimacy level (including the commitment level) of the other aspects of the relationship?
4. How should we go about discussing "hot button" topics in the church when we are educating young people? Or do you feel we should not try?
5. What is your sense of how the church served your educational needs around sexuality as a young person? What of that would you like preserved and what would you like changed?

6

The Gift and Singleness

Julie Nash

A Personal Journey

I write not as a great theologian or exegete but as a single Christian who has wrestled with the question of how I can truly claim and embrace my sexuality as a gift from God with integrity and authenticity. I do not claim to speak for other singles or other young adults, and I confess I have more questions than answers, but I offer you a few insights from my personal experience, as well as a challenge.

My own interest in the subject began several years ago as I gradually became aware of the inner conflict I experienced between the messages about how I should be behaving as a sexual person and how that actually played out in reality. I was not marching in lockstep with my peers, who were mostly to be found somewhere along the steady dating-engaged-just married continuum.

Over the last few years, that tension has increased as attitudes that did not bother me in my early twenties have become increasingly grating. This is so because I seek to develop a positive self-image in spite of the unspoken rebuke I hear regularly, that I am incomplete, abnormal, and completely missing out on a huge part of adult experience. It has led me on a search to seek alternative voices who are challenging status-quo notions of sexuality in order to develop a broader, deeper, and more holistic perspective.

One of the most compelling questions for me recently has

been, "How do I define myself as a sexual person without engaging in sex?" This is an issue precisely because our society perpetuates some very unhealthy attitudes toward sexuality. Here are some that I have identified:

- Love is equated with sex, and sexuality is reduced to its genital form.
- Sex is considered the litmus test of love: if we are having sex, we are loved; if we are not, we must not be loved.
- A very narrow and rigidly defined set of sexual behaviors is considered normative for all adults to engage in; those who fail to follow the script are considered deviant or abnormal. In other words, there is something wrong with them.
- Sex gives relationships—and the individuals within them—legitimacy within the broader society. They are deemed happier, healthier, and more mature than celibates. They are also deemed full adult members of society.
- Relationships not defined by genital activity are devalued in comparison with those that are.
- Every longing or desire we ever experience should be immediately and fully satisfied.

These attitudes are never stated explicitly, and from a very young age, we absorb and internalize them without questioning them. Unfortunately, if we in the church fail to provide a healthy, life-affirming alternative, we tacitly approve and reinforce societal messages that tell us that sex is the be-all and the end-all. And this is what has happened: we in the church have accepted these assumptions without question.

Within the church, the comparable unspoken message is that "it is God's will for everyone to get married." Though this is rarely stated quite so boldly—at least within the Mennonite church—Christian young people learn early that the best and quickest way to earn full acceptance within the church is to get married. The church has capitulated to society's definition of sexuality. While we endorse marriage as the proper context for full sexual expression, we have failed to provide a serious critique of our society's reduction of sexuality to genital sexuality. I believe this is because we feel very ambivalent about sexuality, and taboos make it difficult for us to talk about it honestly and openly. Furthermore, sexuality cuts to the very core of who we are as individuals, and we fear making ourselves too vulnerable.

I have often encountered an attitude in the church that assumes marriage as the norm, and outside the church that assumes sexually active relationships as the norm; but I find it most hurtful when these attitudes come from family and friends within the church. I have been in a variety of situations where individuals I care about thoughtlessly tossed off a comment that revealed their bias. While I know they had no intention of hurting me, their remarks nevertheless served to make me feel stigmatized and marginalized and very alone.

I have spent time wrestling to understand how such comments could hit me on such a visceral level. I have realized they hurt because they reinforce a notion that I too have internalized—that sexuality is about sex, and if I am not having sex, I am somehow a lesser person than those who are. On a purely intellectual level, my inner feminist reacts with utter disgust and revulsion to such a gross misconception, but on an emotional level, part of me has been conditioned since childhood to believe it.

Linking Sexuality and Spirituality

Through reading, I have come to understand sexuality as being more about who we are than about the behaviors in which we engage. It encompasses who we are as God's beloved children, made in the divine image and endowed with unique skills, gifts, personalities, and temperaments. Sexuality is about that drive within us for connection with others, for community, for the need and the capacity to give and to receive love.

One of the major insights I gained from reading is the under-standing that sexuality and spirituality are integrally linked. This was a huge epiphany for me. I had always assumed that sexuality, if not downright antithetical to spirituality, was its much poorer cousin. I inherited the prevalent dualistic belief that values the mind and soul but largely dismisses the body. Since the apostle Paul uses the same term—frequently translated "flesh"—in various passages to refer either to the physical body or to a state of rebellion against God, I equated the body with weakness and sin. Some recent translations of the Bible have attempted to avoid the confusion by translating the Greek to either "body" or "sinful nature," depending on the context.

I continue to work at learning to see myself as an integrated whole rather than as a collection of dichotomized parts, and am learning to develop a healthy love and respect for my body. Yet there are days when I still struggle, days when I feel insecure and I wish I was in a relationship, wish I was married

- to find greater social acceptance and belonging
- to prove I am normal
- to prove I am a full adult woman who is deserving of love and respect.

The Bible and Singleness

There are lots of passages throughout the Bible that speak about marriage, that proclaim the goodness of marriage, or that use marriage as a metaphor for the love God has for the church. There are fewer passages that deal directly with singleness, although the New Testament affirms a radical new definition of family within the church that is not defined by biological ties.

In 1 Corinthians 7:25-35, Paul validates both those Christians who remain single and those who choose to marry. Those who marry do not sin, and neither do those who remain unmarried. He states that the world as we know it is only temporary; therefore, we need to keep an eternal perspective and not hold too tightly to the things of this world. Paul's primary message is that our first concern should be our devotion to God. While this is a calling for all Christians, Paul asserts that it is easier for those who are unmarried. While those who are married must invest much time and energy in building their marital relationships, as well as raising their children, those who are single have fewer commitments and more flexibility to follow God's call on their lives.

On the flip side, singleness promotes a more radical dependence on God. Henri Nouwen suggested that the unmarried person's primary witness to married persons is this conscious dependence on God. While married persons may look to their spouse to meet their primary needs for love and to strengthen their identity, single persons must look more to God to fulfill these needs. Singleness, then, is a reminder to Christians that the church is our primary family.

In Matthew 19:12, Christ commends singleness to those who can accept it, and in verse 29 promises that those who forsake lands or houses or loved ones for his sake shall have abundant reward. As a single person, I am called to love others just as married persons are. I strive to show that love by being a good listener, by providing encouragement and hugs, and by giving my time, skills, and resources to help others. I am called to pour my energies into a variety of relationships rather than focusing the bulk of my attention on one relationship. I find great joy in spending time with, and keeping in contact with, family and friends across Canada and beyond. Singleness has provided me with the flexibility to study and work in Winnipeg, Kitchener-Waterloo, North Bay, and the United Kingdom without being constrained by the needs of another or tied down with a lot of material assets and financial obligations. In addition, I have room to reflect on questions such as

- Who am I? What do I believe?
- What major life experiences have shaped me?

- What are my strengths and how can I build on them?
- What are my weaknesses and how can I either work toward overcoming them or learn to accept them?
- What are the dreams, passions, skills, and aptitudes God has planted within me?
- How do I hear God calling me to make use of these gifts now?

I choose to be a vibrant, loving, sexual person while remaining celibate, believing that is God's best for me at this time. I do not know whether or not God will call me to remain single for my whole life; but if I discern such a call in the future, it will not change my commitment to celibacy as an unmarried Christian.

Created for Intimacy

All humans are created for intimacy, and it can, at times, be a challenge for single persons to meet those needs. There are days when I crave physical touch and affection. Hugs can be a big help then. Rather than trying to suppress such feelings, I have learned to name them honestly before God and to view them as a reminder that I am fully alive and fully human. I think of Saint Augustine's prayer that says, "You have made us for yourself, and our hearts are restless until they find their rest in you." I also remember that perfect fulfillment is not possible for any human being this side of heaven—popular belief and Hollywood mythology notwithstanding.

However, intimacy does encompass far more than the very narrow definition that is generally assumed in our society. Many people foolishly bypass intellectual, emotional, psychological, and spiritual intimacy in their hurry to get to physical intimacy. To meet my intimacy needs, I seek friends with whom I can be authentic, with whom I can share my fondest dreams and my deepest fears, and I commit myself to cherish their unique qualities as well. I have close relationships with my family members, and my dad's expression of self-giving love and humility is a model I seek to emulate in my own relationships.

I do not expect our society to change its attitudes anytime soon. The world does not know God; people do not understand their incredible worth as children of God; and therefore, they grasp at sex to fill the huge void they feel. Sex is too often a substitute for the lack of real love in their lives.

However, I find these unhealthy messages coming from the church far more problematic, because I expect more of the church. We are a redeemed people: we should know better. And yet we are fallible human beings too. Sexuality is an area in which most or all of us are broken to some degree; we all need God's healing for the wounds we have experienced.

On the one hand, we communicate that sex is the way to fulfill people's needs for love and self-esteem. Yet when people misuse sex in a misbegotten attempt to find the love and acceptance they truly crave, we condemn them for their lack of moral fiber. We treat sexual sins as the most heinous sins a person can commit, though Jesus saved his most stinging rebukes for the self-righteous Pharisees who thought they were doing everything to earn God's approval. Is it any wonder that we are so confused and that sex is such a preoccupation and a stumbling block for us? How do these unhealthy messages benefit any of us?

A Challenge for the Church

Regardless of marital status, we all are exposed to the lie that everyone is having more and better sex than we are. Instead of allowing our attitudes about sexuality to be hijacked by our society, which is endlessly obsessed with sex but knows little of sexuality, the church needs to celebrate sexuality, to appreciate our intrinsic worth as unique persons made in God's image. God made us with the capacity and the need to love and to be loved. We have the opportunity to provide a beacon of true hope and sexual freedom to a hurting world.

Marriage is a good institution that is blessed by God, but it is also a human institution. As such, it is a flawed one, so do not idolize marriage or family values too much. Marriage should be honored by all within the church, but the church should not separate the sheep from the goats, those who are insiders from those who are outsiders. Likewise, sex is a good gift from God, who loves us, but it cannot handle the strain of trying to provide all the love, self-esteem, meaning, and fulfillment we attempt to derive from it. There are other ways of expressing love than sex, and there are other relationships that can provide for our emotional needs than marriage alone.

We need to learn to talk about sexuality—not about techniques and methods and positions, as our society does. We need to acknowledge our own struggles in celebrating this gift from God. We need to begin to articulate a vision of sexuality that embraces and affirms all people, whether they are male or female; child, youth, or adult; straight or gay; single or married, widowed, divorced, or remarried.

I hope for a day when all of us can move beyond the first three letters of the word *sexuality*. I long for a day when the church truly learns to validate singleness as a valuable way of expressing God's love and working for God's kingdom. I yearn for a day when individuals experience true freedom in choosing to marry or to remain single, when singleness is not viewed as a temporary or pitiable state, something to be escaped as quickly as possible. I pray for a day when we are able to embrace our sexuality without mixed feelings, to truly appreciate who we are as whole people and beloved children of God.

Discussion Questions

1. What are some of the unspoken messages we communicate about singleness?
2. What are some opportunities for single people to serve God and the church that could be more difficult for people with families to pursue?

3. What lessons might the married majority within the church learn from single brothers and sisters?

4. All human beings have a fundamental need for love and intimacy. How might the church become a family that fosters true intimacy and vulnerability among all of its members, regardless of marital status?

7

The Gift and Marriage

Willard S. Krabill

We come into the world as single people, albeit extremely dependent on other people for our survival and development. As noted in the previous chapter, persons who are single beyond this initial dependent stage can experience affection, have intimate friendships, and have a whole life of fulfillment. Marriage, however, continues to be a choice for the majority of people in most societies for part of their adult life. Singleness and marriage should be equally valued.

The term *marriage* has held different meanings for people in other times and places as well as among people today. These include the ideas of being "married" in spirit but not legally; cohabitation; common-law marriage; arranged marriage, through a choice not made by the pair; civil ceremony; and a ceremony of religious commitment. In each situation, it is assumed that the couple is identified as a social unit separate from others, at least in living arrangements. It is also generally assumed that sexual intercourse is a part of the couple's relationship.

In this chapter, *marriage* will refer to the lifelong commitment sealed through vows made by the partners to each other, witnessed by others, and legally sanctioned.

Many in today's general society do not regard a marriage license as a prerequisite for them to meet their needs for a more or less "permanent" relationship, personal identity, companionship, economic support, sexual intercourse, or bearing children. So why get married? What does the relationship of marriage and sexuality mean for Christian people?

Why Get Married?

Marriage provides a sense of security and opportunities to share feelings, experiences, and ideas with someone with whom one forms a special attachment. Even younger people still believe that marriage is important for people who plan to spend the remainder of their lives together (Rathus, Nevid, and Fischner-Rathus: 444). Today, in general society, access to sexual intercourse is less likely to be a motive for marriage, because more people than earlier believe that premarital sex is acceptable between two people who feel affectionate toward each other.

Marriage does, however, legitimize and restrict sexual intercourse. This allows the couple to assume that any children the woman bears also belong to her spouse. Marriage provides an institution in which children can be supported and socialized into adopting the norms of the family and its culture. It permits the orderly transmission of wealth from one family and generation to another (Rathus, Nevid, and Fischner-Rathus: 444).

When marriage vows are taken seriously, they really do mean something and are not conditional. "For better or for worse" are powerful words. They imply that the commitment made will endure when the road gets rough and difficult instead of smooth and sensual, when job loss occurs, when the money runs out, and when a diving accident renders a spouse a paraplegic. This kind of commitment surely reflects true love and fosters a sense of security.

Marriage allows people to have the freedom to be themselves and to express feelings without the fear of losing the relationship. This freedom to be open and honest builds trust that is so crucial in forming an intimate relationship.

The public aspect of marriage—a wedding or civil ceremony—helps us define who we are in our couple relationship and in our relationship to the community. The community perceives us as a legal social unit and bestows certain expectations upon us. We expect that publicly-made commitments will lead one to pause before breaking them.

By comparing marriage with the alternative of cohabitation, we may gain some insight for answering the question "Why get married?"

Cohabitation

Some cohabitants never intend to get married, but many other cohabitants consider this arrangement a trial marriage. Two people cohabiting may claim commitment to each other. But until it is validated publicly in the presence of witnesses to whom the couple is accountable, there is something tentative about the commitment. If it is tentative, it is not a total commitment. Either one has made a commitment or one has not. If we say, "Let's try it and see if it works," we provide an escape and remove the incentive to make it work. Marriage cannot be practiced beforehand.

In *The Living Together Trap*, Roseanne Rosen said that although most women enter the arrangement expecting a monogamous relationship, many find their partners cheating on them. They further discover that the men had a prior pattern of living-together ventures about which the women had not been told. This data is not reassuring in an age of widespread sexually transmitted infections like AIDS, herpes, chlamydia, and hepatitis B.

Approximately 40 percent of cohabiting couples eventually marry. The casualty rate for those marriages greatly exceeds the rate for those who had not lived together prior to marriage. One study conducted over twenty-three years found that couples who cohabited before their marriage increased their likelihood of divorce by 50 percent when compared with those who did not cohabit before marriage. Those couples who had cohabited also indicated a lower level of marital satisfaction generally (Axinn and Thornton). These findings have been corroborated in studies since then (Rathus, Nevid, and Fischner-Rathus: 442). Those who are leery of commitment are more apt to stray after marriage as well.

As in so many male-female relationships, the women are more vulnerable. Unequal expectations of the relationship are common. Studies show that women, more frequently than men, enter the relationship expecting permanence. Too often, one or the other is secretly saying, "I'm afraid my love for you won't last, so I want an escape hatch, just in case." When sexual intercourse has been involved, a breakup brings suffering, especially for the woman who, more often than the man, expected this kind of a relationship to last. The data simply is not there to support the notion that cohabitation results in better marriages, less abuse, less violence, fewer affairs, or a less painful breakup.

Thus far in the discussion, we have considered marriage and cohabitation as living patterns involving people in general. What does our biblically based understanding of marriage and sexual intercourse mean for Christian people?

Christian Understanding of Marriage and Sexual Intercourse

The New Testament reveals affirmation of monogamy and marriage and only negative statements about either adultery or *fornication*, the word used in the King James Version to describe unchastity or illicit sex of all kinds, including intercourse outside of marriage. Marriage is affirmed in the New Testament, and sexual intercourse is placed firmly within the context of marriage. But among Christians in North American culture today, an increasing number are staying single, delaying marriage, but still engaging in sexual intercourse. Is the biblical stance on this issue obsolete for people in today's culture?

When deciding whether or not to engage in sexual intercourse before marriage, there are things to consider in addition to the biblical admonition. In this chapter I highlight fourteen reasons for abstinence from my perspective as a Christian physician with a background of many years in family practice, obstetrical-gynecological practice, and college health practice. They emerge from my personal experience and observations. I have had a great deal more than average exposure to the sexual experiences of a wide variety of people, many of whom have been young women, young married couples, and college students.

Reasons to Abstain from Premarital Sex

1. Premarital sex tends to diminish personal happiness and predisposes the participants to sexual boredom. People are "doing it more, but enjoying it less." Many have guilt and anxiety about it. People who believe that "What does the Bible say?" is a relevant and important question will feel especially guilty. It is my observation that those engaging in sexual intercourse outside of marriage are not happier and are not having greater sexual pleasure. Premarital sexual affairs frequently complicate a relationship and lead to painful splitting up.

One's first or early sexual intercourse experiences always carry much meaning. Psychiatrists, regardless of their personal value systems, repeatedly comment that one's initial sexual experience constitutes a significant emotional passage or event in one's life. A couple's relationship is somehow different after sexual intercourse has been a part of it.

The notion that sexual intercourse is casual inevitably lessens its impact, its importance, and its potential for ecstasy. To reduce a life-uniting experience to one of "just another physiological function" is perhaps the greatest of all indictments of premarital sex.

2. Premarital sex is often not the result of a mutual decision. For something as "heavy" as sex outside of marriage, as far-reaching in its consequences, as complex in its meanings, as full of potential for pain as well as joy—for this just to "happen" is really immoral and irresponsible. So much should be considered, so much should be shared, and so honest must be the communication that it cannot be "right" when the couple is just "carried away by passion." In premarital sex, a sufficient dialogue and process of decision making has usually not occurred.

3. Premarital sex usually "takes over" the relationship. It tends to become the focus, and the couple spends less time and effort on getting to know each other as total persons. In one school year, for example, two sexually active college women came to me at the health center to say they had stopped using the pill. They were no longer engaging in coital activity with their boyfriends. Each couple had decided that because their sexual activity had come to dominate their relationship, they would discontinue it. They wanted their doctor to know about this change.

Each person should ask, "Do I want the one I am engaged to or dating to be interested in me because of who I am—the real me—or just because of how I perform in bed?" When the growth of physical intimacies precedes the growth of shared interests, beliefs, intellectual intimacy, emotional intimacy, aesthetic intimacy, and spiritual intimacy, the relationship becomes distorted, and the physical relationship tends to dominate. There are already far too many marriages, as well as single relationships, where there is sex without true intimacy.

4. Premarital sex confuses and complicates communication between two people. People are created for relationship. Singles— male and female—can have meaningful relationships with many people of both sexes. Sexual intercourse is one special kind of relationship between people. To be in a relationship requires communication, so honest communication becomes all-important in considering when, where, and with whom one will have a sexual relationship.

Until the permanence of the commitment is sealed, coitus tends to make one unsure of the message and the motive of one's partner. What is the motive: self-gratification, satisfaction of physical urges, or consideration for the partner's long-term best interests? What message is being sent?

5. Premarital sexual relationships break up far more couples than they strengthen. Personal observation, backed by the results of studies, shows that when sexual intercourse enters the premarital relationship, the odds that the couple will split are increased. Many people cannot handle it. Often a female adolescent gives a classic statement: "When I gave in, he lost interest." At a sexuality seminar on our campus, a discussion question was posed: "What do you say to the person the next morning in the dining hall line?" It is sad to see the frequency with which a couple that might have developed a long-term partnership breaks up after premarital sex begins.

6. *Premarital sex denies one the opportunity for the most meaningful sexual experience of all.* We look forward to knowing that two people are coming together in full sexual union after saving that special gift—that portion of their being—for the occasion of final commitment and celebration. That will not be possible for those who engage in premarital sex.

People will be shortchanged if they arrive at the celebration of marriage, of sacred promise, and have nothing special left to share by way of physical union. For all young people, we covet an experience of being able to achieve unity of spirit, mind, purpose, and the promise of life together, and to seal it at marriage as a unique expression of physical unity with a sexual expression not previously shared. That is special!

The uniqueness of human sexual intercourse can best be realized within a permanent, exclusive relationship of complete trust and security. If this potential for ecstasy is misused, one is cheated. The sexual expression that could do so much to seal and enhance a marriage tends to become more of a physical exercise than a celebration of true love, commitment, promise, and trust.

7. *Premarital sex impairs one's sense of community.* One's decision about sex outside of marriage is not really a "do your own thing" issue. When it is perceived that way, both the relationship and the community are shortchanged.

Great experiences are made greater when we can publicly share them. We all have a human need for celebration. Sexual intercourse can be a wonderful milestone in life. When this life-uniting experience begins, people desire and need the shared joy, affirmation, celebration, and support that goes with Christian marriage. To ask that this new relationship be secret and unannounced diminishes and stresses the relationship (Smedes: 146).

8. Sexuality involves all of life: emotional, mental, social, spiritual, and physical. Premarital intercourse infers that our sexual urges are physical "needs" that must not be denied. We speak of having "raging passions." We say, "We can't be blamed if they just take over, you know." We are not created that way. No one should fall for that line. Scientists even question whether the human has a sexual instinct in the way animals do. We have sexual appetites and urges, but the satisfaction of them is not essential to physical or emotional health.

In medical practice, we often hear statements like these: "My husband needs it." "My boyfriend has to get it somewhere." Desires it? Yes. Has to have it? No. People (male or female) survive and are healthy without experiencing sexual intercourse. One of the secrets of a positive and mature life is the experience of being able to forego or postpone something. This is one of the secrets of happiness for anyone, married or single, living a fulfilled life in spite of many unfulfilled desires.

9. Premarital sex is unfair to the physical relationship. Premarital sex tends to be detrimental to the realization of full physical enjoyment. It often occurs in settings "where no one will find out" and is often done with guilt and in a hurried manner. This frequently produces tension. With tension comes less relaxation, less confidence, and less enjoyment. With tension and anxiety, the male may experience premature ejaculation, and the female may have discomfort and frustration.

Premarital sex may predispose one to sexual dysfunction. It frequently is detrimental to the eventual achievement of the best physical sexual adjustment. One hears people claim that premarital sex enhances early sexual adjustments within marriage. Such statements are increasingly being questioned in the medical and psychological professions.

Performance pressure often sneaks into premarital sexual relationships, and it may carry over into many marital relationships. Couples may think they have not "made it" unless they do it "right" or achieve orgasm. This kind of pressure can be detrimental to the relationship.

10. Premarital sex contradicts what human history tells us. It is presumptuous to suppose that we know better than millennia of human experience, mediated through our Judeo-Christian heritage. This cumulative experience has demonstrated that it is best to reserve sexual intercourse for covenanted marriage. Premarital sex did occur in past centuries, but the recommended sexual codes have persisted. Would our sexual codes have endured so long if they were not valid? Human experience speaks loudly.

11. Premarital sex tends to produce spiritual anxiety, thus risking God's disfavor. The Scriptures do not view fornication with acceptance or favor. There has been controversy over the meaning of the word *fornication* in the Bible. Does it apply to engaged couples having sex, or does it refer only to promiscuity and other forms of illicit sex? But the whole tenor of the Scriptures—the high status assigned to marriage and the condemnation of adultery—affirms a sex-within-marriage position.

New Testament scholar and professor Howard Charles writes in his paper "Sexuality in the New Testament" that in the New Testament, "coitus is set firmly in the context of marriage. . . . Nowhere in the New Testament is there a formal discussion of what constitutes the real nature or essence of marriage." However, Charles goes on to conclude that

> the conception of marriage to which we are led by these materials has a foundation covenant which is consummated by coitus and which inaugurates an interper-

sonal relationship between a man and a woman having the potential of embracing all areas of their lives. Both Jesus and Paul intend marriage to be permanent and regard fidelity in coitus as obligatory on both husband and wife. It is in the context of a permanent contractual or covenantal relationship involving an ongoing shared life between a man and a woman that coitus is to have its place both expressing and implementing the marriage union. (Charles: 11)

Details of what the Bible says about premarital sexual union and celibacy can be found in chapters 5 and 6 of *Sex for Christians* by Lewis Smedes. He expresses well the viewpoint reached through my personal Bible reading and experience.

12. *Premarital sex detracts from the meaning of marriage.* A decline in the stature of marriage is evident in society and also in the church. Extramarital sex contributes to the tentativeness of marriage and the trial-marriage kind of thinking. The meaning of marriage suffers when persons have sexual intercourse while engaged, while living together unmarried, or outside a marriage. The finality and the irreversibility of the marriage commitment constitute its significance and its potential value, giving it strength and enriching the sexual expression and message.

I asked a patient whose marriage was floundering and near breakup, "Are you having sexual intercourse with your husband?" "No," she said, "there's nothing for it to say anymore." It is the message, not the physical sensation, that is uniquely human about our sexuality.

13. *Premarital sex is costly.* What was created by God for our pleasure often becomes our pain. Today many say sexual intercourse outside of marriage is okay as long as no one gets hurt. Who is so wise that he or she can predict who will get hurt? Which motorcyclists, riding without helmets, are going to have their heads smashed? Which in a group that uses alcohol will be the one out of ten who ends up addicted and alcoholic? When people decide to experiment with sexual intercourse outside of marriage, which ones are going to be hurt? The hurt may only be perceived in the future, and no one can accurately predict it.

Another frequent observation from my medical practice is that, for those who had sexual intercourse before marriage, the frequency and intensity of intercourse sharply diminished after the ceremony. Might this have a relationship to the earlier-mentioned research findings that living together prior to marriage increases the likelihood of eventual divorce?

14. Premarital sex risks pregnancy and sexually transmitted infections (STIs). One might have expected a physician to present this reason first, but thirteen other important reasons were given before these obvious ones.

In the literature about prevention and treatment of STIs, one rarely reads about the only reliable method of prevention: having only one sexual partner through fidelity within marriage and abstinence outside of marriage. If each person would confine her or his sexual activity to one partner, the STI epidemic would be terminated. This is not likely to happen soon. Hence, we need to recognize the tremendous toll experienced by individuals and society as the epidemic of STIs, which includes AIDS, continues to grow.

The United States National Center for Health Statistics reported in the *New York Times* on October 5, 1996, that for the first time in nearly two decades, the rate of births among single women declined in 1995; and for the fourth year in a row, the teenage birthrate dropped (Holmes). "In 2006, there were 42 births per 1,000 women aged 15-19. The rate has dropped by 32% since 1991, when it was 62 per 1,000, but increased 4% between 2005 and 2006" (Alan Guttmacher Institute: 2). The trend is reversing itself again. We need more study to discover why this is happening. Despite the dramatic decline for more than a decade, the number of births to teens is still too high.

When children are born to an immature parent or parents, the negative results are well known: mothers too often drop out of high school, live in poverty, and experience lives filled with more difficult challenges and less ability to reach their full potential. Children more frequently are born prematurely, have low birth weight, and suffer poor health. They have a greater incidence of abuse, neglect, and learning difficulties. They more often are raised by only one parent. (Chapter 15 will include more on this.)

We can assume that people who engage in premarital sexual intercourse do not expect to acquire STIs or become pregnant. Yet many do not use condoms to help prevent STIs and additional birth control methods to prevent pregnancy. Many adolescents do not use contraceptives, because of their personal attitudes toward sex outside of marriage. They often have the illusion that STIs or pregnancy "can't happen to me," or they think that sexual intercourse must be by impulse and that to prepare for it is wrong.

As many married couples will testify, no contraceptive method is foolproof. Sexual intercourse outside of marriage is particularly immoral if those who engage in it are not ready to accept responsibility for the consequences, including pregnancy. Since a great many persons in extramarital relationships are not ready for pregnancy, that is still a valid reason for abstinence.

In Support of Covenantal Marriage

These fourteen reasons reveal my personal position regarding premarital sexual intercourse. They all have meaning for me, but not all have meaning for others. I believe our sexuality is a good and beautiful, God-given dimension of our being and our personality. It is a serious matter to misuse sex for selfish purposes, out of bounds, or in any nonmutual or exploitative way. In 1 Corinthians 6:18, Paul says, "Flee from sexual immorality."

I do not believe, however, that sexual sins are unforgivable or unique. I believe that the sins of the flesh (carnal nature) are not limited to sex acts; lying, jealousy, and cheating are equally serious. I believe that sexual sins are not sins because they are sexual but because they are hurtful. I have seen beautiful examples of forgiveness and starting over in those who have been guilty of sexual sins.

I believe one can start over in one's sexual practice and lifestyle. Where there are wounds, not all the scars are erased and not all the memories are eradicated. One can, however, become a virginal person (male or female) in God's sight once again.

I urge that sexual intercourse always be a mutually decided event. For premarital sexual intercourse to just "happen" is especially sad. When unmarried persons decide to become sexually active—and some will—they should be responsible enough to use a birth control method. I will continue to be a friend, confidant, and professional adviser to those persons. But when I am asked for my opinion, I must share as I have here. I believe that premarital sex is not the best way to go. We will be happier and closer to God's will for our lives if we keep sexual intercourse within the marriage covenant relationship.

It is rewarding to note how following biblical guidelines serves our best interests. Covenantal marriage is the most satisfying. Abstinence before marriage and monogamy within it would eliminate worry about unwanted pregnancies outside of marriage, STIs, most HIV infections (AIDS), and the emotional pain that derives from multiple sexual partnerships. Why do we ignore the guidelines? They work. They really do.

We must challenge persons who choose marriage not to take their cues from general society's attitudes toward permanent relationships or the marital example of many public figures. Better cues are available from the teachings of Jesus, from those who take their Christian commitment seriously, from the wisdom of those who have experienced the trials and rewards of long-term marriage, and from the examples of those who after forty, fifty, sixty, or seventy years remain loving and faithful till death parts them.

Of course there will be conflict, but couples can experience the reward of resolving conflict. The ability to work things out is remarkably improved when walking out is not an option. When we can walk away from conflict, we do not grow.

Think of two mature, fully committed Christian people exchanging their marriage vows, surrounded by a supportive community of people who love them and share their faith and values. They are in an ideal situation to nourish and sustain their marriage commitment. Avoiding commitment is the prevailing ethos in the society at large. It is not easy to form solid bonds and maintain one's vows in an environment where relationships frequently fall apart. "Christians must begin to live joyfully and faithfully in their marriages—right in the midst of today's marital chaos. . . . Our society desperately needs marriages built on a biblical foundation that combines freedom and sacrifice" (Sider and Sider: 38).

Marriages are special blessings for the church. In turn, the church can bless and strengthen the commitment. Christian marriage also affords a spiritual intimacy—a shared faith, a shared worldview, and a shared sense of God's leading and presence. All these foster a depth of intimacy that is difficult for non-Christians to comprehend. When the church family can celebrate and support the union, another level of extended family is added to support the commitment and to empower the couple as a new home is established.

Within this new union, commitment to God is paramount, and commitment to each other has been blessed by the faith community. Thus the gift of sexuality can flourish and be expressed in myriad loving ways. Within a monogamous, committed, covenant relationship not preceded by premarital experimentation, the marriage partners will be able to be themselves and learn to make love together. They will not be on trial with each other, will not be compared with previous partners, will not feel they have to perform, and will have the freedom to experiment endlessly. They can say no as

well as yes, laugh at themselves, and love each other unconditionally. (Chapter 12 will say more about keeping excitement
and romance alive in marriage.)

Marriage is an excellent choice for those who are ready
and able to make a lifelong commitment. After that commitment has been made, the meaning of sexual union is multiplied
and made celebratory and joyous to a greater extent than otherwise possible. The supporting Christian community wants to
and is in a good position to affirm its members' engagements
and celebrate their marriages.

Discussion Questions

1. What is it about a premarital cohabitation relationship that
   increases the odds of divorce by 50 percent if that couple
   eventually marries?
2. What is observed in marriages that discourage some young
   people from entering that kind of relationship?
3. Why does premarital sexual intercourse often complicate and
   confuse communication in a couple's relationship?
4. What do you think is essential to safeguard a marriage?

8

The Gift and Same-Sex Orientation

Willard S. Krabill

Homosexuality. Apart from *abortion*, there are few words that elicit a more emotional response or that are more divisive and polarizing than this word. This is true in communities large and small, in Congress, and especially in Christian faith communities. Nearly all Christian communities are wrestling with this issue, especially regarding the acceptability of gay marriage. In *The Good Book*, Peter Gomes observes that this issue has become so central to right conduct and belief that any compromise is considered capitulation to error (145).

On this area of sexuality, one can justifiably ask, "What more is there to say?" So much has already been said and written about homosexuality. The polarization emerges from differing interpretations of biblical texts, the "unnaturalness" (for the large majority of people) of same-sex attraction, and a rather pervasive discomfort and insecurity that people have, not only about discussing sexual matters, but also about their own sexuality.

Frequently, people who are "different" seem threatening to others. Gomes states, "More than any other social or theological issue of our day, this one engages us at our most fundamental level of existence and raises disturbing questions about our own sense of identity, of morality, and of the nature of settled truth" (144). I have read many books and unpublished papers by writers on all sides of the issues. Equally sincere interpreters use the same biblical texts and draw contradictory conclusions.

It is conceivable that when and if the twenty-first century turns into the twenty-second—and perhaps sooner—the contents of a chapter on this topic would be quite different. In other words, our understanding of this topic is incomplete. As we live, study, do further research, pray, and discern in our faith communities, we hope new insights will clarify our understanding, give us all more-loving attitudes, and decrease or eliminate the polarization present today. As with any controversial topic, it is wise to keep an open and inquiring mind when considering it.

This chapter is not intended to be a complete or final study of homosexuality. Its purpose is not to prescribe a position on the issue of gay marriage, but to suggest that we keep the issue in perspective. We should not let homosexuality dominate our study of sexuality or be a litmus test of one's orthodoxy.

This chapter will not repeat the broader examination of homosexuality found in *Human Sexuality in the Christian Life* (chap. 2, sect. 7:104-20). We recommend that readers study it.

Chapter 2 in this book provides a discussion of relevant scriptural passages. For the purposes of this chapter, we will identify some definitions and contexts, areas of general consensus, and areas of continuing disagreement. These will be followed by a personal response to the issue, some observations, and the identification of future tasks for Christians regarding the homosexuality issue. This chapter does not prescribe a particular position. It is an appeal for an attitude or stance that allows Christians to remain in fellowship and loving dialogue even while disagreeing on homosexuality.

Definitions and Context

It is important that we discuss homosexuality in the context of our overall sexuality. As noted earlier, we are sexual throughout life, regardless of our life's situation. In the Genesis story, sexuality was not added to the human design *after* sin occurred. We are whole creatures—body, mind, and spirit. These whole beings are (in God's good wisdom) sexual beings. We do not *have* bodies; we *are* our bodies, just as we are mind and spirit.

Jesus came to us in a body—a physical, sexual, male body.

If we believe that, as God's Son on earth, he was fully human, we must accept that he had to deal with male-female interaction as we do. When he spoke of the attraction of one sex for the other, as in Matthew 5:27-28, he no doubt knew about this from personal experience. It is reasonable and scriptural to assume that Jesus experienced sexual attraction and had erections and wet dreams. Hebrews 4:15 says he was "tempted in every way, just as we are—yet was without sin."

Any discussion of homosexuality today must note the variety of identities and terms currently used. We must do this if we wish to recognize the importance of these variations as real to those generally marginalized by the dominant culture. In this chapter we use the terms *homosexual*, *gay*, and *same-sex oriented* interchangeably, not intending to favor one term, even though many in the gay community do prefer a term for various reasons.

The term *lesbian* refers to a female same-sex-oriented person. I will use *homosexual* or *gay* to refer to either or both the male and female same-sex-attracted person. A *bisexual* person is erotically attracted to (or has more than usual identification with) members of both sexes.

This chapter cannot deal with all the variations in sexual affinity and behaviors. For instance, those who consider themselves transgendered often cross the usual (for most of us) boundaries of the expected gender roles for men and women. They have a more fluid sense of traditional male or female identity. Since homosexuality is a major issue dividing society and the church, our focus in this chapter will be limited to that variation.

Homosexuality is defined from a variety of perspectives: psychological, biological, sociological, medical, and political. I served on the study committee that developed the study guide mentioned above, *Human Sexuality in the Christian Life*. We defined *homosexuality* as the emotional, erotic, and physical attraction toward people of one's own gender. Note that the word *attraction*, not the word *behavior*, is used in this definition. Homosexual people, just like heterosexuals, may or may not act on those feelings of erotic attraction: they may be celibate or may be sexually active.

Much confusion occurs in the church and elsewhere when we use the term *homosexuality* and do not clearly say whether we are referring to an orientation and attraction or to certain behavior, meaning genital activity. It is often assumed that anyone calling for Christian charity toward homosexual persons is thereby condoning promiscuous, cruising lifestyles. This assumption is both inaccurate and unfair.

There are some who incorrectly define the word *homosexual* to mean same-sex genital activity. This denies the reality of same-sex orientation apart from genital activity and unfairly makes the term *celibate homosexual* into nonsense.

When homosexuals and homosexuality are discussed in church conference settings, it is apparent to me that the various participants do not have the same images in mind. One person assumes that all homosexuals frequent gay bars and bathhouses and are sexually promiscuous. Another thinks of the friend, son, or daughter who is a committed Christian, reads the Bible, prays, teaches Sunday school, claims salvation through Jesus Christ, and is knocking on the door of the church and asking, "May I come in too?" Or "Can I remain in the church?"

The single word *homosexual* or *homosexuality* cannot be used to capture both of these images; misunderstandings will occur. We have to be more precise in our language, meanings, and dialogue. It is important to note that there is no one typical homosexual any more than there is one typical heterosexual. In both worlds, there is a spectrum of feelings and behaviors. Our sexual roles and the degree to which we experience male or female attraction vary from person to person and from time to time during our lives. In 1953, Alfred Kinsey tried to illustrate this by describing a continuum on a scale of 0 to 6, with 0 indicating exclusively heterosexual orientation, and 6 referring to exclusively homosexual attraction (Rathus, Nevid, Fischner-Rathus: 289).

Few people are exclusively heterosexual in terms of having no affectionate feelings for persons of their own sex. Most of us would find ourselves between the scale of 1 and 5, and the majority of us 1 or 2. There is a midpoint category called *bisexual*. Bisexual persons experience erotic attraction toward persons of both sexes. Considering this scale, it becomes even clearer that when we speak about homosexuality, we must be aware of the range of feelings. We need to specify whether we are referring to an orientation (which most medical scientists believe we do not choose) or a behavior (over which we do have choice).

We also need to keep the issue of homosexuality in perspective. Homosexuality is only a small part of the sexuality issues that should concern us. It is not, nor should it be, the big issue or even the sexuality issue for Christians. So often, after I speak to groups on sexuality, the first question raised in the discussion period is about homosexuality. That issue then takes up the remainder of the period. Perhaps we do that because it is safer to talk about other persons "out there." On other sexuality issues, the discussion gets too close to home, too close to our inner sexual selves, where we may feel insecure.

Actually, we who are heterosexuals have a tremendous agenda of sexuality issues of our own with which we should and must be working. Even in the church, we observe a steady decline in the level of commitment required for marriage. In the church we have sexual abuse, incest, marital rape, pregnancy outside of marriage, and a steadily increasing rate of casual sexual intercourse outside of marriage.

Some church members purchase or view pornographic materials. Television and much of the music industry are damaging our witness. We observe the "scoring" mentality in the dating practices of some Christian young people. We have adultery, sexism, and the chronic problem of men and women viewing each other primarily as potential sex mates and as bodies, rather than as persons, as friends, or as brothers and sisters in the church.

Yet we focus so much of our attention and wrath on homosexuality. Why are we more offended by "unnatural sex" (homosexual activity) than we are about aggressive, uncaring, exploitative "natural sex"? Many Christians whose own heterosexual behavior is crude and exploitative, who are unable to talk about their own attitudes with even a spouse, get hostile and emotional when the subject of homosexuality arises. Even though this kind of emotional reaction is a reality, most people can agree on many aspects of the homosexuality issue.

Areas of General Consensus

The following are points on which we generally do agree, or at least should be able to agree:

1. There is much diversity among homosexuals. There is no stereotype that fits all. There is no typical homosexual any more than there is a typical heterosexual.

2. We usually cannot identify by dress, mannerisms, or speech who is same-sex oriented. Even psychological testing may fail to identify that individual. Homosexual persons do have in common their experience of discrimination; for that reason, most are closeted and invisible (not recognized as such). Gay persons are truck drivers, football players, farmers, policemen, clerks, and homemakers. They are in the professions and many other areas of endeavor. They are our relatives, friends, coworkers, and people with whom we worship in many of our congregations. If we say we do not know any gay persons, it is almost certain that we are just unaware that we do know gay persons.

3. We can agree that we should not define gay persons by their sexual orientation. Joe is a pastor, Jane is a teacher, and Pete is a farmer; but Henry is a homosexual, or Sally is a lesbian. Although our sexuality is a pervasive dimension of who we are, it is not the sole or defining dimension of our lives, whatever our orientation. I am known as a physician; let us define Henry and Sally according to their character and their roles in society as well, rather than as homosexuals.

4. It is difficult to be accurate regarding the incidence of homosexuality. "Kinsey's data suggested that close to 10 percent of the U.S. population was gay or predominantly gay, a number that dramatically exceeds current estimates" (Rathus, Nevid, Fischner-Rathus: 289). In fact, many parts of the Kinsey research methods are being challenged today. It is unlikely that we can acquire accurate data, because so many gay persons are closeted and have not come out publicly, justifiably fearing discrimination and even violence.

5. Homosexuals are not the "scum of the earth." Famous persons who reputedly have been gay include Erasmus, Leonardo da Vinci, Michelangelo, T. E. Lawrence, Willa Cather, William James, Queen Mary II, Walt Whitman, Tchaikovsky, Frederick the Great, Sir Francis Bacon, and Christopher Marlowe. In modern times as well, we are learning of well-known, contributing persons who are of same-sex orientation. The world has been enriched in the past and is being enriched today by the contributions of homosexual persons.

6. Homosexual orientation is not contagious. We do not "catch" it by associating with homosexual persons. It is important for people to understand that neither adults nor children are at risk of acquiring a same-sex affinity in school, church, or elsewhere from colleagues, teachers, or others.

7. Homosexual persons are not per se molesters of children, nor are they predominantly violent. In fact, most are quite the opposite—very gentle persons.

8. One same-sex erotic experience does not define one as homosexual. There is that broad spectrum of sexual preference; during our lifetimes, we move back and forth along this continuum. There is much needless anguish among persons who at some time (often in adolescence or while in an all-male or all-female environment such as single-sex colleges, the military, or prison) had an erotic homosexual experience and fear that it defines them for life. It is not helpful for the sexually obsessed media culture of our day to prey as it does on the sexual identi-

ties and sexual attitudes of insecure adolescents and to imply that people thereby "discover" who they are.

9. Not all homosexual persons want to change their core sexual attraction. Some try to change; many do not. Some consult psychiatrists or other therapists; some never do and do not want to.

10. We should be aware that many homosexuals are married to persons of the other sex and are often parents. Frequently they have married in an attempt to prove to themselves that they are not gay. They probably tried to avoid societal discrimination or to live up to family expectations. Many of these marriages eventually dissolve.

11. There are many homosexual people in our churches— often hidden, hurting, and afraid.

12. Although we do not know the cause of same-sex orientation (see the next section), most people agree, based on research and the life stories of homosexual persons, that it is usually not a consciously chosen condition any more than heterosexuality is consciously chosen. Although many in the religious community dispute this, much evidence shows otherwise. Again, we do make choices on what behavior we follow.

In spite of these many points about homosexuality on which most people can agree, there are also some where people strongly disagree.

Points of Continuing Disagreement

The following three major points of disagreement are present in the church and in general society.

1. What causes same-sex orientation? There are various theories, but, as noted above, the causes are not known. Some believe it represents a developmental arrest around the age of puberty. Others believe it is caused by some hormonal abnormality yet unidentified. Some say it is genetically caused and that someday we will discover the gene for homosexuality. Some believe it is environmentally caused, arising out of disorder in family dynamics.

There is no agreement in the medical-scientific community as to the cause of homosexuality, but there seems to be increasing evidence that there is at least a genetic link of varying degree. Studies on twins and other research suggest that homosexuality is inborn in some way, but nothing conclusive has been determined.

If there is a majority opinion, it would be that the causes of same-sex orientation are multiple and complex, and that a combination of factors along with a genetic predisposition is responsible. Dr. Verle Headings, a geneticist at Howard University, has given much study to this issue. At the time he published results of his study, Headings described the cause of homosexuality as involving many factors and possibly various genetic origins (1024). There has been no further evidence brought to public attention that would counter this hypothesis in recent decades, perhaps due to lack of funding for such research.

If Headings's suggestions are true, it is reasonable to deduce that there is such a complex set of causative factors that the cause may differ from person to person. Perhaps that is why we hear such varying reports from both the religious and the psychiatric community as to its changeability. Possibly, because of its varying causation, some gay persons can change and others cannot, but the depth of change again would vary. Instead of saying homosexuality, perhaps we should say homosexualities.

2. Is same-sex orientation changeable? Most psychiatrists say that they have seen "not one case" of permanent change of core sexual attraction of a person who is a 4, 5, or 6 on the Kinsey scale, mostly same-sex oriented. There are other psychiatrists who claim a 30-percent or more success rate in assisting persons who consult them for help in changing their sexual attraction.

Part of this discord may come from using the same word to mean different things. Are both groups of psychiatrists defining the word *change* in the same way? With many factors of causation, we can anticipate various claims of success in helping persons to change. Some define change as the ability to function sexually in a heterosexual marriage or to refrain from genital activity altogether, even though the person's fantasies remain with same-sex partners. Others insist that change means a shift in one's core attraction and sexual fantasies toward persons of the other sex. Just as with causation, the changeability of sexual orientation remains unsettled and is a source of contention.

3. What is the meaning of biblical materials often cited as referring to homosexuality? Sharply contrasting views persist among Bible scholars; some on both sides even demonize those who hold a different interpretation.

Jesus did not mention homosexuality, and the New Testament has only a few passages that relate to it. Scholars disagree as to whether these passages speak to the issue of gay "marriage" (between two committed, monogamous persons of the same sex in a lifelong covenant relationship). The Old Testament passages denouncing homosexual relations as an abomination also denounce other practices that we routinely ignore. The Bible speaks more clearly and at much greater length on the issues of divorce, prayer covering, and the accumulation and use of wealth.

No language from biblical times had a word corresponding to what we term *homosexuality*. The first usage of the word *homosexuality* in an English translation was in the Revised Standard Version in 1946. In any case, any reference to same-sex eroticism is to sexual activity, not attraction. The understanding of homosexuality as a psychosexual orientation emerged late in the nineteenth century.

Those who believe the Bible speaks clearly on this issue must remember that the texts we read have come down to us through centuries of translation and interpretation, filtered through various languages, and translated through the best efforts of biblical scholars. As Daniel Taylor said in his article, "Confessions of a Bible Translator,"

All translation is interpretation. At every point the translator is required to interpret, evaluate, judge, and choose.
Every text is thickly layered with unique and sometimes
incommensurable features of form, not to mention the
very sound of words. . . . This does not mean that translation is merely subjective, but we should guard against the
illusion that there is a single right way of treating translation in general or any one passage in particular. (76)

In a workshop I attended, one lay church leader said, "What
in the Bible seems to be plain English is often muddy Greek."
Philip Yancey writes,

Those who take up the daunting task of Bible translation step into a force field of tension. On the one
hand, we must keep on arguing about proper meaning
because we so highly value that meaning. On the other
hand, we must recognize that all translation, indeed all
language, contains an element of uncertainty. We dare
not lessen the tension on either end. (88)

So, what does the Bible say about homosexuality? Surely we
must use a degree of humility in our pronouncements. Equally
learned and sincere scholars disagree. We all have our biases and
should admit them. Myron Augsburger writes,

It has been said that what any people of faith believe
is not what the Bible says but what they understand
the Bible to say! This is why we need to admit our perspectives. We test our perspectives by openness before
the Spirit and the Word in the community of faith. (2)

It is my prayer that God will give us the spirit to grow as
hearers of the Word *and* to increase our understanding of the
truth through interaction and discernment with each other.

Personal Responses

In view of all of the above, including the disagreements and uncertainties, what are the implications for our personal attitudes on this issue? The uncertainties and the complex dimensions surrounding the issue of homosexuality call me to sensitivity, to humility, and to compassion.

First, *sensitivity* is born out of the awareness that the person of homosexual orientation is potentially my brother or sister in Christ and, like me, is one for whom Christ died and one whom I must treat with love and respect.

Second, since there is so much about homosexuality that we do not know, I am called to *humility*. What might we learn in the next ten to twenty-five or fifty years from the Human Genome Project (mapping human genes and analyzing human DNA), from biblical scholarship, or from other research? Church people should be wary of making dogmatic pronouncements about the causation or changeability of same-sex attraction, bringing discredit on themselves if later valid research proves them wrong.

For example, if the genetic component of causation is greater than now known, how would that alter our attitudes toward gay marriage? In addition, a broader grasp of the whole of biblical teachings and of God's intention in the original creation and in the new creation may bring us more insight as we listen to each other (Hays; Grenz). Thus, our understanding of the causation, changeability, and the biblical materials is incomplete; this should lead us into an attitude of humility.

Humility is also needed because we who are heterosexual people cannot imagine what it is like to walk in the shoes of our homosexual brother or sister. Lewis Smedes put it this way: "Let it just be said, then, that no matter how sure some heterosexual people are in their moral judgments, they make them in a fog of ignorance about the deeper goings on in a homosexual's life" (64).

Third, I am called to *compassion*. I know of few other issues that have caused such suffering. I must have compassion—

1. For youngsters who grow up feeling different and do not know why.

2. For the adolescent who has almost accidentally experienced a same-sex orgasm and is tormented by the fear that he or she might be homosexual.

3. For gays who are afraid their parents will not accept them if they know of their same-sex attraction.

4. For parents who are in torment when they discover the same-sex attraction of their son or daughter and are plagued by the question "Where did we go wrong?"

5. For parents who do not accept their gay child and rupture a parent-child relationship that should be one of unconditional love.

6. For gay persons who married in an attempt to change their sexual interest, an attempt that failed.

7. For the spouse of the gay person who does not know the orientation of that person in bed beside him or her and cannot understand the lack of sexual interest and the rejection being experienced in the relationship.

8. For the spouse who is locked into a marriage with a homosexual mate and worries about the effect of it on their children.

9. For the husband or wife of the gay spouse who has decided no longer to deny her or his sexual attraction and wants out of the marriage.

10. For the children and the spouse in a family that has broken up because of the departure of a gay parent and spouse.

11. For all those in closets, unable to reveal and share who they really are.

12. For the closeted gay person who has experienced rejection, but for obvious reasons cannot seek understanding or care from pastor, parents, or anyone in their usual support system.

13. For all those who fear their sexuality, are insecure about their own sexual attractions and fantasies, and therefore indirectly influence others to remain in closets.

14. For single people who are assumed by others to be gay just because they never married.

15. For same-sex friends who cannot be carefree in their normal nonsexual friendship for fear of what people will imagine or infer. (Close friends of the same sex find it difficult to form deeply bonded, non-erotic relationships; this is one of the saddest casualties of today's politicized and angrily divided society. Such relationships should be encouraged and affirmed.)

16. For gays who are trying to "change" and cannot.

17. For gays who have "changed" and are called liars by their gay peers.

18. For the homosexual in the pew beside us who listens year after year to harsh utterances from TV preachers and even our own pastors, as well as to the snide remarks and cruel jokes we tell while never suspecting the sexual affinity of the person beside us.

19. For pastors who are hurting because they do not understand why a certain member no longer confides in him or her, not suspecting it is because that person is gay and cannot forget the recent sermon condemning homosexuality.

20. For pastors who are perplexed and frustrated in dealing with gays in their congregations.

21. For church leaders who are trying to bring understanding and healing to the homosexuality discussion but who experience angry criticism for their efforts.

22. For all who are so insecure in their sexuality, in their sexual bodies, in their sexual identities, that this becomes such an explosive issue.

Need we go on? When I consider the issue of homosexuality, I am called to *sensitivity*, *humility*, and *compassion*.

There is an even more personal task for each of us. We need to know some homosexual persons and relate to them. We need to seek out some gay persons and become their friends. If we know people well enough, we can love them. If we really learn to know them and visit their inner thoughts and feelings, we find that we will love them.

Observations and Future Tasks for Christians

As a starting point in resolving the tensions surrounding the issue, it is essential that we first examine our attitudes regarding homosexuality. When our attitudes reflect intolerance, hatred, or fear, we must realize how destructive and disabling they are to the one who exhibits them, as well as to the ones who are the object of them. Our gay brothers and sisters are worthwhile persons, and we owe them Christian love. A people committed to love and justice must be against discrimination and oppression of gay persons.

We can have no part in anti-gay demonstrations. We must protest and reject the attitudes of so-called Christians who display bumper stickers, such as "Kill a Queer for Christ," or who carry signs that say, "God Hates Fags." We cannot join so-called Christians who oppose gay civil rights, which they call "damnable laws sure to hasten America's doom." Christ had much to say about oppression, and a people of justice can have no part in the oppression of gay people.

Second, we will have to learn to live with some uncertainty and ambiguity. The causes of same-sex attraction are unlikely to be known next week or next year. It is hard to live with ambiguity; we want to know everything "for sure." Uncertainty makes us uneasy and tends to give us a feeling that everything is coming unglued. We may think that if we accept any new understandings, everything is up for grabs and anything goes. I disagree. Throughout our lives, we have to deal with life on a moral slippery slope where not everything is clearly right or wrong.

On this slippery slope, we must make moral decisions from the best information and counsel available to us in discernment with fellow believers and in communion with God and the Holy Spirit. Uncertainty should lead us, in humility, into prayer and Bible study and into dialogue with those with whom we may disagree, discerning God's will in community under the guidance of God's Spirit. We must examine more than facts and doctrine; we must also examine our attitudes.

Third, when it comes to sexuality issues, we should always remember that we are all vulnerable. Who of us has a perfectly clean conscience when it comes to our sexuality? We must be careful about judging others. When we read the New Testament, we note that Jesus certainly condemned unrighteousness, but his harshest words were for the self-righteous and their arrogance (Matt 7:1-5). We tend to single out sexual transgressions as somehow being uniquely sinful. God's grace and forgiveness encompass sexual transgressions.

In an address at Goshen College some years ago, Dr. Lewis Penhall Bird said,

> Many Christians seem to assume that the seven deadly sins were fornication, adultery, homosexuality, masturbation, venereal disease, oral-genital stimulation, and abortion. In reality, of course, they were pride, envy, anger, sloth, avarice, gluttony, and lust. All of us must seek the grace of God.

Fourth, we need to work for church unity and fellowship. When it comes to homosexual genital relationships, most Christian groups count this as sin. The major issue being debated has to do with the few persons who want to be a part of the church, who are eligible on all other grounds, but who are involved in a loving, committed, covenantal, and permanent relationship (like marriage) with someone of the same sex. Congregations have differed in their response. I think it is sad when that diversity in response is the cause of breaking Christian fellowship.

We have not broken fellowship with those with whom we disagree on business practices and ethics, on the payment of war taxes, on registration for the draft, on lavish versus simple lifestyles, on the use of alcohol, and on many other issues. Instead, on these issues we keep talking, searching, praying, and striving for the will of God.

Although the issue of homosexuality tends to be divisive, must it be a matter over which we divide our communions?

Personally, I hope not. I believe that, mindful of the inexhaustible grace of God, we need to work responsibly on divisive issues and seek God's will in both our lifestyles and our discernment processes. This will enable us to maintain fellowship with our fellow believers.

Fifth, we must call the homosexual community to Christian attitudes and expression. The homosexual community, as well as the heterosexual community, must face the task of understanding the foundations of heterosexuals' fear and behavior. Closed minds and bigoted attitudes are not helpful, whether displayed by homosexuals or by heterosexuals. If we have attitudes of openness and of seeking truth instead of militant attitudes, we are more likely to understand both sides.

In addition, homosexuals should not expect the church to accept a lesser moral standard from them than it does from its heterosexual members. The church can and should have the same attitude toward sexual promiscuity, for example, whether this involves homosexual or heterosexual persons. It is expected that homosexual people monitor and discipline their thoughts and their behavior. They must hold themselves to the same moral standard that is expected of heterosexual people.

Sixth, honestly searching for guidance regarding the issue of homosexuality may not bring total agreement. However, we should be able to come together in a resolve to find new ways to live out Micah 6:8. We need a renewed commitment to "act justly and to love mercy and to walk humbly with [our] God."

This chapter has encouraged us to do the following:

- View homosexuality in the context of our overall sexuality.
- Narrow the areas of disagreement.
- Avoid becoming emotionally bogged down with rhetoric in areas where there is no real disagreement.
- Use precise language.
- Emphasize the importance of our attitudes.

- Affirm those who have the integrity to deal with this tough question and hear all sides.
- Not break fellowship with those with whom we disagree.

If we withdraw from the struggle of wrestling and discernment, we close the door for possible transformation on either side. This transformation may come through the interaction and openness to which we say we are committed. It is clear that Christian people of goodwill have strong differences on this issue. Our task is to continue to work through it together in loving dialogue.

Discussion Questions

1. If your son or daughter would announce to you that he or she is a homosexual or a lesbian, how would you respond?
2. Why is the homosexuality issue so emotionally explosive in society? In Christian congregations and denominations?
3. We often hear that we should "hate the sin but love the sinner." How have you befriended both homosexuals and heterosexuals in your congregation?
4. Do you feel called to sensitivity, humility, and compassion with regard to same-sex orientation and toward gay persons who claim salvation through Christ? At what points do you agree or disagree with the author?
5. If you are homosexual, are you able to forgive and love those who oppress you by attitude and words?
6. When sincere Christians disagree on interpretation of Scripture, what principles can help us to stay in loving dialogue with each other?

9

The Gift and Cross-Gender Friendships

Willard S. Krabill

In her excellent book *How Can a Man and a Woman Be Friends?*
Mary Rosera Joyce asks, "Is it possible for a boy and a girl [or] a
man and a woman to be friends?" (9). The question implies correctly that sexual difference in our society can be an obstacle to
friendship. Friendship involves a bond between equals; throughout most of history, this kind of bond between a man and a woman was considered unlikely.

Surveys show that most people see same-sex friendship as
different from other-sex friendships. Friendships between women
and men are viewed as more complicated because of potential
sexual tensions, for one thing. We tend to turn to our same gender
for friendship and turn to the other gender for validation of our
worth or desirability; for union, gratification, and possession; or
even for conquest. However, men and women still strive to find
friendship in their relationships with each other as well.

Qualities of True Friendship

In her book, Joyce lists four qualities of true friendship, especially
"other sex" friendship: equality, esteem, affection, and shared
values. Think about those four terms. It becomes evident that
some male-female relationships, even marriages, are not based on
friendship.

Although sexual difference affects friendship, it need not
and must not be an obstacle in forming friendships if we are

to achieve healthy sexuality, experience vital female-male companionship, and understand each other's feelings and needs.

We need to understand our sexuality and our common need for intimacy and learn how to be friends. These accomplishments will help us form a society where it is usual and normal to have as many friends of the other sex as it is to have friends of our own sex. Such a society would be a place where one can feel safe to risk vulnerability or risk falling in love.

We would not need to fear dating a friend. In a climate of male-female friendship (with equality, esteem, affection, and shared values), sexual oppression and exploitation would surely diminish. One would not try to discover how far one could go in making out with a friend or hang nude pictures of a real friend or join in joking about the body of a friend.

Myths About Friendship

One of the myths about friendship is that friends always agree with one another. In his book *On Being a Friend*, Eugene Kennedy said learning how to disagree with a friend begins when one realizes it is not a matter of winning or losing. By recognizing and respecting a friend's point of view, one can learn how to handle differences. Winning and losing are not applicable in friendship.

We need not always agree, but we do need always to listen—as equals who are respected and held in esteem, with affection and sharing of values. Without becoming defensive, men must listen to women's pain from living as part of an oppressive system. Women must listen to men's pain from also living as part of an oppressive system, without blaming or accusing them.

Although complete and constant agreement is not a requirement for female-male friendship, listening and equality are. We have to approach a friendship from equal power bases, fully respecting the worth and the personhood of the other. Clinging or grasping, manipulating, using, dominating or submitting, going along with love to get sex (as men tend to do) and going along with sex to get love (as women tend to do)—these do not characterize the relationship of friends.

Instead, we need to be together in a relationship of trust and respect, with equality, esteem, affection, and shared values. These qualities describe true friendship, healthy sexual friendship, and the kind of relationship out of which romance may or may not grow. In this instance, when I say romance, I am talking about a serious relationship whose foreseeable objective is permanent union.

In any case, however, a romantic relationship that over time evolves out of a friendship with this kind of integrity is a relationship that need not be feared as a threat to friendship. It can be a romantic relationship with a far better chance of survival than a dating relationship that short-circuits true friendship and intimacy, prematurely moves to the physical and the genital, overloads the circuits, and blows the fuse. After experiencing a few such negative episodes, one naturally becomes afraid: afraid to risk, afraid to trust, and even afraid to date.

A healthy sexuality is one that is emotional, mental, relational, and spiritual as well as physical. The physical does not necessarily include the genital relationship; that, I believe, can fulfill its potential for ecstasy only after all other dimensions of friendship, intimacy, and commitment have been achieved. A well-developed sexuality is centered in the head and soul, not in the groin. Even genital sex is not truly human without the elements of love, freedom, responsibility, decision, imagination, sensitivity, and feeling. These all are qualities of the brain, not the gonads.

Some of us have learned about sexuality and other-sex relationships from exemplary models of devoted, loving parents and extended families, and thereby we are blessed. But too many people have learned about sex and sexuality in homes where parents were not friends, were absent, had multiple partners, or modeled infidelity in various ways. Parents may have been abusive, uncles guilty of incest, and on and on. Not all have had the privilege of discovering sex in beautiful and non-exploiting ways.

Surely most of us have learned much about distorted exploitive sex as purely physical passion from the popular culture—visual and written media, music, and various examples. True male-female friendships should enable us to hear the pain of those whose learning about sex was not ideal. Such friendships should enable the already wounded among us to learn that there are women who are not out to exploit us and men who are not out to abuse us.

Given the popular culture, it is a tremendously difficult task to grow into friendships with the other sex, relationships that enable us to fulfill our real intimacy needs. Immature and underdeveloped sexual beings seem to believe that the center of our sexuality is not in our heads but in our groins. This mentality perpetuates the false notion that a healthy female and male who are attracted to each other must either head for bed or frustrate their sexuality. Whatever happened to friendship? A genital-centered view of sexuality binds us in our erotic desires and feelings. But a person-centered view of sexuality frees us for equality and friendship.

We live in an age of compulsive sex. If we are to be freed from the enslavement of compulsive sex, we need to experience true sexual freedom. Men are not really just hungering for women's bodies. Women are not really just hungering for men's bodies. Not really! This can become a dimension of intimate relating, but the real need is for the broader fulfillment of intimacy, closeness, and friendship. True sexual friends are able to touch and hold each other in affirmation without becoming erotically aroused. To be able to do that is sexual freedom.

Friendship as Prelude to Marriage

In the context of our many friendships with persons of the other sex, it may be that after developing a friendship, a couple will choose to marry. That chosen marriage is made secure and great by the quality of the couple's friendship. Their commitment growing out of such a friendship gives their genital union an intensity and a joy not otherwise possible.

A new sense of self and of female-male relationships can be discovered and developed. It is part of our human and God-given potential, and the rewards are astounding. In Matthew 5:27-29 and 6:22-23, Jesus emphasized the importance of the eye, of seeing rightly, and of the relation between seeing and lust. These verses confirm that it is important how we view each other—as objects or as persons, as friends or as sex mates.

Jesus modeled for us what it means to be a friend. He infused friendships with the meaning that makes them true, intimate, and worthwhile. The New Testament presents a model of head-centered, soul-centered sexuality. The greatest value two friends can share is their mutual friendship with God. Love for God intensifies human intimacy and all other qualities of friendship.

Freedom to Be Cross-Gender Friends

Why should we allow a sexually distorted society to define our sexuality and our ways of relating? Martin Luther King Jr. inspired us with his dream of equality and freedom in his famous "I Have a Dream" speech to massed thousands in Washington, D.C., on August 28, 1963. I too have a dream of a society where men and women feel free to be friends, intimate friends, able to relate in equality, esteem, affection, and sharing of values, without feeling any necessity or compulsion to become genital sex partners. I have a dream of a society where men and women would have as many close friends of the other sex as they do of their own sex.

I have a dream of a society where men would not tolerate for a minute the violence done to their women friends by those who rate the bodies of the women walking by. So many gutless, silent men allow such verbal garbage to go unchallenged. I dream of a society whose women are truly liberated and assertive enough to insist they are ready and available for friendship, but not for conquest by the friend. I dream of a society whose men are truly liberated and assertive enough to insist that they are ready and available for friendship, but not for possession or seduction by the friend.

I have a dream of a society where women will not feel driven to find their identity in a man; where both men and women have their relationships centered in meaning and values, in friendship and not in ownership; where women and men share friendships that promote personal growth and transcend rigidly defined roles; where men and women find joy, fun, laughter, and celebration in the company of their friends—friends who do not have to be their party mates or their sex mates.

I have a dream of a society of persons freed from genital preoccupation, who have grown enough in their sexuality to discover that the center of their sexuality is in their heads, not below their belts. I dream of a society where administrative authority is shared, in friendship, between women and men. I have a dream of a society of sexually free persons, free to enjoy their mutual attraction for each other without having to express it in an erotic or genital way. That is real sexual friendship, real sexual freedom, appropriate male-female relating.

What would fulfillment of this dream mean? It would mean the same thing it meant to Martin Luther King Jr. decades ago in Washington, D.C.: "Free at last! Free at last! Thank God Almighty, we are free at last!"

Guidelines for Developing Friendships with Other-Sex Persons Who Are Not One's Spouse

I base these guidelines on an assumption that if one is married, the relationship is solid; an atmosphere of trust and confidence exists, based on conviction and on past performance earning that trust. The guidelines, developed from various sources, are presented as questions to ask oneself in evaluating other-sex friendships with anyone not one's spouse.

1. Is the friendship about something outside ourselves? That is, is it a shared interest about art, music, business, sports,

church life, theology, or something else? If the friendship is not around some *thing*, but rather about *us*, we are getting into a dangerous area where red flags should be raised.

2. Is it an exclusive friendship, or could it be shared with a third or even a fourth party who also is interested in the thing that brought us together as friends? If it is exclusive and could not be opened to a third party, we are clearly dealing with a high-risk situation.

3. Is it an equal friendship? In this relationship, is either person in an advantageous position over the other? Is either trying to impress the other or manipulate the other for any purpose? If one party to the friendship has an advantage or is trying to impress or manipulate the other, there is danger.

4. Can we talk openly with others about our relationship, or is it secret? Do we have to hide the fact that we are friends and are meeting with the other person to share a relationship? Secretive friendships are risky.

5. Is the activity we share and our behavior within the relationship appropriate to friendship rather than courtship? Is it clear and assumed (discussed if need be) that sexual attraction is not acted upon? The friendship must be considered too important to let a sexual undertow drown it.

6. If we are married, does the relationship add to or take away from our respective marriages? Could our spouses be invited along or invited to look on at any time? Would our behavior be the same if our spouses were present? If not, there is danger.

7. Am I jealous of this friend? If so, the relationship is suspect.

8. Do I *need* the relationship, or do I *want* the relationship? Is the friendship something I enjoy and desire, or is it necessary for my emotional needs to be met? If I *need* the other person, again we are dealing with a risky situation; the friendship needs to be reevaluated and reconstituted on a different basis. We should be able to say, "I appreciate you, but I do not *need* you."

Discussion Questions

1. What might contribute to forming a person-centered view of sexuality that frees us for equality and friendship, rather than a genital-centered view that binds us in our erotic desires and feelings?

2. Some people relate more easily with people of the other gender than with those of their own gender. What factors contribute to this? What factors make this difficult for others?

3. How can fulfillment of the dream to have intimate friends in both genders be facilitated and promoted?

4. What steps should one take when the answers to questions asked in the guidelines raise danger warnings?

10

The Gift and Aging

Keith Graber Miller and Anne Krabill Hershberger

People fortunate enough to reach their seventh, eighth, and ninth decades of life have a wealth of experiences and acquaintances just from having lived that long. These memories can enrich our lives immensely, but they are not enough. We all need close friends—those with whom we can relate, be our totally honest selves, and share our deepest thoughts and feelings. When a spouse and/or close friends die, it takes extra effort to develop relationships that allow us to "connect, commit, and care" (Crowley and Lodge: 265). Such relationships are not a given.

This chapter will focus on living whole and rewarding lives as sexual beings in later years of life. Since we are sexual beings from birth to death, what matters to everyone—older people included—is our need for human contact: intimacy. This is critical to good health and quality of life, and its absence is devastating.

Dramatic Increases in Older Adults

In the United States, the number and percentage of older adults is getting larger all the time. Because more people than ever before are living into their seventies, eighties, and nineties, and birth rates are declining, both the number of people over sixty-five and its percentage of the total population have grown rapidly in recent years and will continue to grow. In the United States in 1900, only 4 percent of the population was sixty-five years of age or over. In 1950 older people made up 8 percent of the U.S. population, and by 2000 the figure was 12 percent. By 2050, people over sixty-five will make up about 21 percent of the U.S. population, according to the Congressional Research Service (Shrestha: 13–16).

The population explosion of older people is directly related to dramatic increases in life expectancy. When the United States was founded, the average American could expect to live to age thirty-five. By 1900 life expectancy at birth was 47.3; the average American born in 2010 can expect to live to seventy-eight (U.S. Census Bureau).

Not only are there more older adults than in earlier generations, but these older adults also are continuing to engage sexually. It is wrong to assume that we lose all interest in sex as we age. Although men and women tend to experience a gradual decrease in the frequency in which they engage in sexual intercourse as they age, that does not say that sexual expression and enjoyment are not important later in life. The National Council on Aging conducted a survey of 1,292 people in their sixties, seventies, and eighties in 1998. The survey confirmed that "about half had sexual activity at least once a month, and 70 percent of those who were sexually active indicated that their sex lives were at least as satisfying as they had been when they were in their forties" (Kelly: 194).

In "Grandma's Got Her Groove On," a 2007 *USA Today* article that cited research done at the University of Chicago's National Opinion Research Center, findings included the following:

- U.S. women age fifty-five and older are enjoying sex more than women the same age a decade ago. They are putting more thought and effort into their sex life.
- More than half of those age fifty-seven to seventy-five said they continued to give or receive oral sex, as did about a third of seventy-five- to eighty-five-year-olds.
- Those who had sex with a partner in the previous year included 73 percent of people age fifty-seven to sixty-

four; 53 percent of those sixty-five to seventy-four; and 26 percent of those seventy-five to eighty-five.

- Those who have sexual activity two or three times a month or more included 55 percent of men age fifty-seven to sixty-four; 38 percent of women that age; 43 percent of men ages sixty-five to seventy-four; 26 percent of women that age; 21 percent of men age seventy-five to eighty-five; and 9 percent of women that age.

- Women at all ages were less likely to be sexually active than men. Women also often lacked partners, partly because far more were widowed.

- People whose health was excellent or very good were nearly twice as likely to be sexually active.

Earlier studies also noted ongoing or increased sexual pleasure in older age. A survey of 1,604 people aged sixty-five to ninety-seven, conducted by Mark Clements in 1996, found that 52 percent of males and 30 percent of females were sexually active. "They engaged in sexual activity on the average of 2.5 times per month, although they would have preferred to have sex about twice that amount. During their previous ten sexual experiences, the men reached orgasm about 80 percent of the time, and the women about 50 percent" (Kelly: 193–94). "Human beings retain a full range of emotions—including romantic and sexual ones—throughout the life span. A major reason behind suppression of these feelings in many older people is the societal attitude that such reactions are indeed lost with age" (Kelly: 193).

Aging and Changing Bodies

There definitely are physical changes that occur for men and women as they age, and these can affect their sexual experiences. The following table describes these changes.

Changes in Sexual Response Connected with Aging

Changes in the Female	Changes in the Male
Reduced muscle tension (myotonia)	Longer time to achieve erection and orgasm
Reduced lubrication	Need for more direct stimulation to achieve erection and orgasm
Reduced elasticity in the vaginal walls	Less semen emitted during ejaculation
	Softer erections
Smaller increases in breast size during sexual arousal	Testicles may not elevate as high prior to ejaculation
	Reduced intensity of spasms of orgasm
Reduced intensity of spasms of orgasm	Less need to ejaculate
	Longer refractory period

From *The Kinsey Institute New Report on Sex*, 1990, p. 27. Reprinted by permission of The Kinsey Institute for Research in Sex, Gender, and Reproduction, Inc.

In both men and women, the loss of subcutaneous fat (fat just under the skin) causes the skin to sag, including the breasts. One older woman was overheard saying that she used to think of her breasts as rosebuds; now she sees them as long-stemmed roses. Weight gets redistributed. There is hair loss in the pubic area, as well as on other parts of the body.

Women reach a peak of sexual responsiveness in their mid-thirties and tend to maintain this level throughout the remainder of their lives, given regular sexual activity. In spite of the physiological changes related to endocrine imbalance (noted in the table above) the potential for orgasm remains high and in some cases continues to increase well into a woman's later years. In the post-menopausal period of life many women experience a kind of liberation as they enjoy freedom from the worries of pregnancy and childbearing.

> People who have been sexually active early in life often continue to be throughout life, as long as their physical health permits. . . . Many seniors say that the capacity for sexual pleasure increases with age, even if frequency and intensity of sexual activity do not. . . . For some people diminished interest in sex can be a liberating and welcome change that aging brings. (Weil: 254–55)

On the other hand,

> No one knows how many couples struggle with a loss of sexual intimacy because one or both of them has Alzheimer's Disease, Parkinson's Disease, diabetes, heart disease, multiple sclerosis, severe arthritis or has suffered a stroke. Invasive surgical procedures, antidepressants, blood-pressure medications and other prescription drugs also can affect the sex drive. But many people face this problem. (Pope: 8)

Prostate surgery, for example, has caused many men to be unable to have an erection or ejaculate. For other reasons, some males experience erectile dysfunction (limited blood circulation to the penis), which can make sexual intercourse impossible.

> Sex may be the one experience where a healthy spouse and an ill partner can restore the emotional equilibrium of their relationship, making it less of a nurse-patient model. Even if the ill spouse can only manage a back rub or neck massage, it can have a marvelous restorative impact on the care-giving spouse because it's a small but symbolic effort to rebalance the relationship. (Cohen interview in Pope: 8)

One spouse, who had lived in a situation where illness

prevented the couple from engaging in sexual intercourse, said,

> What we went through was hard, sad, and painful, but looking back, our relationship really did get better. It was a different kind of love, a deeper kind, but it was just as strong as when we were younger and physically active. (Pope: 9)

Some physicians fail to inform older patients about sexual side effects of medications for conditions such as arthritis and high blood pressure because they assume sexual desire does not continue in older people. Then when drugs decrease the sex drive or responsiveness, older adults just assume that this is part of aging, and so they go into a downward spiral in sexual activity when they could be maintaining an active sex life.

When couples experience sexual problems, help is available (physicians, sex therapists, books), but a starting point is to maintain open communication with one's partner about sexual needs, anxieties, and difficulties. "In some cases . . . education or referral for counseling and behavioral strategies may be effective. In others, medication may offer the most effective treatment strategy" (Lacy: 25), though medicines—such as those for erectile dysfunction—may not be the first route older adults should pursue. Teacher and journalist Sally Feldman wrote in the *New Humanist*, "Currently more money is being spent on breast implants and Viagra than on Alzheimer's research. So in the very near future there should be a large elderly population with impressive breasts and magnificent erections, but no recollection of what to do with them."

Longevity and Sexual Engagement

For those *able* to engage sexually, recent studies also have suggested that doing so in our later years actually contributes to extending our life. A study already in the 1970s at Duke

University suggested that for men the frequency of sexual intercourse was associated with lower death rates and for women the enjoyment of intercourse was correlated with longer lives. A more recent study published in the *British Medical Journal* found that the death rate from all causes for the *least sexually active* men was twice as high as that of the *most sexually active*. The decade-long study included one thousand Welsh men ages forty-five to fifty-nine and involved placing the men into three groups: those who had sex twice or more a week, an intermediate group, and those who reported having sex less than once monthly. A similar pattern of longevity and frequency of orgasm was found for all causes of death, even when researchers factored out differences in age, social class, smoking, blood pressure, and evidence of existing coronary heart disease at the initial interview. The researchers suggested not only a correlation but also a *causal* relationship between engagement in sexual activity and longevity (Davey Smith, Frankel, and Yarnell: 1641–44).

At the same time it is true that many older adults who are willing, able, and desirous of having sexual relationships cannot because of lack of a partner. Statistics concerning people in the United States indicate that in the sixty- to sixty-four age bracket, there are eighty-eight men per one hundred women. Above age seventy-five, there are only fifty-five men per one hundred women. Among those over the age of eighty-five, there are forty men for every one hundred women. Nearly twice as many older men (78 percent) are likely to be married than older women (40 percent). For men over eighty, about 40 percent say they are still sexually active with a partner. For women over eighty, only 10 percent are still sexually active with a partner (as cited in Kelly: 195).

Even when one is in a relationship in which sexual intercourse is a possibility, adaptations to former patterns may be needed as one ages. Some of the changes that may occur include diminished libido; greater desire for touching, snuggling, and caressing than for intercourse itself; and choosing to make love at peak energy times rather than late at night, as may have been an earlier pattern.

For the many older people for whom a relationship that includes sexual intercourse is not a possibility, the need to relieve sexual tensions may be resolved in alternate ways. These alternative behaviors can be misunderstood, misinterpreted, and consequently troubling to some.

For example, a person who craves the touch of another person and uses appropriate opportunities to satisfy this need should not necessarily be labeled "dirty old man" or "watch out for that woman." It would be very helpful and appreciated if younger, as well as older, people would recognize this need and freely offer their affirming touches and hugs to those who get precious few of these on a regular basis. So much can be communicated in a caring touch. "I like being with you." "You are worthy." "You are touchable."

A very natural and readily available way to relieve sexual tension is physical self-pleasuring. In the past, this has been vilified and considered a pejorative activity by many people who did not understand the healthy and positive role it can have. Nor do most of us know how common self-pleasuring is, even into our older years. Some studies suggest that about 40 percent of women and 50 percent of men in their sixties engage in self-pleasuring.

We mention self-pleasuring in this context where older people have no sexual partner; however, it has been found that the majority of both men and women, whether married or single, find this to be a satisfying sexual release throughout their lives. In Roger R. Hock's book *Human Sexuality*, he lists a number of benefits derived from masturbation, based on the research of many scholars. These include sexual self-discovery, release of sexual tension or frustration, enhancement of sexual interactions with a partner, resolution of a variety of sexual problems (part of treatment programs), orgasm, relief from stress, relief from menstrual pain, compensation for a disparity in a couple's levels of sexual desire, and safe sex (Hock: 205).

Slow and gentle manipulation of one's erogenous zones of the body can satisfy sexual desire and lead to a climax in orgasm. Our bodies are incredible, responsive creations that can serve us well no matter what our situation in life may be. Self-pleasuring is helpful to many people, but it does not fulfill the longing for meaningful interpersonal relationships. In fact, Gary Kelly has indicated that as we age and become less genitally oriented, we actually have the potential of rediscovering our larger sensuousness. "Older people consistently report the sexual satisfaction they gain from kissing, caressing, holding, cuddling, and other types of lovemaking that involve both spiritual and physical intimacy" (Kelly: 198). This is how one woman who still had her husband expressed this point:

> I have been a very fortunate person. The man I married I still love dearly. We both respect each other and try to keep each other happy. We don't have sex as much as we used to but we kiss and hug and hold each other a lot. (Koch and Mansfield: 5)

Developing Intimacy, Embracing Aging

Some aging adults live in nursing homes or assisted-living facilities. In many of these facilities, there is a lack of personal, private space for couples to share intimately. There may be roommates or staff who are constantly in and out of the room. Some facilities are making allowances for couples who wish to have privacy to engage in sexual activity by providing private spaces for them. Much more sensitivity to the needs of institutionalized older people and creative planning are needed in this area.

Chris Crowley and Henry S. Lodge indicate that to live fully, older people need to invest some personal energy and attention. The integration of exercise, emotional commitment, reasonable nutrition, and a real engagement with living in one's daily life is the kind of needed investment (34). Emotional commitment may or may not involve a physical sexual relationship, but it certainly will go far in fostering meaningful intimacy with others and bring richness to one's life. "This effort might be called becoming the person you long to love" (Livingston: xvii).

Ralph Waldo Emerson once wrote, "As we grow old, the beauty steals inward" (cited in Livingston: 127). One commentator interprets Emerson's statement as suggesting that certain attributes of character replace the good connective tissue that is the sole property of the young.

The message of this chapter should be clear: interest and participation in sexual relationships is not limited to the young, nor should it be. Even though significant losses may be part of the older person's life experience, the potential for rejuvenating, life-enhancing relationships fosters a belief that Robert Browning's words in "Rabbi Ben Ezra" still ring true:

> Grow old along with me!
> The best is yet to be,
> The last of life, for which the first was made.
> Our times are in his hand.

Discussion Questions

1. Why has it been difficult for younger people to acknowledge and affirm the sexual vitality of older people?
2. There is a fine line between offering affirming physical contact (hugs, patting) and invading another person's personal space. How can this line be determined?
3. Livingston suggested that to live fully, older people need to invest some personal energy and attention to "becoming the person you long to love." What might this entail?
4. One person quoted in this chapter indicated that after her husband became ill and they could no longer have normal sexual relations, it was sad. But they developed a different, deeper love—just as strong as before. What factors facilitate this kind of development?

5. If you were managing a long-term care institution, how would you provide privacy for your residents and their spouses to have conjugal relations?

11

The Gift After Losing a Spouse

Rachel Nafziger Hartzler

This chapter is written from the perspective of a single-again widowed person whose husband died unexpectedly more than ten years ago. Can one write about sexuality as God's gift in this circumstance? Can sexuality be a gift to those who do not have a sexual partner? After a decade of experiencing a wide variety of emotions, concentrated study, spiritual reflection, and prayer, today I live well. I experience love, community, friendship, family support, creativity, joy, and delight. My life is full and satisfying even though I sleep alone.

God's gift of sexuality is indeed a gift, even for single people. Sexuality is energy, perhaps the greatest human energy, and it is part of a driving force that prompts us to be creative. Whether we are single or married, celibate or partnered, young or old, we express our sexuality in the deepest way with acts of healing, blessing, reconciliation, and co-creation with God.

I have come to embrace my sexuality as a gift from God. However, I do not see celibacy as a gift. Even though some say that the grace of God and the grace of creation develop the natural gift of celibacy, for me celibacy is a discipline. It is a discipline that has both spiritual and practical dimensions and can be joyfully practiced, even though it is challenging at times.

While a student at Associated Mennonite Biblical Seminary in 2003, I conducted a study of widowed people. The results are reported in my master's thesis essay and in a book published by Herald Press in 2006: *Grief and Sexuality: Life After Losing a Spouse*. This chapter incorporates some examples and summarizing concepts from the collected data, referred to here as the Living Well Study.

Single and Single-Again Adults

There are many single adults in the world and in the church. In 2007 there were nearly 93 million unmarried people in the United States over age eighteen. A 2008 U.S. census report yields the following (U.S. Census Bureau):

2008 U.S. Census	Never Married	Married	Widowed	Divorced	Total Single
women	22.5%	56%	10%	11.5%	44%
men	29%	59%	3%	9%	41%

The range of what single-again people experience after losing a spouse is great. Some widowed people say that their sexual desires died when the beloved spouse died. Others are shocked to find that intense sexual feelings occur soon after the death of a spouse—even an unexpected death. Some single-again people are relieved that a bad sexual/genital relationship has ended and that there is possibility for a new and better relationship, perhaps with a level of intimacy not experienced in the marriage that ended. A divorced person who is still in love with the rejecting ex-spouse may have intense sexual desires when thinking about (and especially when seeing) the person who left.

Whether single-again out of choice or not, formerly married people will likely have a new agenda regarding sexual expression. It has been suggested that people who have been accustomed to sexual relations might experience greater genital and physiological tension than people who have not been genitally active with another person. This is suggested but not documented in literature.

After years of research and countless interviews, I have concluded that, with the possible exception of the first months of being single-again, the intensity of sexual desires has little to do with present or past marital status, gender, orientation, or even age. Making good choices about sexual activity has more to do with self-understanding, education, maturity, and the quality of intimacy in a person's life than with age, gender, or even religious commitment.

Certain truths can help one to live well as a single, sexual, celibate person:

1. Sexuality and spirituality are deeply connected.
2. The basic sexual longing is for intimacy.
3. Intimacy can be experienced in friendships that are not romantic or genital.
4. There are healthy ways to respond to sexual desires without a genital partner.

Sexuality and Spirituality

Sexuality lies at the center of the spiritual life, and "one of the fundamental tasks of spirituality . . . is to help us to understand and channel our sexuality correctly" (Rolheiser: 193). After the first few months of intense mourning following my husband's death, I began to sort through my feelings by praying, reading, reflecting, and journaling.

I recognized a deep longing within myself, a longing that had been partially filled by the intimate relationship that Harold and I enjoyed. I began to wonder if my deepest longings and desires were really for God, and if the reason I was not totally satisfied with my marriage was because another person can never completely fill one's desires. I discovered a parallel in sexuality and spirituality. Both are a longing to know and be known by another, in one case by another human being and in the other case by God. I discovered Richard Rohr's *The Gate of the Temple: Spirituality and Sexuality*. Rohr's words were rays of illumination, and I began to see loss as an invitation to spiritual transformation. For me the invitation was to examine my deepest longings and to open myself to a deeper intimacy with God and a new call from God.

Donald Goergen examines theology and sexuality and says that "sexuality is an indication that we are not created self-subsistent beings. We are created incomplete by ourselves, relational beings, in need of others. God does not intend us to be alone" (58–59). Becoming independent is not our goal in life. Rather, we live to give and receive love. Love is at the root of Christianity, and sexuality is a gift from God that exists to make human love possible. God's plan is that not only do "two become one" but that in God's reign we will all be one, as Jesus and his Father are one. Sexuality is part of God's divine plan.

John S. Dunne clarifies that "our mind's desire is to know, to understand; but our heart's desire is intimacy, to be known, to be understood. To see God with our minds would be to know God, to understand God; but to see God with our hearts would be to have a sense of being known by God, of being understood by God" (39). Our sexuality and our spirituality both draw us into intimate relationships.

The desire to be intimately united with another is grounded in God's image. Relationship is at the heart of what it means to be in the image of God. An intimate relationship between people is a human expression of a relationship with God.

Intimacy

Although sexual arousal is often understood as an indication of a need for genital intercourse, the basic need is really for intimacy, relationship, acceptance, and affirmation. There are many kinds of intimacy, including spiritual, emotional, intellectual, and physical intimacy. Physical intimacy can be genital or nongenital, romantic or nonromantic.

The psalmists, mystics, and other thoughtful people describe a longing for God within the souls of all people. Some describe the desire as longing for union. From the Latin root of the word *sex* (to cut off) comes the idea that sexuality is an awareness of having been cut off. We are cut off when we are born, and being cut off is experienced as very painful. Ronald Rolheiser calls it "an aching loneliness and an irrational longing" (193–94). All our lives we long for union with another, with God and/or other humans. We need human relationships so that we can know God. Rohr says that relationships can be sacraments, ways to come to God. We cannot know the love of God unless we know the love of another human (Rohr: 1988).

Obviously, the fact that God made us sexual beings does not mean that God intends for us to respond to every sexual instinct or impulse by finding a sexual partner and having genital intercourse. God also made us *spiritual* and *thinking* beings with a great capacity to make decisions to control our instincts. (Other animals have little if any capacity to control their instincts.) We are relational beings, and there are powerful connections between being sexual beings and relational beings.

The late Dr. Willard Krabill helped generations of students and patients learn that needs for intimacy are far greater than needs for sexual expression. But it is sexual longings that draw people into relationships that can become intimate. Our sexuality includes all those activities that stem from and lead to the fulfillment of one's need for intimacy (Clark: 19).

A person without relationships may exist, but hardly lives. Rather, that person exists in the process of dying. This is seen vividly in babies who "fail to thrive" when they have inadequate human contact. It is well documented and acknowledged that human babies as well as babies of other mammals need parent or surrogate-parent interaction to stay alive. It is not so well recognized that this phenomenon continues throughout life. In chapter 3, "The Gift and Intimacy," Krabill says, "Intimacy is not only desirable; it is also a real need for everyone at every age."

A mystery in the cycle of sexuality, relationships, and intimacy is the fact that we can know ourselves only in relation to others. Rohr says, "We know ourselves only in mirrors, only in relationship. God's life is always mediated. We wait in darkness, unaware of ourselves, living in illusions and shadows as C. S. Lewis says, 'until we have faces'" (Rohr 1979: 22). Our sexuality draws us into relationships where we can learn to know ourselves and experience intimacy. As we know ourselves better, we will be better equipped to respond in healthy ways to our sexual desires.

The role of various kinds of intimacy within marriage is illustrated by responses in the Living Well Study. Widowed people were asked, "What did you miss most about your spouse in the first months after his/her death?" The following options were offered, and people were asked to rate them, with one being what was missed most.

____ my spouse's overall companionship
____ my spouse's physical presence
____ our emotional intimacy
____ our sexual intimacy
____ our physical (but not necessarily sexual) intimacy
____ other

"My spouse's overall companionship" was missed most by 68 percent of respondents. "My spouse's physical presence" was missed most by 18 percent of respondents and was rated second most-missed by 33 percent, all but one of whom had rated "my spouse's overall companionship" as number one. Only one person rated "our sexual intimacy" as number one, while 4 percent rated "our sexual intimacy" as the number two thing missed most. Fourteen percent rated it as number three, and another 14 percent rated it as number four. Interestingly, 57 percent of respondents did not check "our sexual intimacy" as something that was missed. This suggests that when reflecting back on a marriage, sexual intimacy was not nearly as important as other kinds of intimacy.

Sexuality in Widowhood

To try to determine the range of what is "normal" regarding sexual interest following the death of a spouse, the Living Well Study asked what changes in intensity of sexual desire widowed people had experienced.

Of those who answered this question, 16 percent said they did not note any changes in the degree of sexual longings after the spousal death, while 11 percent said specifically that the degree of sexual longings decreased. Responses included "No husband = no sexual longings"; "My sexual longings were tied to my spouse so closely that after the death those feelings were gone too"; "At first I lost all interest! A new relationship cautiously revived it."

Another 22 percent gave fairly neutral responses to the question about sexual longings, noting the presence of sexual desire but not commenting on whether it increased or decreased. Some typical responses follow:

- I would enjoy intimacy, but I don't crave sex most of the time.
- Sexual longings have not been prominent in my conscious awareness. I have enjoyed them when they have come, remembering my husband, but there is also a heightened sense of loneliness and loss at those times.
- For the first three years it seemed there were so many major crises that these needs did not seem important. When I first began to date, it was reassuring that these feelings were still a part of me.
- The unfulfilled longings still exist.
- I am not aware that my sexual interest changed much; the "opportunity" changed.
- I enjoyed sex when married but have never felt like I couldn't live without it.
- I don't know which is more difficult: being single—never having experienced sex and wanting to—or being widowed and wanting to again.

- A young horse is always ready to run. If there's not open field, you just keep him penned up!

Of the respondents, 21 percent said or implied that their sexual longings increased or continued to be intense after spousal death. Responses from people who experienced increased sexual desires or intense interest include the following:

- For the first few months I did not think about sex at all. Then it hit me like a tidal wave—great waves of sexual desire. I was very angry and frustrated. I had a lot of serious situations in my life that demanded time and energy, and this was very inconvenient. After loss of appetite, sleep, and energy, and after advice from counseling, I began to masturbate. At this point I masturbate more frequently than we had intercourse.
- After a few months I felt a stronger sexual drive than I had in years.
- I thought about sex then more than I did or do when married.
- I didn't realize sex was so important until I suddenly didn't have it anymore.
- They were still quite intense.
- Definitely more desirous.
- My sexual interest or drive picked up.
- I awake from dreams with sexual longings.
- I have continued interest in a long-term sexual relationship.
- I became more aware of how touch-deprived I am and how therapeutic it is to be held and hugged.

Even though the previous responses indicate that sexual intimacy is not the most missed thing, 11 percent stated that they very much miss the sexual relationship they had, saying:

- I deeply miss sexual intimacy.
- I have intensely missed our sexual relationship and our mutual sexuality.

Stephen Shuchter suggests that increased sexual interest, which sometimes follows the death of a spouse, may be a response to the loss of the many layers of intimacy that typically occurs with a spouse's death. Since the height of intimacy occurs in the sexual relationship for many couples, "the newly bereaved person may turn toward sexual relationships to create the illusion that they have again achieved such intimacy and saved themselves from pain" (111).

While this is likely true for some people, feelings of intense longing may occur in part due to the profound sense of emptiness a widowed person experiences after the death. Feeling disconnected from God as some people do after the death of a loved one, there may be a tremendous sense of longing to be loved and accepted, to know and be known; and there may be some relief of the intense longing when one's personal barriers melt away, as happens at the time of orgasm.

It is a complicated process to detach sexually from a deceased partner. But why is the death of a spouse, this event that occurs for nearly half of all married people, a huge issue? Why are the effects so profound? Perhaps just as there is mystery in the two becoming one in marriage, so there is mystery in the depth of the pain that occurs at the time of the death of a spouse. Freud's work on this subject is summarized:

> When a love object dies, the task of grief is to "decathect" or detach the libido from an object no longer capable of meeting one's needs, so that one may reinvest in a new object. This process of "mourning" is very demanding because the mourner rebels against the loss and is reluctant to abandon the original attachment. (Billman: 80)

Nongenital Intimate Friendships

To live well we need friendships. In fact, we need relationships to live. We were created because of God's passionate desire for relationship with humanity. God also created us for relationship with God. Created as we are in the image of God, we need relationships with God and with others. Indeed, it is in relationships that we learn to love, and it is love that gives meaning to life (Rohr: 1988).

As noted in chapter 9, friends are people who share values, feel affection for each other, experience equality with each other, and admire each other just as they are. Friends are important and extremely significant in that they help to shape who we are and who we become. People who experience friendship in a monogamous, lifelong, covenanted relationship are indeed fortunate and blessed.

For single nonpartnered people, nongenital intimate friendships are exceedingly important. In the Living Well Study, respondents said that longtime friends provided the most important support following spousal death. Family, church-family members, and other widowed people also gave important support.

Because widowed people repeatedly report that many former friends, especially couples, do not remain supportive after a spouse's death, the Living Well Study asked about relationships with the couple-friends people had before the spouse's death. Of those who responded to this question, 37 percent said all their couple-friends stood by them, 40 percent said most of their couple-friends stood by them, 11 percent said that some of their couple-friends stood by them, and another 11 percent said that only a few of their couple-friends stood by them.

Asking why the widowed person thought only a few friends stood by after being widowed elicited responses such as, "They didn't know what to say," "They don't know how to include a single," and "Because of their own hurt." Other respondents thought that former friends made unwarranted assumptions. For example, they assume that a widow is "after" another's husband or that a widowed person would not want to spend time with married people. As a result of not being included with couples, some widowed people said they felt alone or left out, which added to the sense of loss. Others chose to avoid spending time with groups of couples.

On the positive side, the fifty-two people who said all their couple friends stood by them gave reasons such as the strength of the friendship, things shared in common, and deliberate effort on the part of the widowed person. As a result of sustained relationships, people described feeling blessed, loved, supported, respected, valued, grateful, normal, protected, safe, comforted, strengthened, and encouraged.

More observations about friendships in the Living Well Study follow:

- Friends are extremely important to me. I'm not sure what I'd do without them.
- It's great to be in groups who aren't all widowed or single.
- I find that my new younger friends energize me.
- Widowed friends are helpful and seem to build strong ties.
- I have learned that there may be a need to exercise a certain caution in relating to the husbands of couple-friends, not because of attractions I have felt, but concern about being misunderstood.
- They say, "Call me any time." But I don't easily do that— especially married friends. It is better if they call me.

This deficiency of other-gender friendships was described in various ways. One widow in her forties referred to needing to pay all the men who help her. She pays her attorney, her psychotherapist, and servicemen. In one sense she even pays her pastor. She said, "I don't want to get married again, at least not now, but I would like to have a male friend so I can hear a male perspective on things in life." Furthermore, the man needs to be single so that the friendship is not complicated by his wife. Another woman who has since remarried said, "I missed male input. I remember wanting male relationships, not for romance, but just to be with them. It made me feel more complete."

Same-sex friendships are also important. Numerous women in the Living Well Study referred to the importance of friendships with other women. Although needs for intimacy can be met in same-sex friendships, many single people are interested in and/or seek intimacy with people of the other sex. Relationships with those of the other sex can be intimate without being genital.

Responding to Sexual Desires

One of the most important and most pressing questions for our society today is how to respond to sexual desires in healthy ways. The answers offered by North American culture to any desires are immediate gratification, individualism, and consumerism. The world needs some countercultural answers to the messages about body-centeredness and impulsive genital intercourse, and the church is poised to offer them.

A selfish, impulsive, undisciplined response to sexual desire is to have genital intercourse with the person with whom desire is aroused, even if a relationship does not exist. Responsible, thoughtful, and disciplined people will seek other responses when sexual desires are aroused. Following are healthy ways to respond to sexual energy for people who do not have genital partners.

Reflection on sexual desires. God created us with the capacity for reflection and the freedom to make choices. How we respond to sexual desires is extremely significant for ourselves and others, and it deserves our best reflection and careful choices. A sexual desire may represent the need for intimacy, but when intimacy needs are met and satisfied in other ways, the desire for physiological genital experience is lessened. This has been confirmed by widowed people surveyed.

Needing to have sexual intercourse is a result of an unbalanced sexuality within the self. "Anyone who thinks that genital intercourse is necessary to a sexual relationship, or necessary for physical, emotional, or mental health, lacks true sexual freedom." Sexual freedom is increased for those who have friendships that include equality, esteem, affection, and value-sharing (Joyce: 31–32).

Mary Rosera Joyce explains that an immature person who lacks self-knowledge and self-esteem tends to experience a stimulus-response reflex. An understanding of one's deeper sexuality, strengthened by self-esteem, will "cause the stimulus-response reflex to develop into a stimulus-reflection-response process" (27). Reflection helps a person to create or associate some meaning with the stimulus or feelings, and then to make a decision about a response, rather than letting a response simply emerge from the stimulus without thought or reflection. Simply put, reflection is using one's brain. And after all, the brain is the human being's primary sexual organ.

There is a difference between unexpressed sexual urges and repressed sexuality. Sexual repression is a way of blocking awareness or consciousness of an impulse, of burying it alive. With immediate gratification (a reverse form of repression), the impulse is born dead. What an impulse needs is integration with conscious reflection (Joyce: 36).

The alternative to repression is expression—not thoughtless, outward expression, but thoughtful, inward expression and integration with consciousness. "An erotic impulse actually needs and wants inward sexual expression before it is ready for outward expression." To become sexually mature, one must learn inward sexual expression, that is, to turn feelings and urges upward within the body, to let the impulse "flow into the head," to become part of one's conscious reflection. Inward expression is totally positive. It is a connecting process that could also be called the "centering" of erotic feelings (Joyce: 36–38).

This process is assimilation, not sublimation or repression.

"An erotic feeling is assimilated in consciousness, not by being digested, but by being integrated with self-knowledge and esteem, and in this way is transformed while remaining itself." When an erotic urge moves toward its own consciousness-raising center, it can have some kind of lasting meaning in its outward expression (Joyce: 39–40).

This mental work is not just a matter of self-control or of self-management. It is a quiet, loving self-process. Erotic desires can be welcomed into one's mind, received, felt, understood, and integrated into life's meanings and values. Repression or possession is not needed. One can touch and hold erotic feelings without possessing them (Joyce: 41).

Reflecting on erotic feelings is a natural process of human development. It is at the heart of true sexual freedom. When one experiences sexual freedom, one can "see with mental eyes and touch with mental hands," allowing physical eyes and hands to become less possessive and more tender (Joyce: 36–38).

Sexual centering results in sexual freedom, allowing one to embrace the gift of sexuality and choose an outward expression to an erotic impulse, an expression that is loving to self and other. A sexually free person has developed a capacity for true sexual friendship, and at the same time, the capacity to choose genital abstinence.

Living with inconsummation. In *The Holy Longing*, Rolheiser presents a model for healthy and holy sublimation of sexual desires, a way to modify or divert the impulse for sexual/genital activity to other disciplined activities. "Living with inconsummation" is in contrast to fulfilling a desire, in this case a sexual desire, by consummating or achieving that which is desired, in this case genital union with another person. Living with inconsummation begins by recognizing the expansiveness of sexuality. "A mature sexuality is when a person looks at what he or she has helped create, swells in a delight that breaks the prison of his or her selfishness, and feels as God feels when God looks at creation" (192). Choosing to live with inconsummation is one way to overcome separateness with nongenital, life-giving activities.

The concept of "living with inconsummation" recognizes that all desires cannot be met on this earth. When one does not have all desires met, it is easier to identify with the poor of the world. Sexual incompleteness can be solidarity with the poor. Understanding the time in which we are living, the already but not yet, may help one to work harder to help bring about the reign of God. Mature sexuality is "about giving oneself over to community, friendship, family, service, creativity . . . so that, with God, we can help bring life into the world" (Rolheiser: 198).

Inconsummated sexual energy may help one turn to solitude—where spiritual reflections may lead to greater well-being. One might think of living with inconsummation as living an unfinished symphony, of living with tension as Jesus did. Jesus carried the tensions of hatred, jealousy, and anger until his life was consummated in death, and then forgiveness, compassion, and love were offered to the world. Rolheiser says that "only someone who can live with the tension of an unfinished symphony will truly respect others" (224).

Living with inconsummation is holy sublimation. One of the Living Well Study respondents said, "Sublimation can be sublime—NOT!" Perhaps some sense of the transcendent can occur as one is sublimating sexual energy, but probably not without introspection and intentional effort. We may come to know that although we do not have the whole symphony, we do not need the whole thing. In some sense, none of us will have the whole symphony on this side of heaven.

An integration of sexual energy, heart, head, and spirit. An integrated model of responding to sexual desires involves both heart and head work. It begins with recognizing erotic feelings, sexual longings, and sexual energy anywhere or everywhere throughout one's body, but often centered in the pelvis. After one has recognized erotic feelings, one can figuratively (and almost literally) draw the feelings up into one's heart. There the energy can be transformed from a desire to almost possess the other to copious feelings of unselfish love, tenderness, and compassion—feelings that usually "come from the heart."

Along with the heart work, one can also draw the energy into one's head and reflect on its meaning as described above. The feelings of desire can be held alongside the unmet longings of the world. One can choose to live with inconsummation of sexual desires, either for a period of time or for a lifetime, and participate in some kind of holy sublimation.

It is heart work, head work, and spiritual work to reflect on the energy that is part of the longing to know and be known, and to reflect on the similarities of the longing for union with God and the longing for union with another person. Thus this work becomes an integration of one's sexuality, both the physical and emotional aspects—particularly aspects of love, one's intellect, and one's spirit. These intersect with and relate to God's Spirit.

Celibate sexual expression. Although the topic of masturbation or self-pleasuring is covered very well in other chapters of this book, a few data from the Living Well Study follow. The survey of widowed people included the following question: "If you have been celibate for periods of time, what have you done (or do you do) with your sexual energy?" Of the 105 who responded to this sexual energy question,

- 59 percent say they try/tried to channel sexual energy into wholesome activities
- 21 percent say they stay(ed) busy
- 19 percent use(d) it as an opportunity to learn about self
- 18 percent have talked about it with close friends
- 6 percent remain(ed) frustrated
- 55 percent say they masturbate(d)

When feelings of guilt or shame are removed, masturbation may be understood as a gift. It can be an opportunity to enjoy the beauty and mystery of sexuality, this greatest of energies that God created in humanity. Thanking God for the gift of sexuality as experienced in an act of self-pleasuring will offer peace of mind and a greater understanding of oneself as created in the image of God (Perito: 91).

"From Your Valentine"

Before being widowed, I gave valentine cards to my husband and children. Now I give valentines to my grandchildren and mother. During the past ten years, I have made valentine cards or selected store-bought cards and then made a beeline toward the checkout counter. I imagine that lingering in the aisles overflowing with special gifts for sweethearts is not a favorite pastime for most single people.

But I recently learned Saint Valentine's story. Although there are variations of this story, some believe that Valentine was a priest in Rome in the third century. The emperor had difficulty getting young men to participate in the army and decided if he would make weddings illegal, he might have more volunteers. Father Valentine secretly continued to officiate for weddings. He was imprisoned for going against the emperor and was martyred on February 14, about the year 270. One of the stories about Saint Valentine is that his jailor, observing that the prisoner was a man of learning, brought his young daughter, Julia, to Valentine for lessons. Valentine read her stories, taught her arithmetic, and told her about God.

Before he died Valentine wrote a last note to Julia to thank her for her friendship and to urge her to stay close to God. The note was signed, "From your Valentine." My dream is that someday everyone, young or old, single, married, or single again, will have at least one intimate friend with whom to share mutual messages of acceptance, affirmation, and love. I also dream that, in addition to having an intimate human relationship, people everywhere will be able to imagine and come to know that intimacy with God is more to be desired than any other gift we might ever be given.

Discussion Questions

1. What similarities do you see between spirituality and sexuality?
2. If you are widowed, what do you think about the responses to the Living Well Study regarding what aspect of living together is missed most?
3. What do you think about the statement "Four essential qualities of friendship are equality, esteem, affection, and value-sharing"?
4. What do you think about the statement from Mary Rosera Joyce: "An erotic impulse actually needs and wants inward sexual expression before it is ready for outward expression"?
5. What reactions do you have to the idea of living with inconsummation?
6. How would you describe an integrated sexuality?

12

The Gift and the Sensuous

Anne Krabill Hershberger

Can we seriously consider sensuousness to be a divinely approved aspect of God's gift of sexuality? Augustine of Hippo and other early-church leaders, drawing on the dualisms of their cultures, effectively convinced Christians that body and soul were distinctly separate entities in the human being and that the soul was good and the body was bad. Ever since, we have had a hard time accepting what we experience through our bodily senses as positive contributors to human well-being.

This tragic error has been countered in recent decades with new insights about the wholeness of human beings—an integration of body, mind, and spirit. However, we still do not give much public credence to the positive role sensuous experiences can have in our relationships with each other.

We know the biblical story of the woman whose tears fell on Jesus' feet. She then wiped his feet with her hair before pouring expensive perfume on him (Luke 7:36-39, 44-50). As we ponder this drama, we have often been led to think about the economic issues related to her act. She used this extravagantly expensive way of doing what was otherwise culturally common in that day, washing the feet of guests as an expression of hospitality.

Simon, the host of the occasion, had failed to offer this common act of hospitality when Jesus arrived. But he was quick to suggest that the perfume the woman used should have been sold and the money given to the poor. He saw excess and waste in the woman's expression of her love for Jesus.

Less often have we given thought to the meaningful, sensuous impact this act likely had on Jesus. Here is the visual image of a caring woman whose love for Jesus moved her to tears, whose long hair was used to express her love through touch, and whose perfume filled the room with pleasant fragrance. In Matthew's account of this story, Jesus said, "She has done a beautiful thing to me." He promised that wherever the gospel is preached throughout the world, this story would be told and her memory would be perpetuated (Matt 26:6-13).

Our culture has given *the sensuous,* meaning qualities that appeal to the senses, a bad name among Christians because of the way culture exploits what should be beautiful and reduces it largely to *the sensual,* meaning gratification of physical appetites. People are often presented in a sensual way, as ends in themselves, or to sell products or distorted values.

Instead of portraying males and females with all their diverse and interesting characteristics, our society promotes a stereotypical image that few can realistically emulate. Society's message is that we, especially women, are not acceptable unless we "fix" ourselves—"fix" our skin, size, hair, lips, eyes, nails, breasts, clothes . . .

In various media, scantily clad women with pouting expressions and well-toned, weightlifting men perpetuate stereotypical sensual images. Much as we may resist this kind of presentation of the human, we cannot deny that sensory experiences are meaningful to us in many ways; they can be particularly significant in our relationships with each other.

Most people find spiritual uplift in the *sensuous* experience of being in a natural setting and viewing the beauty of flowers, trees, streams, animals, mountains, rocks, and all of God's creation. As we feel the wind against our skin while running, biking, or sailing, we sense goodness in our lives.

We also recognize the spiritually enriching experience of seeing, hearing, and/or participating in thoughtfully conceived, effectively communicated, and well-crafted artistic expressions in the areas of visual art, music, theater, and dance. But all these examples do not reflect how our senses can serve us well in our relationships with others.

As affirmed above, we are all sexual beings all the time, and we relate to each other sexually in all our interactions—some of us as females and some as males. Again, we are referring to sexual relating much more broadly than the act of sexual intercourse. What role does sensuousness play in these nonspecific sexual relationships?

What different people consider pleasing to their senses will vary significantly. Yet in general, most people will respond well to others who take the time and trouble to be clean and well groomed, and who wear attractive, well-fitted clothing. The narrator in the film *The Sexiest Animal* says that human beings are the only animals able to choose their own plumage—and do we ever choose plumage! Fine weaves, coarse weaves, bright colors, dark colors, soft and silky, hard and bulky, formal design and casual style, clothes made for action, and clothes made for ceremonies of dignity.

What can be sensuous about all this is the appropriateness and attractiveness of how we present ourselves. We are drawn to people who care enough about themselves and others to enhance the human landscape by presenting themselves in the most attractive way they know and can muster.

It is important to take seriously the biblical admonition in Matthew 6:31 not to worry about what we shall eat, drink, and wear. The body is more important than clothing. However, carefully selected clothing fabric, design, and fit can accentuate our positive features and be an aesthetically pleasing "gift" to the people with whom we relate. This gift can express Christian principles. Well-fitting and well-chosen clothing sends a more important message than expensive, high-fashion clothing. Clothes need not be the latest style to please the senses, but neither do they need to defy contemporary design.

More potentially pleasing to the senses than our clothing is the body language and social graces we use in each interpersonal encounter. There can be something quite sensuous about a friend-ly smile, handshake, hug, and direct eye contact while maintaining respect for personal space.

Positive sensations come to us when persons with whom we are in conversation are not easily diverted by the presence or activities of other people in the area. We show respect for a dialogue partner if we refuse to put aside the current focus when "more-important" people come into view. Introducing each person in the immediate environment and kindly excusing oneself when needing to leave a conversation—such things all have something to do with sensuousness. They feel good.

Not everything that feels good is appropriate, however. Caring about one's personal appearance and developing social skills require discipline to avoid two extreme attitudes. Some people tend to criticize the efforts of others who try to present themselves in positive ways, almost priding themselves in appearing in nonpleasing ways and behaving in a socially inept manner. At the other extreme, some people seem to flaunt their physical bodies and apparel, send inappropriately tempting and sexually seductive messages, and exude an almost smothering "friendliness" when relating to others. Neither this attitude nor this behavior becomes a Christian.

For a Christian whose life is focused on allowing Christ's love to flow through self to others, the senses are key in this communication. Loving touch, caring eye contact, empathetic listening, fragrant flowers, or tastefully prepared food—these all send a message: "You, my friend, matter to me. You are worthy to receive love." How beautiful! How sensuous!

Let us move from the arena of general human interactions to a specific relationship that holds romantic meaning for the individuals involved. The level of sensuous expression also is likely to become more intense. A dating relationship often is initiated by sensory stimuli: "the sound of his voice," "that wonderful smile of hers when our eyes meet." When two people enjoy each other's company and are most happy when they are together, opportunity exists for them to develop a relationship of true intimacy, with all the ingredients described in chapter 3.

Here again, the senses play an important role in the relationship. The conversation as well as the type of touching will become more personal. At this stage, before experiencing intense degrees of passion, it is so important for the dating pair to decide how far to allow physical interaction to go. It is no secret that couples often find touch communicating their deepest feelings for each other in ways that words cannot.

Consider the following levels of commitment. Make two photocopies of the form (on the next page). Ponder the degree of physical interaction with which you are comfortable and which you think is appropriate for each type of relationship.

On one form, record the letter before each of the physical expressions in the "self" column beside the level of commitment where you believe it best fits. Ask your friend to do the same in the "friend" column of another copy of the form.

Compare your responses. Do you agree in your opinions? Discuss your differences before you find yourselves in the heat of passion. This could be very important to your relationship and to your lives.

How can the gift of sensuousness bring joy and be an enhancement to the sexual relationship of a married couple, committed to each other for life? When beginning a relationship with another person, no one knows what life experiences will come. Some of these may bring dramatic changes, with potential for great joy or major distress. However, one of the greatest threats to a satisfying long-term sexual relationship may actually be a lack of drama in the relationship—a sameness or routine year in and year out. Creative sensuous experiences are important in fostering a deepening appreciation for each other.

Popular magazines present many articles and suggestions to prevent or respond to monotony in a long-term relationship. One often sees advice like "put more sizzle or excitement into

Levels of Commitment	Self	Friend	Physical Expressions of Affection
Casual attraction			a. Holding hands, light embracing
Good friends, non-monogamous			b. Casual, closed mouth kissing c. Intense, open mouth kissing
Going steady, monogamous			d. Horizontal embrace, clothed e. Above the waist petting, clothed
Considering engagement			f. Above the waist petting, unclothed g. Below the waist petting, clothed
Announced engagement			h. Below the waist petting, unclothed i. Nude embrace
Marriage			j. Oral-genital sex k. Sexual intercourse

your marriage" or "surprise him tonight." The specific suggestions given by the popular media as to how this can be done may or may not fit with Christian values, but the basic concept is important. Creative use of the sensuous is significant.

The sensuous experiences that mean so much in the dating relationship need to be continued in marriage, but in new and perhaps unpredictable ways. In their book *Sizzling Monogamy*, Earl and Rose Smith use the term *comfort zone* to analyze what happens at different times in every intimate relationship. Usually, *comfort* would sound like something desirable for which to strive. In an intimate relationship, it can mean being at ease with each other. But comfort can also mean being chronically bored with each other as you settle into everyday life and slowly let the romance in the relationship die.

The Smiths say this experience is inevitable. Yet a couple can recognize when being in the comfort zone is becoming a potential threat to the relationship and then do something about it. In their marriage seminars, they counsel many people who are looking for more-fulfilling relationships. The Smiths recommend that couples indulge in "a marital affair with their mates"—not an extramarital affair with someone outside the marriage relationship. Capitalize on the features that make an "affair" appealing. These seem to be the elements of escape from everyday routines and responsibilities, and secret rendezvous in romantic settings, spawning excitement and fun.

Many books, articles, and television and radio talk show hosts have discussed how to keep the romantic spark in a marriage—how not to take each other for granted. The Christian would start with love and commitment as basic to an enduring relationship. Sometimes Christians, however, think that simply having these in place ensures a happy marriage. They may give limited attention to some of the very human elements that can be so enriching to the relationship.

We humans have been given a gift of the sensuous to enjoy and therefore should not neglect it. Speakers and writers regularly make the point that arousing the senses is important and then list various elements, such as the following.

Create an uncluttered atmosphere with candlelight, beautiful music, and pleasant fragrance. Present yourself to the most-important person in your world in a way that says that you care deeply about him or her. Such memory-making ingredients help to build a happy marriage. We can add caring conversation and true listening—not so much about life's struggles as about the richness of life together. Thereby we can enrich the soft caresses, kissing, and physical expression of love. We add to the excitement when we have fun creating such intimate times and building into them some mystery and anticipation and perhaps a bit of mischief.

Is there a place for the sensuous when Christians relate as sexual beings with each other? Indeed there is. Are there boundaries to respect in expressing and satisfying our sensuousness? Of course there are. Is it possible to control our human appetites for sensual stimulation? Yes, it is not only possible but also essential that we do so, with respect for God's good gift of sexuality and the quality of our relationships.

This ability to control is part of what makes us different from other animals. It is part of what makes life more abundant and enjoyable. May God give us the insight to enjoy this good gift, enrich life for others, and honor our Creator in all our attitudes and behaviors.

Discussion Questions

1. Many experts agree that a lack of comfort with our sexuality adds to our fear of enjoying sensuous pleasures. How can we help ourselves to become more comfortable with our sexuality and with sensuous pleasures?
2. Social graces are obviously lacking among some people, even among some Christians. How can congregations and individuals, including parents and teachers, facilitate the development of social graces in themselves and others?
3. When the "sizzle" or romance is no longer experienced in a marriage relationship by one or both partners, what might be done to help restore this?
4. When some persons exude too much "sizzle" for comfort as they relate to others, how might we respond in a helpful manner?

13

The Gift Expressed in the Arts

Lauren Friesen

Works of art and the ability of an individual to find expression in the arts have become significant factors in the development of human emotions and knowing. On a routine basis, we are exposed to many art experiences and participate in those events as spectators, creators, critics, or consumers.

Artistic expression and viewer response involve sensuous components, even though the experience of an entire work of art is more than just a series of sensations. These sensory elements may focus on the composition of units of color, composition, sound, rhythm, and line; or even on sensuous or sexual imagery. Significant art evokes emotions that form a unified and whole experience.

Similarly, sexual arousal engages the total personality in feeling and thought. Significant art evokes from a viewer a consequent degree of response (emotive and cognitive—knowing with awareness and judgment). Repeated viewing continues to sustain or even increase the high level of attention. When sexuality, sexual images, or sexual feelings are expressed in the arts, we can experience these in new ways and with enhanced understanding and appreciation for our embodied selves.

The first part of this chapter will explore the nature of artistic expression and how it can communicate. This is followed by examples of the arts expressing sexuality.

Many art forms are highly complex, such as abstract painting or symbolist theater. Others give the appearance of being more simplified and therefore more accessible to the public. But whatever the level of sophistication, there are a number of central questions that apply to all works of art. These questions center on epistemological and ontological issues—on how we know something and on how something exists: What do we learn from the experience of art? What qualifies an object to be called a work of art?

Such questions aid in providing a framework for understanding the relationship between a work of art and its sensuousness. The sensuousness of a work of art creates an aesthetic event for the creator or observer of the work. It also serves as an analogy for meaning that is beyond (transcendent to) the work itself.

Sensuousness (Feeling) in Art

The sensuous element in art is an integral dimension in the experience of the work. Music involves sound and rhythm, painting engages the eye, poetry elicits a lively interaction between the word and cadence, and theater stimulates response from nearly all five of the human senses. These sensuous elements in art engage the mind and body in a response that is an analogy to human sexual response, says the philosopher Arthur Danto. The common bond between art and sexuality is the presence of passion, which guides much of life and thought.

These passions, so common to human experience, are a major element in artistic expression and knowing. Even though artistic knowing is not limited to emotional arousal, it certainly explores the depth of human feeling. Danto separates art from "mere" human emotion in the sense that appreciation for art is learned behavior; we acquire the ability to access the feelings in a work of art. These feelings are not in conflict with intellectual knowledge; instead, they may form the basis for rational thought, as Susanne Langer asserts (74 and following).

The artistic expression of passion is accomplished in many subtle and some not-so-subtle ways. Art is the exploration into the context of feeling and form, of passion and abstract thought. Langer claims that these two dimensions form a dialectic: one cannot be achieved without the other.

In this fashion, art fills a void in human knowing that cannot be supplied by more-cognitive disciplines, no matter how much they discuss art. That void in the knowledge of human feeling is not filled if education programs explore only cognitive disciplines. Aesthetic education provides an understanding of sensuous arousal through art; by analogy, those feelings are also aroused through human sexual response.

The artist expresses human feeling in multiple ways. As the philosopher Benedetto Croce reminds us, artistic knowing differs from other forms of knowing. Art challenges us with infinite possibilities; forms of (empirical) knowledge based on observation or experience involve the learning of finite truths. These infinite possibilities are made possible through art and are associated with the wide latitude of knowing that the artwork arouses in the viewer.

According to Croce, the more complex the sensuous and intuitive responses to an art object, the more significant the work will be (85). This perspective was already suggested by Immanuel Kant in his *Critique of Judgement* (146).

The artist explores the complexity of feeling by employing material substances, such as paper, ink, wood, metal, paint, fabric, and dyes. These objects are not the work in and of themselves, and yet the artwork could not exist without them. The artist explores the limits and possibilities of expression with mundane objects. Sometimes this results in minimal use and manipulation of objects. A painting may just use the color red and the sensuous response that red evokes. A poem may use word sounds that do not make intelligible statements.

It is a surprise to many viewers of art that such minimal works, employing so few material substances, still express an infinite range of feelings. Other works employ a wide range of substances with multiple colors, shapes, and sounds to create the desired aesthetic effect. Whether the artist has elected simple elements or complex ones for expression, the effect can be similar in the sense that our feelings may be deeply engaged by either method.

When artworks engage our feelings, we turn our sole attention to them; it is not simply in looking at a work of art but in "dwelling in" it that we become engaged with the art (Polanyi: 18). *Dwelling in* a work of art implies the capacity to withhold critical judgment until the viewer has imaginatively entered into the world that the artwork creates. Entering into a work of art opens one to be emotionally and intellectually changed by a musical composition, painting, play, or dance.

The emotions of the viewer need to become fully engaged to shift from being an analytical "observer" to being altered emotionally by the sensuous experiences the artwork provides. A relationship is formed between the art object, the creator of the art, and the viewer. It is a relationship that impacts the viewer's capacity to feel and to think.

Art as Transcendence

Profound experiences of art are not limited to sensuous moments. Those works that open up worlds to the viewer-listener also, by analogy, imply an existence beyond the art object. When we engage our senses in a composition, such as Brahm's *Requiem*, we experience, not just the work itself, but also the world it creates, within which we momentarily dwell and have our being. When a work stimulates our senses at our basic level of experience, it also lifts us beyond the sensuous and into the realm of the ontological, the domain of being.

A reading of the text of the *Requiem*, while essential to the entire work, is not the experience of the musical event, which is created by hearing it produced musically. The same can be said of the musical composition too; it is neither just an assemblage of notes on paper nor a sequence of measures played by an orchestra. Instead, significant music provides a unified sensuous experience that creates an aesthetic world into which the listener enters and dwells. When we dwell in an artwork, we come to recognize a state of being and existence beyond our immediate sensory world. Our reflection on these aesthetic moments, in turn, also provides us with insight into human sensuous and sexual experiences.

The transcendent dimensions of art are dependent, though, on the experience of actual objects (in aesthetic discussions, music is a created "object"). The sensuous experience works as a whole unit and is a requirement for aesthetic experience and transformation. The transcendent dimension in aesthetics emerges from response to an artwork. Without the actual object, aesthetic experiences would be impossible.

While nature may provide beauty and pleasure, it does not thereby provide aesthetic experiences, because these moments require human-made objects. As materials are shaped and transformed into objects of meaning and significance by the artist, they become instruments for aesthetic experiences to transform human perception.

Emotional Dimension in Art

The aesthetic world is also an emotional dimension. The arts not only "cause" an emotional response in the listener, but also deal with greater complexities. Langer has outlined the possibility that artistic experiences articulate human emotions and reveal their shapes. She assumes that human feeling has been formed by cultural and artistic development, and that art reveals both the feeling and structure. Langer claims that our feelings are an "ordered" part of our beings and that art alone gives expression to the complex connection between emotion and form (90).

According to this perspective, a work of art is a "window" to our emotions and their shapes. Works that repeatedly engage us emotionally will provide the most profound learning experiences. We learn to recognize an emotion we may not have noticed before the artwork reveals it to us, such as the birth, growth, and death of feelings of joy, anger, or sexual response.

These feelings and their presence and power form a sensuous aspect of being human. Recognition of such feelings is the foundation for knowledge; emotion forms the basis for rational thought, Langer says. Emotions are part of human existence, an ordered dimension of our lives, and art provides a direct "window" through which we perceive and express feelings.

Art that engages the viewer will provide a significant degree of sensuous pleasure. This does not imply that it will necessarily be decorative or that all art needs to be beautiful. Art arousing sensuous pleasure provides experiences that stimulate and frequently, though not always, are pleasing to the senses. Some works of art may stimulate through unpleasant or even grotesque sensations. Even these works provide a degree of "pleasure," but not because humans enjoy the grotesque. Instead, aesthetic pleasure is derived from the depth of feeling that a work of art evokes, not in limiting the kinds of feelings.

In Victor Hugo's novel *The Hunchback of Notre Dame*, the hunchback is not a pleasant figure. Yet he envelops us with his personality, which cannot be separated from his physical deformity. The pleasure in reading this novel or seeing the movie based on it comes, not from superficial beauty, but because we emotionally dwell in the suffering of the protagonist.

In her play *Twilight: Los Angeles 1992*, Harvard University professor Anna Deavere Smith has portrayed key figures from the Los Angeles riot of 1992, also known as the Rodney King riot. She has created the script of the play from interviews with many participants in the riot. Smith has condensed each person's statements into a poetic form, but the language, rhythm, and tone of each character is retained.

A wide spectrum of characters inhabit this play: participants in the Reginald Denny attack, Mayor Bradley, Police Chief Gates, and many individuals from the black, Asian, Latino, and white communities. Smith performs each character and creates distinguishing features for each one: a costume piece, accent, tone of voice, rhythm, or movement.

The experience of the play is an encounter with the persons active in the riot and affected by it. This collage of personalities creates a world within which the audience can dwell and begin to feel the various emotions coming from each character. The audience is led through a landscape of emotional possibilities: anger, fear, compassion, remorse, jubilation, anger, and many more.

As the wide range of emotions and the swift alteration of personalities and impressions flow from the stage, the context and causes for the riot begin to emerge. It becomes a world unknown to many people in the audience. Yet, through the sensuous experiences of these characters and their words, the audience can enter into their experiences. The play serves as a window to the nature and depth of their feelings.

Even so, the play is more than a litany of impressions and emotions. By juxtaposing stories from various ethnic groups and organizations, Smith also provides an experience that transcends each individual story. During an evening in the theater, this play creates the context of the riot, brings it into focus, and provides foundations for new thoughts about it.

Smith does not merely vilify or excuse the rioters; this is not a lament for the victims. Instead, she presents their stories and allows us, the viewers, to dwell in their experiences so we will be able to discover new dimensions from that cataclysm. This enables the audience to make judgments about that event and avoids the simplistic tendency to moralize about victims of urban decay.

From many different perspectives, Smith presents the feelings of pain and joy, frustration and hope, and anger and forgiveness. In doing so, she has developed a play that liberates the viewer from being ensnared by those same feelings. In this sense, art becomes transforming: it can change our feelings and thoughts about significant issues as we dwell in the artwork. Many in the audience at the Goshen College production (March 1997) commented on how the play impacted their understanding of the riot and changed their feelings about it.

Poetry also opens up emotional worlds for the reader. Experiences of transformation and new understandings of life can emerge from the aesthetic experience. The sharing of art is the act of compassion toward those who need meaning and significance in their lives. The words of a poem create an experience that forms a unified moment where feeling and thought intersect. They establish a series of emotions that enables the reader to take residence in the image made by the poem, even though that image may shift from line to line.

Art as Experience

The American painter Mark Rothko also wanted to make worlds in which viewers can dwell. There were times when he would sit for hours in front of an unfinished painting and become absorbed by the painted image, like a mystic contemplating the eternal. He sought for a way in which the painter could express emotions directly and evoke a similar response in the viewer.

With his large red, blue, or black canvases, he did not want to paint a "suffering figure" to illustrate the suffering of others. Neither did he paint lonely landscapes to express the feeling of isolation. Instead, he wanted an image that would lead us, the viewers, to a *feeling* of suffering or one of isolation.

By painting shapes on large canvases, he sought to have the color itself express feeling, to stimulate a more powerful experience than works using recognizable figures to represent a feeling. Rothko says, "People who weep before my pictures are having the same experience I had when I painted them" (Breslin: 325). He wanted the viewer to come into direct "contact" with color and thereby gain a certain feeling from the work instead of having a recognizable image as an intercessor.

This process of painting large "blocks" of color so that the viewer can dwell in them was a spiritual (transcendent) enterprise for Rothko. In my conversations with Dr. Breslin (at the University of California-Berkeley, 1994), he stated his personal belief that Rothko had intended a "spiritual" dimension for all of his work, not just his late "chapel paintings."

In the 1950s, Harvard University commissioned Rothko to paint a series of murals for the new Holyoke Center. When

Nathan Pusey, Harvard president, went to New York to examine the finished works, Rothko showed him five large canvases painted in various shades of eggplant, with hints of blue, red, and pink. Rothko asked Pusey for his comments. After a long, long pause, Pusey said, "I think they are very sad."

This direct path to the emotion that Rothko wanted to portray opened the door of conversation between the artist and Pusey. After extensive dialogue, Rothko offered that the first three paintings (respectively) represented the feelings of Maundy Thursday, Good Friday, and Easter—with hints of pink for Easter expressing the glimmer of hope in resurrection. This abstract expressionist painter had grounded his work on the belief that art provides a direct experience of human emotion and, at the same time, provides the potential for a transcendent one. Art, for Rothko, was a discipline through which he explored spirituality, the shape and content of spiritual feelings.

If the arts provide meaning and value and do not exist just to decorate walls, then a pragmatic question remains: How does art accomplish this? The motif of making meaning, as Frank Kermode has so aptly stated, is the artistic act of making the invisible visible (130).

Art makes things visible by presenting objects in an altered relationship. This is the definitive element in the modern quest for meaning and value. The task for the artist and for those who view art is then an enormous one: opening windows onto life and exposing the raw emotions that reside there, as the first step in transforming what is meaningless into something meaningful.

Embracing Life Through Art

Art is unique, not only because it expresses feeling, but also because it has the capacity to explore all of life's dimensions. The ambiguities and complexities of life are recurring themes in significant art. Art has the capacity to embrace all dimensions of human experience and to provide experiences that transform the viewer and creator of the art.

The theme of sexuality, appearing early in the chapter, is a significant component in this constellation of human perception, feeling, and meaning. Whether the models in the painting or the characters on stage are nude or fully dressed, they are always rooted in their sexual identity. That fact gives significance to their words, actions, and feelings.

The sculptor who shapes the human figure with clay or bronze is exploring what many consider to be the most daunting challenge for an artist: the rendering of the human form. Similarly, the poet who writes of a specific love or an occasion of loss, is opening a window and providing knowledge of love for all who elect to enter that room.

Some choose to close the portal to these direct encounters before they have an effect or even alter the viewer. The exploration into human feeling opens the possibilities that all emotions become legitimate for artistic expression, including the pleasures of the erotic.

There is a distinction, an important one, between pornography and the erotic. Pornography is an explicit act of degrading another person or that person's image. Human sexual response incorporates erotic pleasure and desires as a valid aspect of sexual expression. In comparison, as Gloria Steinem has noted, pornography is rooted in a desire to dominate or subjugate women (Francoeur: 642). (See chapter 15.)

Artists have often explored various dimensions of sexual desire and expression. Plays frequently present the mutual attraction of two persons for each other and their sexual feelings. Shakespeare's *Romeo and Juliet*, where the principals do not even kiss on stage, is a love story examining the power of sexual attraction and the beauty of desire. Even the long-standing enmity between their families, the Capulets and the Montagues, is not as powerful as their desire for each other.

This power to evoke human passion has intrigued artists and audiences through the ages. As with many other artistic explorations, artists have frequently been ambivalent toward political and religious taboos on this subject or exploited those taboos. But it is not merely an intrigue with erotic passion that informs much of art focusing on sexual desire.

Significant works of art portraying the erotic dimension of sexuality are exploring the connection between the aesthetic image and the nature of human experience. This connection is a powerful one within the imagination. As Danto suggests, it combines two experiences that are highly similar: the arousal from sexual attraction with the arousal from an aesthetic experience. It is somewhat understandable that viewers who do not have an appreciation for the complexity of art will not be able to understand the connection between these similar modes of stimulation.

The playwright Ron Penhill presents erotic themes in *Love and Understanding*, viewed by this chapter writer in its premiere, at London's Shepherd's Bush Theatre, on May 27, 1997. Penhill presents the body and the erotic as metaphors for exploring the themes of love's variations and commitment. The play contrasts two relationships: one that is kind and considerate but devoid of passion, and another that is explosive and filled with emotions.

The action of the play demonstrates how simple kindness and emotional distance eventually give way to passion and sexual desire. The characters have a moment of "understanding" when they realize that passionate attraction is at the root of commitment and that erotic pleasures are a significant and necessary element in expressing love. The erotic themes in the play form a metaphor illuminating the search for love, conveying meaning beyond the mere appearance of the body.

The playwright might have chosen other means to express this theme, but it is significant that he chose not to do so. He presents the viewer with the challenge to dwell in the erotic and loving world of this play. As the title implies, the object is not simply to present eroticism on a stage but to provide an experience that transforms the characters and thereby also alters our understanding of human personality and love. The element of transformation through erotic awareness is at the heart of this play. The action of the play, then, is built on the risks connected with sensual love. It contrasts those feelings with the human tendency to strive toward a serene life, one lacking erotic pleasure.

In the final scene, the play does not endorse one type of love (erotic) and condemn another (serene and platonic); instead, it portrays the limitations of both. The characters come to an understanding that a committed and loving relationship is strengthened in the presence of both dimensions: passion and commitment. The characters recognize their need to be "liberated" from their previously held and limited perceptions of love and passion. They realize that healthy, passionate love requires commitment.

In the confessional conclusion, the characters acknowledge to each other their own mistakes in action and judgment. The portrayal of this disclosure enables the audience to participate in that moment of recognition. For the play, however, the confessions come too late, and the broken relationships cannot be healed. By dwelling in that disclosure, the audience is able to transform its own understanding of the connection between committed love and the presence of passion.

The play confirms Aristotle's ancient view that the depth of human feeling, when expressed in exaggerated means through art (tragedy), would lead to human wholeness (catharsis). The feelings that works of art evoke and express are closely connected with human well-being.

A contemporary writer, Martha Nussbaum, has developed this theme further. In *The Therapy of Desire* (especially the chapter "Emotions and Ethical Health"), she argues that while art does provide a sense of wholeness, it is also the foundation for ethical behavior. Humans learn to feel the distinctions between good and evil through art. An "emotional" appreciation for art serves as a form of therapy, a road to emotional health.

These examples of artistic expression are meant to illustrate the infinite and creative possibilities for gaining insight and appreciation for sexuality as a significant dimension of life. Art is also an important part of the foundation for culture and learning because it stimulates reflection (thought) and feeling (passion), while insisting that living faithfully involves the integration and expression of both. This prospect, a life centered on expressive commitment and fulfillment, is the function of art in human experience, and surely a phenomenal aspect of God's creative work in us.

Discussion Questions

1. Many thinkers have said that the arts have the capacity to communicate universally to all humans, especially across gender lines. Do you believe this? If so, why? Give examples.
2. How does art make the invisible visible? How might you relate this to an understanding of sexuality as expressed in the arts?
3. Why does a song, painting, poem, or other art form have the capacity to move us so deeply, not only emotionally, but spiritually and physically as well? Can you recall any artwork that created such a transcendent moment for you? Why do you remember it?
4. Some works of art feature the erotic as pleasurable and constructive. How is this different from pornography and its effect in destroying human well-being?
5. Not all art that engages the viewer-participant in sensuous ways may be considered "beautiful." Do insights gained through effective and yet unattractive aesthetics allow the artwork to become "beautiful" because the insights increase your understanding? Explain your reasoning.

14

The Gift and Celibacy

Sue L. Conrad

A Personal Journey

Over the past decade, when asked by various professors, churches, high schools, and others to share my personal perspective on singleness or, more importantly, on my decision to practice celibacy as a single person, I was not sure I had much to share. Was my perspective different from most others?

I was brought up in a strong Christian household with a father and mother who proposed, and at times imposed, very strong sexual ethics on all of their four children. We were taught to be proud of who we were as persons, that we were whole persons from the very beginning of life.

I could talk to my father about almost anything related to relationships or the biological aspects of sexuality. His openness and frankness encouraged me always to have an open attitude concerning sexuality, from an emotional as well as a physical perspective. I am blessed to have had such an upbringing and am grateful that I can attribute my healthy views on sexuality to my family, my church, and my friendships. I now realize I am in a minority, even in many Christian circles.

Yet despite all those wonderful, supportive experiences growing up, as with all things, there comes a point when we need to make decisions for ourselves. Our beliefs, which surely emerge from our heritage, also are influenced by the world around us.

Today's world definitely does not promote celibacy. And that lack of promotion goes beyond TV and movies: it is also found in our churches. When was the last time you heard a clear call for celibacy outside of marital vows? Surely we see that broader society does not embrace and, in fact, even ridicules celibacy. While the church highlights biblical reasons for celibacy, it does not always add the emotional, physical, and spiritual reasons that create a positive, healthy individual when celibacy is practiced outside of marriage. All of these things impact the decisions we make. If we have not processed all these factors or decided where we stand on sex outside of marriage, we can easily get confused regarding the difference between a desire for sexual satisfaction and a desire for intimate relationships. Ronald Rolheiser says,

> Popular culture today teaches that one cannot be whole without being healthily sexual. That is correct. However, for the most part, society thinks of sexuality only as *having* sex. That is a tragic reduction. Sexuality is a wide energy and we are healthily sexual when we have love, community, communion, family, friendship, affection, creativity, joy, delight, humor, and self-transcendence in our lives. Having these, as we know, depends on many things and not just on whether or not we sleep alone. (195)

I write this chapter as a thirty-nine-year-old, heterosexual, never-been-married, female virgin. I have never had genital intercourse with another person nor have I had oral-genital intercourse. I have never regretted these decisions, but there are days when I wonder what I am missing. Is this really what God intended for me (and other single people), and why does the church feel so passionately about keeping sex within marriage, yet so rarely talks about it?

When asking these questions and experiencing my own sexual temptations (I have done more than just hold hands), I have decided that celibacy is indeed God's call to all persons who are outside the covenant of marriage. I also believe that single people are not the only ones who should read this chapter. Married people also will go through times of celibacy (voluntarily or involuntarily) in their marriage. The following thoughts on the gift of celibacy can be applicable in one way or another to all people.

Defining Celibacy

Celibacy is defined in many ways. It can refer to an absence of sexual activity in one's life, a hatred of sex (Norris: 51), a life-style without genital sexual expression (Sheridan: 34), or a state of voluntary singleness (Hershberger: 75). At times, celibacy is defined as the state of not being married or an abstention of the vow of marriage (Sammon: 101). It is important to acknowledge the distinction between *celibacy* and *chastity*. While sometimes the two are understood to be synonymous, *chastity* is defined as purity, decency. In this chapter, *celibacy* is defined as abstaining from sexual intercourse.

Biblical Celibacy

What does the Bible say about celibacy? Most Christians point to two prominent men in the New Testament in reference to celibacy, Jesus and Paul. Many interpretations of 1 Corinthians 7 explain Paul's attitude toward celibacy as the preferred state for those who are able. Jews were strongly encouraged to marry, and although the Jewish culture was very influential during Jesus' ministry, both Jesus and Paul were advocates for the single life.

The Old Testament makes very clear that sexual intercourse was intended for procreation, but texts such as those within Proverbs and Song of Songs allow us to see sex and sexuality beyond the role of procreation. It also indicates specific, appropriate contexts for sexual relations (marriage) and certain responsibilities and obligations that accompany sexual intercourse.

Perhaps the most compelling argument for keeping sexual intercourse within the covenant of marriage is found in the biblical account of creation. God created us as sexual beings, and God called us "good." Sometimes we forget this. Our sexual attitudes and actions may not allow us to celebrate this fact. In Genesis 1–2, Adam and Eve become one flesh.

> One-fleshness both is and is not metaphor. It captures
> an all-encompassing, overarching, oneness—when they
> marry, husband and wife enter an institution that points
> them toward familial, domestic, emotional, and spiritu-
> al unity. But the one flesh of which Adam speaks is also
> overtly sexual, suggesting sexual intercourse, the only
> physical state other than pregnancy where it is hard to
> tell where one person's body stops and the other's starts.
> (Winner: 37)

Based on the creation account, sex was created within a covenanted relationship. God's yes to sex within marriage is the only time when the full commitment that accompanies inter-course can be fully realized. When we attempt to simulate that sense of intimacy outside marriage, we are denying ourselves the full sense of unity that comes when all the aspects of "one flesh" are experienced. God's vision for healthy sexuality found in Genesis, including sexual intercourse within marriage, is foun-dational for how we read the remainder of the Bible in regard to sexuality.

The New Testament offers some carry-over of the strong Jewish affirmation of marriage found in the Old Testament. However, "there is evidence of an early dethronement of marriage from its all important place within Jewish society" (Brown: 120). Jesus, John the Baptist, and Paul all are examples of single, suc-cessful living. Although the call for singleness is not widespread in the New Testament, "it is univocal" (Yoder: 75). Jesus' single life-style modeled an alternative to the Jewish customs of marriage. Most Jewish men would have been married by their thirtieth birthday (Nelson in Brown 1986: 97). Yet Jesus did not force this nonmarital lifestyle on his followers, for we know that some of his disciples were married. While still honoring the marital bond, Jesus showed that marriage was not the only important thing in life and that there were more important things than meeting one's sexual needs (Hershberger: 75).

It has been argued that Paul's call for celibacy had more to do with his time and his understanding of the second coming of Christ than with an actual call for a sexual ethic. It was commonly understood in the Christian community of Paul's time that Christ's return would come before the next generation. Therefore, procreation was not important, and a call to celibacy seemed quite possible. However, if Paul proposed celibacy only for this reason, it does not *disallow* it as an appropriate Christian ethic to follow even now. "What a text *means* normatively for ethics in the ongoing life of the church need not be contingent in all respects on what it originally *meant*" (Cahill: 72).

The Greek word *porneia*, or "sexual immorality," found fifty-five times in the New Testament (see, for example, Gal 5:19; Rom 1:24; 1 Thess 4:3-5; Col 3:5, 1 Cor 5:9-10; 6:9-10; 7:2) is translated in various forms: *prostitution, fornication, adultery, lust, unchastity,* or *impurity* (Cahill: 64). For those persons who translate *porneia* as "fornication," these texts often are cited as some of the most explicit teachings concerning celibacy in the Bible. Yet some still debate what *fornication* means. Most Christians would interpret such texts to prohibit sexual intercourse outside of marriage and conclude that this is an important element of a Christian sexual ethic.

However, some biblical scholars claim these Scriptures do not address premarital sex as fornication (Comsia and Rolfe: 58). Such references, some suggest, were intended for sexual relations with prostitutes, not for men and women in loving relationships, even those outside the marriage bond. It can be argued that what Paul proposed had more to do with issues of community and what sorts of members the Christian community can have within it to build the body of Christ than with pointing out *specific* sexual acts as sinful (Cahill: 64). Daniel Comsia and David J. Rolfe also propose that a couple fornicates, not based on sexual relations outside of marriage, but because of a lack of willingness to add commitment to sexual relations and have sex based purely on present desires (59). Accordingly, fornication, based on this interpretation can occur in marriage and does not necessarily limit itself to the physical sexual behavior of a couple.

In the Bible, "sexual conduct is highly regulated but seldom prohibited" (Hawthorne: 116). Few churches today teach all the sexual codes that are presented in the Bible (for example, the instruction in Ruth that a man whose brother has died must impregnate the widow). In fact, some might argue that much of what is taught about sexual ethics from a biblical perspective does not, in fact, contain any specific teaching from the Bible (Hawthorne: 116).

However, few would argue that biblical standards, explicit or not, are as sexually permissive as modern society's standards.

As a result of this debate about interpretation, some biblical scholars profess that there is no explicit prohibition regarding sexual intercourse between unmarried, consenting adults, in either the Old or New Testaments (Nelson 1994: 81). Do we then declare that sexual intercourse is acceptable and perhaps even encouraged (for example, Song of Songs) as long as the two consenting people are in a committed, loving relationship? Or do we say that such a sexual ethic of premarital sex can be developed, but not based *solely* on biblical interpretation?

Nelson proposes that while no specific biblical text prohibits premarital coitus, Christians need to look at the overall ethic taught in the New Testament (1994: 81). "It presses us to do our ongoing theological-ethical work in ways that attempt faithfully to discern the in-breaking reign and grace of God in our present contexts" (1994: 81). But what are those foundations, and how do we express the grace of God through our sexuality? "Surely," continues Nelson,

> they include such affirmations as these: the created goodness of our sexuality and bodily life; the inclusiveness of Christian community, unlimited by purity codes; the equality of women and men; and the service of our sexuality to the reign of God . . . (expression in acts

shaped by love, justice, equality, fidelity, mutual respect, compassion and grateful joy). (1994: 82)

In essence, we must ask, how does my sexual behavior contribute to or detract from the work of the Christian community and my dedication to God? Choosing to restrain from sexual intercourse outside of marriage could say more about a person's commitment to Christ than about one's sexual activity. When one chooses to make a strong commitment to Christ and the church, along with it comes other commitments. The statement is strong when many areas of one's life, both personal and public, can profess a personal commitment to Christ.

A noticeable void in many Christian circles is a theological perspective on the meaning of singleness or celibacy. The Catholic Church has long taught, thanks in part to Augustinian influence, that sex is acceptable only within marriage and for procreation purposes. As a result, any thought of sex in any other way is sinful (Sipe: 33). This understanding of sex, sexual thoughts, and human sexuality is unhealthy and unrealistic. Do we want to develop a statement of sexual ethics that discourages one's true identity and faithfulness to any religiously influenced ethic?

Making Room for Celibacy

It is not unusual for single persons within a church community to feel discouraged or inferior due to their nonmarital status. "Singleness is a challenge [to the Christian community] because it represents unfinished theological and ethical agenda" (Yoder: 95). If singleness is indeed better than marriage, as some biblical interpretations might propose, and if as Christians we constantly strive to do our best within the Christian call, why are we so discouraging of the single life?

The understanding that marriage is better than singleness is instilled in very young children. This was evidenced in my four-year-old niece. Recently she and I were planting flowers in my backyard and talking about worms, flowers, soil, and shovels.

Suddenly, without any provocation, she stood up and stomped her foot saying, "Aunt Sue, you *have* to have a husband! Why aren't you married?"

I took a breath and decided this was an opportune time to teach my niece about a countercultural view of life. Calmly I said, "Ava, not everyone needs to be married. Many people are happy without a husband or wife. Besides, you wouldn't want me to be married to someone who is mean, nasty, grumpy, and unkind to me or you, would you?" She seemed intrigued and responded, "No." I said, "Neither would I. I would be happy to have a husband but only if he were fun, kind, happy, generous, and a really good man . . . and a good uncle to you."

The wheels were turning in her mind. She seemed to understand. I did not want her to think that I was opposed to the idea of marriage. Rather, I wanted her to realize that not everyone needs to be married and that marriage should be a choice, not a requirement. I continued, "So, if that kind of man would come along, I would consider dating him and maybe marrying him. Do you know of any men like that whom I could meet?"

She liked this idea of matchmaker and thought long and hard. Finally she exclaimed, "Yes! I do!" *Wow*, I thought. Maybe this educational lesson will turn into more than just an education for my niece; maybe she'll introduce me to a potential mate. I asked, "Who?" Proudly she declared, "My daddy!"

I smiled, grateful that she had such a good view of her dad (my brother-in-law) and said, "You're right, he is all of those things, but I'm not sure how your mommy would feel about that. He's already married." Returning to reality from her matchmaking visions, she sheepishly smiled and said, "Oh yeah, I forgot."

Persons without marriage partners cannot, nor should they, deny their sexual feelings and interests. Humans cannot control how they *feel* (sexual arousal), but they can control how they *act* on those feelings. Sexual feelings are no different from other human feelings (such as anger or jealousy), and how we respond to them is a matter of choice (Sammon: 80). This is where the church needs to claim a moral teaching. Humans will naturally, as sexual beings, think sexual thoughts; how they act on those sexual thoughts will determine how they are following the moral teachings of the church or, perhaps, a broader, universal sexual ethic.

Ethics and theology are innately intertwined. It is questionable whether sexual ethics can be taught within the church without having a theology of sexuality and celibacy. "When a more developed theology of sexuality emerges, it will not be based on pleasure, negatively or positively, but on the nature of quality of relationships with all life" (Sipe: 34).

Is celibacy natural? In other words, can persons be fully human without having sexual intercourse at least one time in their lives? Some people believe that the only way for sexual beings to fully express their sexuality is through sexual intercourse. Sexual intercourse fulfills sexual needs but also can fulfill emotional, physical, spiritual, and willful aspects of the individual (Rosenau: 415). It encompasses the whole person and fulfills not just our sexual urges but also our needs to be loved, touched, affirmed, and needed. Not to have intercourse, or to practice celibacy, can appear to be unnatural or abnormal, especially in our sex-crazed culture. Society also implies in so many ways that romantic relationships will lead to sex. If someone willingly chooses not to have sex, society wonders if this person cannot develop friendships, is too obsessed with himself or herself, or is not attractive enough for anyone to desire him or her.

Furthermore, even within some Christian contexts, persons who do not marry and procreate, and who implicitly practice celibacy, are considered abnormal. "I am convinced that we will never fully understand celibacy until we free it from analogies to marriage. Celibacy is a reality in itself, not merely the absence or negative of something else" (Sipe: 59). Similarly, the concept of discouraging premarital sex gives a negative focus to sexual ethics. Perhaps we need to change our language and not focus on a negative sexual ethic, but rather focus on the purpose of sexual intercourse. Rather than saying, "You cannot have sex outside of marriage," we could say, "Sex was created for marriage" (Winner: 25).

The Role of Christian Community

Although celibacy is often considered to be an individual, personal issue, the role of Christian community is vitally important. Issues of sexuality must be included within the context of community. "Both married and single people need to be in close relationships with females and males as we attempt to develop our divinely created nature in the image of God" (Heggen: 190). In the same way that we offer counseling and support to married couples, we must be prepared to help single persons with their struggles. If we expect nonmarried persons in our congregations (and our broader world) to practice sexual abstinence, we must be prepared to support them through loneliness and other struggles associated with a lack of physical intimacy. "The celibate needs others who can nourish and sustain his or her capacity for the celibate engagement" (Sipe: 185). Community is critical to the celibate because it is in community that one's identity is born.

Sexuality as revealed in Scripture must be interpreted by a community. Of course, individuals still may do their own interpretation, but value is found in discussing with others. "The Church as a whole is the bearer of Scripture and tradition means that *all* the faithful—not just the bishops, ministers or theologians—have the privilege and call to wrestle with the word of God" (Jung and Coray: xx).

Not only can celibates gain from their community, communities can receive much from celibates. While secular society might consider celibates to be social oddities because they defiantly oppose some practices of the sexually obsessed culture, the Christian community should welcome their unique perspectives and gifts for the broader community. "This is the purpose of celibacy, not to attain some impossibly cerebral goal mistakenly conceived as 'holiness,' but to make oneself available to others, body and soul. Celibacy, simply put, is a form of ministry—not an achievement one can put on a résumé but a subtle form of service" (Norris: 52).

Community is also important to celibate individuals in that those who practice celibacy give up the opportunity to have their own biological children. For that reason alone, community can be all the more valuable to the celibate. Celibates can offer time, perspective, and energy to families, while families can offer community and inclusion to celibates.

Henri Nouwen proposes in his book *The Wounded Healer* that it is in our woundedness, or our weakness, that we can offer ministry to those around us. Society proposes that those without mates are weakened and not whole. Many within the church have adopted such a philosophy and attitude toward single people.

> Most of us maintain a partial illusion that if we only find the right companion and sexual partner, he or she will erase that ache in the center of our soul called loneliness. Experience teaches us that love involves inevitable risks, separations, conflicts, and losses that are only intensified by the depth of our loves. (Sipe: 77)

This is perhaps where the bridge between celibate persons and married persons in our congregations can be found. Celibate individuals, through their ethical choices of sexual abstinence, know the struggles between loneliness and intimacy and can offer comfort and guidance to other people when they are recovering from the all-too-common grief in human/sexual relationships. Yet most single people do not want sympathy for their life circumstances or decisions. Rather, they want community and support. One single person said to a married person, "Don't feel sorry for me because I am single, but do realize that my life is different than yours and we can talk about ways that would help both of us live more fully in the kingdom of God."

Celibates will feel more welcomed in a community where people share their thoughts and experiences about sexuality and sex openly. Sharing with each other about the value of celibacy along with the thrills and challenges of married sex is a gift that the Christian community can offer to each other.

The Role of Self-image

A healthy practice of celibacy requires a positive self-image. This can come from believing that each of us is created in the image of God, that we are made for God's purposes and goodness in the world, and that God desires joy and happiness in our lives. When we believe this, we will be less inclined to enter into a relationship where our bodies, minds, and souls are not honored and respected.

Yet sometimes we feel shame about our bodies, especially if we have not felt loved fully and completely by another person. Some people have been taught that sex and sexuality are dirty or mysterious, not something to be discussed. When we are taught these things, especially by our parents or church, we are more likely to enter into unhealthy relationships and struggle with questions regarding sexuality.

Moving Beyond Judgment

When failings occur, Christians seem to judge sexual sins more harshly than many other sins. Great disappointment is expressed when someone breaks a vow of celibacy. Perhaps this is due to the integration of sexuality and spirituality. Or perhaps it is because our sexuality is, in essence, who we are. Rolheiser writes,

> Sexuality lies at the center of the spiritual life. A healthy sexuality is the single most powerful vehicle there is to lead us to selflessness and joy, just as unhealthy sexuality helps constellate selfishness and unhappiness as does

nothing else. We will be happy in this life, depending upon whether or not we have a healthy sexuality (192).

When sexual sin occurs, it seems as though everyone has an opinion or a piece of advice concerning the situation and the sin. "Let's take a first step toward a realistic outlook on human sexuality and stop idealizing the virtue of chastity [and celibacy], instead let's pledge to agree that the virtue of charity is at least as important" (Sammon: 70).

Can one who grew up in the church, was taught that sex outside of marriage is always wrong, and has remained a virgin demonstrate charity with friends who have had premarital sex and feel no remorse? In fact, they really enjoyed it. It felt good and right to them. We struggle with our feelings because our heads tell us that premarital sex is wrong. Yet for some, their experience of premarital sex is joyful and positive. How do we rectify this incongruity?

> In insisting that premarital sex will make you feel bad, the church is misstating the nature of sin and the nature of our fallen hearts. The plain, sad fact is that we do not always feel bad after we do something wrong. To acknowledge that premarital sex might *feel* good is not to say that premarital sex *is* good. It is rather to say that our feelings are not always trustworthy. (Winner: 89)

Just because we *feel* good in the act does not make it right. God wants us to have full, joy-filled, pleasurable lives, and has created guidelines for us to follow so that we can live to the fullest, with minimal pain inflicted on ourselves.

Celibacy as Spiritual Discipline

Practicing celibacy is a spiritual discipline. Like all disciplines, it takes practice, deliberate thought, and attention. Eventually, it offers us great insight into the Divine. Unlike the spiritual practice of prayer, however, if we skip "practicing" celibacy one day, we are less likely to go back and pick up where we left off and move ahead.

Practicing celibacy needs to be *part* of a broader sexual ethic that enhances the goodness of God's creation and celebrates our bodies. If being a virgin is one's *only* understanding of sexuality, other important aspects of life are being missed. There is the possibility of failing to live life as a fully sexual person. "To organize one's Christian sexual ethics around virginity is to turn sexual purity and sexual sin into a light switch you can flip— one day you're sexually righteous, and the next day, after illicit loss of your virginity, you're a sinner" (Winner: 154). While the hope is that persons will be able to continually practice the discipline of celibacy, one's sexuality cannot hinge on that alone.

Celibacy is a choice and a gift. "Those who do [accept the gift of celibacy] find that they've received a wonderful agent for integrating their sexuality and spirituality and realizing that goal of both: union with God and others" (Sammon: 103). Persons who choose celibacy are still able to find union with others, just not through sexual intercourse. When one chooses celibacy, boundaries are placed on sexual activity. It is because of those boundaries that sexual sabotage can be avoided, whether by oneself or by other people who may attempt to use and/or abuse sexual intercourse as revenge, manipulation, rebellion, or punishment (Rosenau: 416–17). The gift of celibacy also encourages one to explore other elements of the spiritual life that can enhance a person's identity as a sexual person, as Jesus did.

When we begin to see both sexual intercourse and celibacy as a gift and not a curse, punishment, or mandate, we no longer need to feel ashamed or embarrassed with our state or another's state. Perhaps a better theology might not identify sexual intercourse or celibacy as a gift but rather as an integral part of our sexuality. Our theology of sexuality should view our sexuality as a gift from God, not just the act of sexual intercourse, though that is *part* of the gift. When the emphasis is taken away from the act of intercourse and focused on the overall view of human sexuality, the gift is broad and inclusive of *every* human being. Society makes it difficult for single people of all ages to believe that sex is not something we should want. This is where the church must be countercultural. Is it too naïve to believe that the church could tell its unmarried members and participants that celibacy is a gift? If we truly believe that our sexuality is God's good gift to us, we can successfully celebrate each individual, married or single.

Children and Youth and Celibacy

Children are often taught in the church setting that our bodies are temples. Most often this refers to taking care of one's body with exercise, good food, sufficient rest, avoiding alcohol, drugs, junk food, and maintaining good, healthy habits in general. Rarely is this analogy made to celibacy. If we take our bodies and treat them as temples, we will be mindful of how we use them in sexual ways too. Reserving our sexual activity only for those things that are God-inspired, such as sexual intercourse within marriage, is appropriate as a facet of respecting one's personal temple. With the rise of sexually transmitted infections, it is appropriate that we encourage such behavior, not only for our emotional health, but for our physical well-being as well. If we can celebrate and embrace our sexuality and the many ways it is manifested, we can truly honor the gift of our Creator.

Broader society has initiated some efforts to incorporate celibacy into the practice of the teen population. An example is the "True Love Waits" campaign. The goal of this initiative is to encourage teens to practice sexual abstinence until marriage. On the surface, this approach is valid and should be encouraged. However, it supposes that every teen *will* eventually have a wedding night. While it encourages celibacy, it still proposes that marriage is the preferred, encouraged, and normative state. Again, until we separate marriage from the issue of celibacy, we will continue to struggle as a community of faith in regard to a theology of sexuality.

The reasons for choosing celibacy as an adult may not be persuasive to a teenager, especially when they are bombarded with highly suggestive sexual messages on every front every day. However, single persons, regardless of age, can be taught the importance of self-respect, personal health, and fidelity to personal commitments. For unmarried Christians of any age, celibacy can be taught and encouraged. Modeling healthy, wholesome sexual values and providing church-based sexuality education can help. Everyone, especially teenagers, must be encouraged to talk about sex, to examine the pros and cons for remaining celibate outside of marriage, and to make a clear decision about one's sexual intentions before being in the "moment" with someone. For all of us, no matter what our age, when we are in a physically intimate moment, feeling passion, excitement, sensations, and energy, we will be incapable of objectively deciding, at that very moment, if we want to engage in sexual intercourse with this person. Only when the decision is made prior to the encounter will we be confident that the best decision is made for that time.

Conclusions About Celibacy

When celibacy is a choice rather than a mandate, I have concluded that it does not emerge out of rebellion. Celibacy seems to be the right choice outside of marriage—*not* because God says explicitly, "You shall not have premarital sex," but because God wants us to live within community, true to ourselves, faithful to the vows of marriage *and* to God as Christians. While those who are married make a commitment before God and the community to sexual intimacy only with each other, single persons within the church could also make a similar commitment, one of celibacy in their single life, to God and the community in a public way. And, just as a marriage vow is celebrated and affirmed, so should such a vow of celibacy. Whether the sexual commitment is to sexual fidelity with one's spouse or to celibacy as a single person, our fidelity (and this commitment to God's fidelity of love in our lives) can and must be affirmed, supported, and celebrated. Stephanie Paulsell writes,

In our day, when "sexual freedom" seems to signify only multiple sexual partners, it is good to remember that postponing or refusing sexual relationships can also be a gesture toward freedom. It is good for young people, whose sexual selves are still unfolding, to know that delaying full sexual expression might preserve for them the freedom to live into a deeply satisfying sexual life as adults. It is good for couples practicing the discipline of sexual fidelity to remember the freedom that unfolds over time when two people remain committed to one another's pleasure in a context of trust and faithfulness. It is good for those living with—or without—a sexual relationship to remember that the erotic dimension of life is not dependent on sexual intercourse. (144)

Communities still struggle with single persons within their midst, not quite sure how to deal with their sexuality. Will this single person be a threat to my marriage? How should I touch him? What is wrong with her that she is still single? We are guilty of being influenced by our society, one that is obsessed with sex. As much as Christians try to proclaim they are countercultural, there still is the influence of the media, which tell us to look, act, and feel beautiful and sexy . . . for the sake of drawing sexual attention and possible partners for sexual intercourse. Until communities learn to embrace all humans as sexual beings and realize that sexual intercourse is not the *only* way to express sexuality, we will continue to struggle.

Recently, a single friend wrote about her church service the past Sunday.

There were at least six announcements regarding engagements, upcoming weddings, and anniversary celebrations, which are good to celebrate and applaud. I kept wondering, though, when I'll be "applauded" if I never get married. When do we affirm single people for who they are, for the big "milestones" in their lives?

Might applause be forthcoming if she informed her church that she was committing herself to a life of celibacy outside of marriage?

Kathleen Norris applauds, in new ways, the value and the power of "celibate passion" (53). Jesus demonstrated this celibate passion that Norris defines. "Refraining from genital relationships, nevertheless [Jesus] was deeply in touch with his own embodiedness, his feelings, his sensuous capacities, his eros. All this is evident in his relationships with others, both women and men. It is evident in the passion that pervaded his life" (Nelson 1986: 102).

Rolheiser encourages Christians not to focus on Jesus' choice of singleness and celibacy, but rather to ask the question, "'What did Christ try to reveal through the way he incarnated himself as a sexual being?' If asked this way, the answer to the question will have the same meaning for both married people and celibates" (209).

Jesus was indeed a passionate, expressive person. He did not seem to feel sorry for himself or focus on his singleness. Jesus demonstrated a successful life for single adult living. He needed quiet time as well as time with a diverse group of friends. We can also assume that Jesus had needs for intimacy, sexual expression, and intense companionship—but even as a sexual being, Jesus was able to find sexual expression through, as Norris writes, "celibate passion."

Even in his times of loneliness or desolation, Jesus seemed to crave emotional intimacy more than sexual and physical intimacy.

> Among many other things, through his celibacy, Christ was trying to tell us that love and sex are not always the same thing, that chastity, waiting, and inconsummation have an important role to play within the interim eschatological age we live in, and that, ultimately, in our sexuality we are meant to embrace everyone. (Rolheiser: 209)

In our "I want it and I want it now" culture, the practice of celibacy allows us to practice the spiritual discipline of waiting and patience. This is a good practice that all people could improve on, single or married.

How can celibate persons best focus their sexual energies? The challenge of exploring celibate passions and seeing sexuality in new, healthy ways brings its own satisfaction. The celibate lifestyle still has its challenges. All people have sexual desires, of course. However, the desire to practice celibacy as *part* of sexuality, given to me as a gift from God, is a way to express commitment and fidelity to God as my Creator.

Discussion Questions

1. In what settings have you heard celibacy or abstinence promoted or discouraged? Have you ever heard explicit teaching on celibacy in the church? Why or why not?
2. Do you think celibacy is an important sexual ethic for Christians? Why or why not?
3. The author supports the "True Love Waits" campaign's call to abstinence but does not support the framework of the campaign, which presupposes that everyone will someday be married and have sex. Do you agree with this? Why or why not? What are your thoughts in regard to campaigns that promote abstinence among teenagers? Are they helpful or a waste of time?
4. What can married people gain from reading this chapter? What can married people learn regarding celibacy?
5. What new insights do you have after reading this chapter?
6. If you are single, what do you wish to tell married people about your life that you believe they currently misunderstand or overlook?

15

The Gift Misused

Willard S. Krabill and
Anne Krabill Hershberger

It is clear that many people are not choosing to live according to God's intention. Among the greatest concerns of people in our churches and in society at large is the disturbing awareness that something has gone badly awry regarding love, sex, marriage, and commitment. All around us, we see debris and victims from the distortion of our sexuality.

There are many broken marriages; abortions; pregnancies of the unwed; teenage parents; and abused men, women, and children—especially abused women and children. There is much sexual inequality and harassment, coercion, and rape. Sexually transmitted infections abound, along with sexual ignorance and misunderstanding. Less observable but equally painful is the inner world: disillusionment experienced by teenagers and others; guilt feelings; loss of self-confidence, good reputations, and the confidence of one's mentors and friends; social discrimination; psychological damage; and lack of spiritual accountability.

We believe that our sexuality is a good gift from God. So then, why are these things happening?

In general, our society ignores or disrespects God and a Christian lifestyle. This paves the way for the development of many sexual problems. The "god" that usually claims our allegiance is a love of self and what we think will satisfy us. It is then not a large step to disrespect other people.

Added to this is a constant bombardment of overt or covert

messages to "do what feels good," "get it wherever you can," "go with the flow," "get out when the going gets rough," "show her who's boss," "score whenever and wherever you can," "be sexy or miss the good life," and on and on. We clearly have been influenced by a society obsessed with one dimension of our sexuality—the physical; people equate intimacy with sexual intercourse. That is faulty and is only the beginning of our problem with society's influence.

In Romans 12:1-2, Paul warns us,

> Don't let the world around you squeeze you into its own mold, but let God re-mold your minds from within so that you may prove in practice that the plan of God for you is good, meets all His demands, and moves toward the goal of true maturity. (Phillips)

Too often, when it comes to living our sexuality, we have not heeded this warning. We have allowed ourselves to be molded by the sexual influences of our society. When we try to identify some of the influences in our sexual understanding and mores, we rarely think first of home and church, even though these are crucially influential in many areas of our lives. When we consider current influences, we tend to think first of the usual culprits leading our popular culture: many stars of stage, screen, and television; parts of the music industry; and purveyors of violence, sadism, pornography, and computer sex.

We think of some advertisers who use blatant and demeaning sexual innuendoes. They are culprits, to be sure, and we should keep trying to counteract their activities and messages with conviction. In their greed and selfishness, they are destroying our families, corrupting our children, objectifying women, and misusing God's gift. We could justifiably continue to indict these usual culprits, but in doing so, we would let ourselves off too easily.

Consider the societal characteristics behind these usual suspects, the factors we allow to have such influence in our lives and the lives of our children. How has the world squeezed us into its mold?

Consumerism

Consumption defines western society. Consumer capitalism strongly influences the other values in our society. With it comes the bombardment of advertising, which coaxes us to consume more and more. Consumerism has sanctified choice—choice of new products, new brands, and new pleasures, keeping us perpetually dissatisfied. Gradually, our wants become our needs, and our needs become our demands for all kinds of temporary pleasures that we are led to believe will make us happy.

Excessive consumption of things is bad enough, but consumerism as a "character-shaping" way of life should concern us most. In *Christianity Today*, Rodney Clapp stated,

> The consumer way of life fosters a number of values contrary to many Christian virtues. Can we simultaneously seek and to some degree realize both instant gratification and patience? What about instant gratification and self-control? . . . A central virtue of biblical faith is fidelity. Christians aspire to be . . . faithful to one particular God, not to a succession or collection of gods. Likewise, Christian . . . marriage is an exercise in the virtue of fidelity. A Christian marries and commits him- or herself exclusively to a particular mate—"till death do us part."
>
> The consumer, on the other hand, marries because marriage will serve his or her interests, as he or she understands them at the moment. Commitment in the Christian way of life is an ideal and a goal; commitment in the consumer way of life is more . . . typically a temporary good. Marriage in the consumer ethos is too often open to reevaluation. If at any point it fails to promote the self-actualization of one or another spouse, the option of ending the partnership must be available.

In the Christian way, lifetime monogamy makes sense. In the consumer way of life, serial monogamy (a succession of mates, one at a time) is a much more sensible practice. (29)

It is idolatrous to suggest that human fulfillment comes from accumulating more possessions or "possessing" more people. Sexual conquests are admired. Sex appeal sells everything from toothpaste to automobiles. Recently, a cancer-detection ad on the back of a Christian magazine headlined, "Before you read this, take your clothes off." Then in fine print, it counseled how to do bodily self-examinations. (25)

In *Love and Living*, Thomas Merton wrote about "Love and Need: Is Love a Package or a Message?"

Love is regarded as a deal. . . . We come to consider ourselves and others not as persons but as products—as "goods," or in other words, as packages. . . . Life is more interesting when you make a lot of deals with a lot of new customers. . . . We are biological machines endowed with certain urges that require fulfillment. If we are smart, we can exploit and manipulate these urges in ourselves and in others. We can turn them to our own advantage. We can cash in on them, using them to satisfy and enrich our own ego by profitable deals with other egos. (29)

The casualties of consumerism include simple living, deferring immediate gratification for the sake of long-term goals, patience, generosity to others, modesty, restraint and self-discipline, and wholesome male-female friendships.

We western Christians cannot escape the consumer culture. Even though it is counter to our values, to a great extent we have bought into it. Nevertheless, we can and must resist it. This resistance must be a joint effort between young people and adults. Young people are not likely to defy the culture of their peers until their parents and mentors exhibit some conscientious objection to the consumerist system.

Individualism

Consumerism and individualism go hand in hand. The individualist insists, "What I do, where I go, with whom I associate, and what I acquire—these are my business and mine alone." This attitude is not new. In the Old Testament book of Judges, two identical verses describe a period of disorder: "In those days there was no king in Israel; all the people did what was right in their own eyes" (17:6; 21:25 NRSV), as they "saw fit." In Proverbs 21:2 we read, "All deeds are right in the sight of the doer, but the Lord weighs the heart" (NRSV).

The apostle Paul begins Romans 14 with instructions against judging one another. He writes about being tolerant of those with differing opinions and those who are at different stages of maturity. Then he says, "We do not live to ourselves, and we do not die to ourselves" (v. 7 NRSV). How true.

Christians are all a part of a body. We are a community that looks out for one another. We should be ready to curb our interests for the sake of the community. What I do in private, in my home, in my bedroom, in my sexual behavior—in a real way, that is not just my business. Each of us is a contributing member of our collective witness. Even our private acts are building or tearing down a community.

In myriad subtle ways, each private life and behavior collectively creates the pattern of habits, attitudes, and behaviors that tell the world around us, "This is how it is done here, in this community, in this family." Like it or not, we do not and cannot live in total privacy. Our private behavior does influence our public witness.

The health of a community, especially a faith community, depends in part on the health of the sexual relationships within it. So we in faith communities have much sexual agenda with which to deal.

Secularism

The religious, moral voice has been muted in the public square. United States society, established with separation of church and state, has evolved into one where the religious voice is often ignored or even not tolerated, as we note from repeated court and school board decisions. Part of it is the fault of the churches themselves. We have been so contentious over the years, so intolerant of each other's views, and so sectarian and divisive. The courts and government bodies maintain that religious convictions have to contend with all other forces in trying to influence public policy. Even with First Amendment rights, Christians often feel they cannot be effectively heard.

Politicians do profess faith and woo blocks of religious people. Yet in large measure, religion has become privatized. In *Christian Century*, Martin E. Marty reflects on this idea:

> Assemble mixed company. Make any assertion you'd like about the pope, one or another side of the Southern Baptist Convention, Mormons, Christian Scientists, Jews, the Nation of Islam, Jesus, Joseph, and Mary. Then listen to the fights you've started between the religious. You can't blame politicians, textbook writers, or playwrights like Suzanne Hannon for avoiding all subjects that get close to religion. Hence, a culture of disbelief. Hence, a secular society. (879)

We Christians thus bear some of the responsibility for taking God out of the textbooks—except for a few hints of religious history—and for removing references to religion or church from children's television. That voice is especially missed when the subject is sex. Here we have a wonderful gift (sexuality) given by God to all members of the human family, and yet the religious voice is silenced. Without the religious, moral voice dominating the discussion of sexual values and mores, should we be surprised that our society has assumed the sexual character it has?

Dualism

Dualism is the persistent notion that we can separate spirit and body. Although in recent years the church has made long strides in viewing people as whole beings, dualism still rears its head. We have made great progress in viewing our sexuality in positive ways, as a wonderful gift from God, yet sexual sins are still considered to be worse than any other. The term *immorality* is used much less often in connection with destructive business practices than it is in referring to negative sexual practices.

We still have some fear of our bodies, especially our sexual bodies, as being dangerous. We think, "My body may cause me to sin." We still hear the same old excuses: "Well, I couldn't help it." "I had this overwhelming urge, this uncontrollable passion." "It's not my fault. He tempted me beyond my human capacity to resist."

When we engage in some illicit sexual behavior, we do not leave our souls parked outside in the driveway. What my body does is "all of me" doing it. I am a whole person. I am fully accountable for my body's activity. I am spirit, mind, and body. I am responsible for all my behavior. The body does not run on automatic pilot.

Some studies have shown that regular church attendance and an increased level of religious devotion result in reduced rates of extramarital sex and sexually transmitted infections among young people. But even so, the rates of these are too high among Christian young people.

Dr. C. Everett Koop, former surgeon general of the United States, has said that teenagers will develop strong Christian standards only when Christian parents teach their children early and appropriately about sexuality, sexual behavior, and the moral, ethical, and religious reasons governing it.

Body, mind, and spirit are interconnected and interdependent, and each influences the others. Because of this, we can avoid the dualistic understanding of who we are as sexual beings and be the whole people we are meant to be.

Idolatry

Our society has made sexual fulfillment (as the world defines it) an idol. Sexual intercourse has become the marker for human happiness. Sexual activity without commitment, without covenant, is the standard. We have also made an idol of physical beauty, and we disregard the quality of the person. When people, particularly females, try to meet an unrealistic standard of "beauty" set by a sex-crazed culture, there are long-term negative effects. This can be extremely damaging to one's self-concept.

One aspect of the idolatry is the worship of "sexual freedom"—but it is not freedom. True sexual freedom is realized best within a committed covenantal, exclusive relationship, where we can enjoy the freedom to be ourselves:

- to not be on trial
- to not have to perform
- to not be compared with previous partners
- to learn together
- to trust that my beloved is fully committed to me alone
- to say no as well as yes
- to laugh at ourselves.

Such experiences compose true sexual freedom. In *The Search for Intimacy*, Elaine Storkey says that so much of the sexual activity in our society takes place under conditions that exclude intimacy. Examples are rape, multiple sexual encounters, adultery, and pornography. These violate the spirit of intimacy. She challenges the church to "help re-establish the wonderful humanness of sex" (190).

Too many turn to this idol—sex, coitus, sexiness, casual coupling—to fill the void in their lives. Yet they end up with their real need still unmet and only greater loneliness and fractured feelings to show for it. Our society's sexual preoccupation is a false god, an idol, and it distorts our understanding of who we are, who God is, and the purposes for which we were created. Living our sexuality in accord with God's purposes for sexual union is the only way to find real joy and true sexual fulfillment. That purpose for sexual union is spelled out in the New Testament, where sexual union (sexual intercourse) is placed firmly within the context of marriage.

Consumerism, individualism, secularism, dualism, and idolatry—we must reckon with these five characteristics of our society in exploring our sexual understandings and mores today. We can test our behavior by asking, "What works?" The consumerist, individualist, secular, dualist, and idolatrous behaviors of our genitally focused society that we see around us are not working. We see altogether too many losers. Later in this chapter we will return to the question, "What works?"

Identifying these five traits of our society can give insight on how our culture spawns attitudes that permit

- language that ignores or insults at least half of the human race.
- suggestive remarks, off-color jokes, and actions that make persons to whom they are directed feel uncomfortable and devalued.
- the production, sale, and purchase of photos, print materials, films, videos, computer software, and Internet sites meant to be a sexual turn-on, that exploit and objectify the bodies of both men and women, but especially women.
- relating to others from unequal power bases and coercing others to "do as I say."
- seeking instant sexual gratification regardless of its effect on ourselves or others.
- breaking commitments, and thus destroying the trust of others.

Let us look at the destructive nature and effects of such behaviors and recognize that all people have had some experience in each of these areas and are in need of forgiveness in relation to them.

Exclusive Language

Consciousness has been raised in recent years, in some settings, to use pronouns in speech, writing, and song that include both women and men in the messages sent. The use of masculine pronouns to represent the whole human race is insensitive to women and is no longer acceptable among people who recognize the pain of exclusion.

Christian people have an obligation to use the most sensitive manner possible in helping educate others who have not recognized this pain. Modeling the use of inclusive language may be the most effective educational approach. Use of exclusive language has a long history and will take time to change. We are making progress.

Sexual Harassment

Where does good fun and harmless teasing cross the fine line to become sexual harassment? This is not an easy question to answer, because the particular circumstances are crucial in deciding. In addition, our sense of what constitutes harassment differs. However, in another sense, the question is not that hard to answer. In making this decision, start by respecting the golden rule: "In everything, do to others what you would have them do to you" (Matt 7:12).

Answering some pertinent questions can help to guide our behavior: Does this comment or action foster or damage self-esteem in the other person? Does it respect the person's character or exploit the person's body? Is the speaker or actor thinking or caring about how these words or actions might affect the other person or only considering how he or she is portraying himself or herself among like-minded peers? Is this a loving thing to do or say?

Some men say, "I never would have been offended by what I

said to her, but she sure was." Are men and women coming from such different places and life experiences that we really cannot predict how persons of the other sex will respond to the same stimuli? To some extent, yes. However, it is important to learn to be sensitive enough to read the body language of another person.

When a person becomes uncomfortable, that person inevitably gives cues that indicate this. Many people have been known to develop a creeping blush from their upper chest to their neck and face. Some will just become silent, lose eye contact, or move away from the setting. Others engage in useless movements of their hands and bodies, sometimes called fidgeting. We have all seen people who get teary-eyed when embarrassed. Some assertive types will begin a loud, accusatory, verbal barrage in response to offensive treatment.

It is much more effective and educational not to attack but to state clearly, "I do not appreciate being spoken to or touched in that way. Please do not do that anymore." This communicates clearly that I have a problem with what has just occurred. Whether or not it seems like a problem to the perpetrator of the harassment, it is not acceptable to me. This allows me to own the problem and not accuse the other of being a bad person.

If that approach is not effective in stopping the assault, further steps can be taken, such as keeping a record of specific harassment experiences (who, where, what, when, and who witnessed them), bringing the problem to the attention of people in positions of authority, and using existing channels or help to establish ways of dealing with these infractions.

Sometimes we contribute to sexual harassment by means other than speaking or doing. Laughing at raunchy jokes; giving a thumbs-up or thumbs-down expression as an evaluation of someone's body; posting online or on our walls seductive pictures that objectify the people portrayed; playing and listening to suggestive music; or spending hours with pornographic materials in print, film, or the Internet—these all contribute to becoming part of the problem and not part of the solution.

Pornography

It is estimated that the pornography industry in the United States has grown to a twelve-billion-dollar-a-year business and is larger than the combined revenues of all professional football, baseball, and basketball franchises (Faith & Life Resources: 4). There is an element of subjectivity in trying to define pornography, because visuals, print, speech, and live contact (as in strip clubs) intended to arouse sexual desire depend on what is in the mind of the producer as well as the beholder. Pornography is often equated with obscenity in that it is degrading, harmful, abusive, or humiliating to those involved. However, as U.S. Supreme Court Justice Potter Stewart said when asked to define obscenity, "Although he could not define obscenity, he knew it when he saw it" (Rathus, Nevid, and Fischner-Rathus: 633).

All of us, being human and therefore sexual, find sexually explicit imagery to be titillating, and we may be tempted to search for it. Once involved, some people find themselves addicted and needing to spend more and more time with pornographic materials to fulfill their sexual appetites—never getting enough.

Sexually stimulating material is not always pornographic. There often is confusion about the distinction between pornography and erotica. Pornographic materials portray degradation, humiliation, objectification, exploitation, and often violence and aggression toward others. Erotica is material that reflects the spirit of love known as *eros*.

James B. Nelson, a widely published Christian sexual ethicist, says that *eros* (from which the word *erotic* is derived) is one of many words the Greeks had for love. "It is that part of human loving that is born of desire and hunger. Eros feeds me, fills me, makes me more alive." He reminds us that we are bodily people and as such we are "hungry all the time—born to be erotic" (1997 lecture at Goshen College).

Erotica is sexually stimulating material, but in a positive context. In erotic presentations, "sex is portrayed as part of the broad spectrum of human emotions present in intimate relationships. The people involved are shown to be complex human beings with a variety of nonsexual feelings in addition to sexual ones. . . . Erotica reflects a balance of mutual respect, affection, and pleasure" (Kelly: 445).

When misused,

> the erotic . . . has been made into the confused, the trivial, the psychotic, the plasticized sensation. For this reason, we often have turned away from the exploration and consideration of the erotic as a source of power and information, confusing it with its opposite, the pornographic. But pornography is a direct denial of the power of the erotic, for it represents the suppression of true feeling. Pornography emphasizes sensation without feeling. (Lorde: 76)

There remains some ambiguity about the role of erotica in the lives of sexually healthy Christian people. We do get some help in determining this in a general way from Scripture. Paul said, "Live by the Spirit, and you will not gratify the desires of the sinful nature. . . . The fruit of the Spirit is love, joy, peace, patience, kindness, goodness, faithfulness, gentleness, and self-control" (Gal 5:16, 22-23). Enjoying bodily pleasures is certainly part of what it means to be human. The ability to control those appetites is also a part of what is expected of human beings created in God's image.

Eroticism is in stark contrast to pornography. Our college sexuality classes learn about how some pornographers go to extremes of exploitation to sexually stimulate others, or more accurately, to sell their products. The students often become incensed that society allows these people to be so highly rewarded for their despicable acts. One wrote in her journal, "Women are made to feel like a piece of meat—nothing more!" Another said, "The limit for me comes when children are portrayed in sexually seductive ways to satisfy adult sexual cravings."

Christians must be alert to the insidious evil of pornography that is permeating the minds of so many people. One of the most popular venues for producing and utilizing pornography today is the Internet. Luke Gilkerson said about the Internet, "[It] is a modern day Gyges' ring: it makes people invisible and anonymous, and thus holds out a formidable temptation for everyone to live as they please." Gilkerson goes on to say that when he discovered the world of Internet pornography, he was an easy target and developed an addiction that was one of the hardest things he had ever experienced. He was looking for cheap thrills, "held back only by social norms and religious sentiments" (Pure Life Ministries).

Mary Pellauer describes pornography well when she says,

> Aside from the instances in which it explicitly portrays sexual violence, porn also purveys almost total misinformation about human sexuality. The scenes in porn are endlessly repetitive—boring is a generous judgment. There are no persons, only cardboard caricatures—persons reduced to bits of flesh. There is no intimacy, and no social or personal drama. Further, messages about sexuality that ignore or deprecate *women's* sexuality convey misinformation about *human* sexuality. (350)

We need to help young as well as older people avoid being seduced into a lifestyle that makes room for such garbage. Who is using the Internet in this way? The average age of first Internet exposure to pornography is eleven. The twelve to seventeen age group is the largest consumer of Internet pornography. Twenty-five percent of search engine requests are for pornographic sites. There are 4.2 million pornographic websites (12 percent of total websites) and at least 10 percent of Christian men—and a third as many Christian women—are compulsively attracted to porn (Faith & Life Resources: 4). "A total of sixty-five million unique visitors use free porn sites, and nineteen million unique visitors use pay porn sites each month" (Carnes: 6).

It is gratifying to see that on our Christian college campuses so many students, once they are informed, are moved to consider taking action and speaking out against pornography in their local communities. Countering this kind of multibillion-dollar enterprise will demand constant vigilance and effort on the part of all Christians. Helpful approaches to deal with such addictions are in the next section.

Sexual Addiction

We have much to learn about sexual addiction, but it generally refers to sexual behavior that has become an overwhelmingly intense obsession. It can cause major distress and interfere with normal living. "Some people use sex to manage their internal distress. These people are similar to compulsive gamblers, compulsive overeaters, or alcoholics in that they are not able to contain their impulses—and with destructive results" (Carnes: 5). Not all sexologists believe in the concept of an *addiction* to sex or the use of twelve-step programs to help people with sexual compulsions. This section, though, refers to sexual addiction as a true addiction.

As in other types of addiction, sex addicts make excuses to justify their behavior, blame others, and deny that they have a problem. "For some people the sex addiction progresses to involve illegal activities, such as exposing oneself in public, making obscene phone calls, or molestation. However . . . sex addicts do not necessarily become sex offenders" (Web MD/Cleveland Clinic).

The sexual addiction data collected over twenty years by Dr. Patrick Carnes, former clinical director for Sexual Disorders Services at The Meadows, Wickenburg, Arizona, shows that sexually addictive behavior clusters into ten distinct types:

1. *Fantasy sex.* Arousal depends on sexual possibility.
2. *Seductive role sex.* Arousal is based on conquest and diminishes rapidly after the initial contact.
3. *Voyeuristic sex.* Arousal may be heightened by mas-

turbation or risk (peeping) or violation of boundaries (voyeuristic rape).

4. *Exhibitionistic sex.* Arousal stems from the shock or the interest of the viewer.

5. *Paying for sex.* Arousal starts with "having money" and the search for someone in "the business."

6. *Trading sex.* Arousal is based on gaining control of others by using sex as leverage.

7. *Intrusive sex.* Arousal occurs by violating boundaries with no repercussions.

8. *Anonymous sex.* Arousal involves no seduction or cost and is immediate.

9. *Pain-exchange sex.* Arousal is built around specific scenarios or narratives of humiliation and shame.

10. *Exploitive sex.* Arousal is based on target "types" of vulnerability such as clients or patients (5–6).

"The goal of treatment is healthy sexuality . . . and true recovery involves a clear understanding about abstaining from certain sexual behaviors combined with an active plan for enhancing sexuality" (6–7). Successful treatment plans include good addiction-oriented therapy, a twelve-step sexual addiction group, early family involvement, spiritual support, and a healthy lifestyle (6).

In a discussion with 190 sex addicts about what had helped them the most in their recovery 87 percent said, "A higher power"; 85 percent said, "The couples twelve-step group based on sexual addiction"; and 69 percent said, "A friend's support" (6). How often do our Christian outreach programs consider serving this population?

Sexual Coercion

When sexual decisions are made from unequal power bases, coercion is likely to result. It may be overt, as in the case of sexual abuse and rape, or it may be subtle, as when sexual favors are an unspoken expectation after someone has spent a significant amount of money to entertain another. These examples reflect the power-holder's self-centeredness and lack of respect for the other person.

The negative things that result when sex is forced on another against that person's will are well known to those who have survived such events:

- The victims question their personal worthiness.
- They feel that somehow they themselves brought about the event.
- They have a feeling of personal violation.
- They lose their sense of what constitutes appropriate boundaries.
- They lack interest in taking care of their physical body and appearance.
- They tend to drift toward sexual promiscuousness.
- The victims cannot view their sexuality in a wholesome way or relate to a loving, caring spouse in a healthy, spontaneous, and unencumbered way.

These and many more negative results have been well documented in numerous studies and personal stories.

Alcohol is often involved when sexual abuse and rapes occur. Our local newspaper reported that a twenty-one-year-old woman in our community was raped early Sunday morning. She said she had been out drinking on Saturday night. Shortly after returning home, two male "friends" came over. They also allegedly had been drinking. One of the men helped her make it upstairs to her room. She says she does not remember anything else until she realized one of the men was having sex with her. The second man then also had sex with her. She says she was too intoxicated to say no or to resist.

Another very serious and too common type of sexual coercion is sexual abuse of children. The American Academy of

Child and Adolescent Psychiatry finds that child sexual abuse has been reported up to eighty thousand times a year. There are far more unreported cases because children are often afraid to tell anyone what has happened. Also, the legal procedure to validate that abuse has occurred is difficult. "The long-term emotional and psychological damage of sexual abuse can be devastating to the child" (AACAP: 1).

Child sexual abuse takes many forms: inappropriately exposing or subjecting a child to sexual activity; oral, anal, genital, buttock, and breast contact; use of objects for vaginal or anal penetration; fondling or sexual stimulation; exploitation of a child for pornographic purposes; making a child available to others as a child prostitute; and stimulating a child with inappropriate solicitation, exhibitionism, and erotic material (Florida Center for Parent Involvement: 1).

Ninety percent of child sexual abuse victims know the perpetrator in some way and 68 percent are abused by family members (National Child Abuse Statistics: 2). It behooves caring, Christian people to inform themselves about this blight in our society and to be willing to intervene when needed for the sake of a child. If ever there is a time to cry out "Lord, have mercy," it is surely in these situations.

Such illustrations of sexual coercion cause many Christians to dismiss the problems as belonging to other people—not me and my acquaintances. Statistics, however, show that battering, incest, and other abuses occur almost as frequently in Christian homes as in the general population. This is difficult to comprehend.

It is a long, complex, and difficult process to try to help persons involved in coercive sexual activities, either as perpetrators or as victims. This is important work that must be done in the most sensitive way possible. The services of professional therapists are needed. It is also urgent to support efforts to prevent sexual coercion. This is where the Christian community should have much to offer through example, education, and the presentation of God's way as a better option. (See chapter 16.)

Instant Sexual Gratification

Unwillingness to control our sexual urges and delay sexual gratification leads to major problems in our society. Here we give attention to two of these issues.

Adolescent pregnancy and parenting. Not the least of these major problems is adolescent pregnancy and parenting. Statistics from Alan Guttmacher Institute reveal that each year in the United States, nearly 750,000 women aged fifteen to nineteen become pregnant. The rate declined 41 percent from its peak in 1990 to 2005; however, the rate started to increase again (3 percent) in 2006. The fifteen-year decline is believed to be due to more consistent contraceptive use and to higher proportions of teens choosing to delay sexual activity. Ten percent of all births in the U.S. are to teens, and 59 percent of pregnancies among fifteen- to nineteen-year-olds ended in birth in 2006. Twenty-seven percent of pregnancies among fifteen- to nineteen-year-olds ended in abortion in 2006. As of January 2010, thirty-four states require that a minor seeking an abortion involve her parents in the decision. Six in ten minors do so with at least one parent's knowledge, and the great majority of parents support their daughter's decision.

Forty-six percent of all fifteen- to nineteen-year-olds in the United States have had sex at least once, and 13 percent before age fifteen. If this occurs without use of contraception, a sexually active teen has a 90-percent chance of becoming pregnant within a year. Fifty-nine percent of sexually experienced teen females had a first sexual partner who was one to three years older, and 8 percent had partners who were six or more years older.

The long-term effects of early reproduction are extensive and generally negative. The odds are stacked against the offspring of adolescent mothers from the moment they enter the world. "Babies born to teens are more likely to be low-birth-weight than those born to women in their 20s and 30s" (Alan Guttmacher Institute: 2).

As they grow, they are more likely than children of later childbearers to have health and cognitive disadvantages and to be neglected or abused. The daughters of adolescent mothers are more likely to become adolescent moms themselves, and the sons are more likely to wind up in prison. (Maynard: 5)

Teen mothers are now more likely than in the past to complete high school or obtain a GED, but they are still less likely than women who delay childbearing to go on to college. (Alan Guttmacher Institute: 2)

People at every age have a series of developmental tasks to accomplish. For the adolescent, these include the developmental tasks of establishing personal identity, separating from parents, considering educational and vocational interests, establishing effective social relationships with peers, and establishing personal values and a workable philosophy of life.

When a pregnancy occurs, the adolescent female's focus necessarily moves from her personal identity to consideration of the new life forming within her. At the very time when it is important to gain distance from her parents, she is forced to become even more dependent on them and their emotional and financial support. Plans for further education and vocational preparation and involvement are often thwarted due to lack of funds and/or childcare needs.

At the time when peers mean everything, a pregnant adolescent or teen parent often is not able to hang out with the crowd. The young parent needs to assume adult responsibilities before being ready or capable of handling them. This often fosters confusion, frustration, anxiety, and anger in the adolescent. Life's script is interrupted and most likely changed forever. "What do I value?" "What is the meaning of my life?" These are questions plaguing pregnant teens, even though they may not be able to verbalize them.

Some women and men who find themselves facing parenthood at a young age are blessed to have loving support from family, friends, church, and/or community resources. The experience will most likely be a maturing influence in their lives. It need not be a negative entrapment, even though this seems to happen for many.

The Robin Hood Study (1996) found that the consequences of adolescent childbearing on both younger and older fathers are not as sharp as the effects on mothers and their children. Yet there were some impacts, especially on younger dads, such as not completing high school and having less earning capacity (Maynard: 5). The male sexual partner of the pregnant teen may or may not assume responsibility or offer financial or emotional support to his pregnant partner. Sometimes he goes on with his life as though nothing significant has happened, ignoring the needs of his partner and baby. Many males will try to become involved in caring for the mother and child, but they may or may not be in a position to be very helpful. Lack of employment, education, or long-term interest may militate against his being positively involved. Marriage may not be a good option when the couple is immature.

When God's way is chosen, people do not need to deal with these negative consequences of adolescent pregnancy. Then the couple delays sexual intercourse until marriage and makes a long-term commitment to each other.

The Christian community can again be instrumental in upholding the better way for young people. But when youth decide to be sexually active before marriage, they are especially in need of a loving, caring community that will provide support of their personhood and worth and will not be judgmental of their actions. In this situation, we need to follow Jesus' example: he loved those whom society spurned and considered sinners.

Sexually transmitted infections. Misuse of sexuality brings a scourge of epidemic proportions to our society—sexually transmitted infections (STIs). There are more than twenty of these, some incurable. These infections usually are transmitted by having sexual intercourse with an infected partner. Having sex with multiple partners also raises the risk of becoming infected, because one really is having sex with everyone that person has ever had as a sexual partner.

Of the 18.9 million new cases of STIs each year in the United States, 9.1 million (48 percent) occur among fifteen- to twenty-four-year-olds (Alan Guttmacher Institute: 2). It has been estimated that at current rates, at least one American in four will acquire one or more STIs at some point in his or her life.

In addition to some STIs being life threatening, they can lead to infertility, ectopic pregnancy, cancer, chronic liver disease, and recurrent or chronic pain. Women, teenagers, and minorities suffer disproportionately from STIs, and the financial burdens exceed five billion dollars annually in the United States.

With these kinds of statistics, Christian parents justifiably can be concerned that there will be a limited number of infection-free persons available for their children to marry.

When STIs are preventable, why do people opt for sexual behavior that brings this kind of physical and emotional risk? The reasons certainly are complex. Nevertheless, young people typically think they are immune: "It can't happen to me."

It is important for people of faith to communicate that God's way is best. If everyone committed herself or himself to one sexual partner for life, the scourge of STIs would end. When a person already has had more than one sexual partner, it is appropriate to begin to hold to the standard of becoming monogamous.

Broken Commitments

As noted in chapter 3, one of the important ingredients of a truly intimate relationship is trust. Trusting another person means that we believe that person will keep promises made. We feel secure in knowing that commitments made are taken seriously and upheld. We know that a person in whom we trust will have our best interests in mind and will use good judgment about divulging anything about us to others. When someone breaks those commitments and promises, the partner experiences a devastating loss of trust. The betrayed partner may never again perceive the other to be quite as reliable, even though confession and forgiveness may have occurred.

In our society, commitments made in marriage vows are often broken through adultery and divorce. There are many reasons for the destruction of marriages.

> Most of those who research the divorce epidemic note that a key cause is over-inflated expectations of emotional bliss and romantic love. . . . While Christians can do all that lies within our power to nurture happy, loving, and joyful marriages, at the same time we must assert that in God's plan, people are not free to go from one marriage to the next, looking for greater bliss. (Gushee: 19)

It is surprising to note that only 20 percent of divorces are caused by an affair, according to John Gottman, professor emeritus of psychology at the University of Washington in Seattle. "Most marriages die with a whimper, as people turn away from one another, slowly growing apart" (Marano). The mundane events of everyday life build or damage love in marriage. Our way of relating in the countless "mindless moments" that usually go by unnoticed establishes a positive or negative emotional climate.

This growing apart is usually not anticipated. Marriage partners may begin to give increasing attention to very appropriate endeavors, like developing careers or raising children, but when they do this, they may end up neglecting their marriage relationship.

Conflicting values also may contribute to the destruction of marriages. Couples often are caught between

> the value of a lifelong marriage covenant and commitment to stable families on the one hand, and on the other,

the value of individual freedom which says each person, male and female, ought to be free to pursue their own dreams, gifts, career. Both American culture and the Christian church are searching for a balance between these two conflicting loyalties. (Sider and Sider: 38)

When faced with this conflict, even the church often settles for an either/or approach. "Legitimate individual fulfillment need not be sacrificed on the altar of 'family values'; nor does the nurture and care of children need to be sacrificed on the altar of selfish individualism" (Sider and Sider: 38). There is a need for

Christian marriages where both partners seek to nurture the other's joy and personal fulfillment, practicing mutual submission. Patriarchy does not work. Self-centered feminism—and its counterpart, self-centered male irresponsibility—do not work. Mutual submission, practiced over a lifetime of joy, pain, struggle, and growth, is just what our hurting homes need. (Sider and Sider: 38)

What works? God's design for our lives works. It is the only design that lives up to its promise. Only God's design can bring us real joy, true intimacy, and true sexual fulfillment. What has been described in this chapter are components of the mold into which the world tries to press us and some of the resulting behaviors from these influences.

Paul says, "Do not let it happen." Refuse to be perpetually dissatisfied, always wanting more. Refuse to settle for that which yields only temporary pleasure. Refuse to be silent in the public arena. Refuse to make sex an idol. Refuse to remain self-centered. We can and must give nonconformity new life, new meaning, and new urgency. We can and must create in our faith communities a sexual counterculture, better than that of the world. With God's help we can do it. This is at least part of what Paul is telling us to do in Romans 12:2.

A passage from 1 John 2:15-17 gives us guidance:

> Stop loving this evil world and all that it offers you, for when you love these things you show that you do not really love God; for all these worldly things, these evil desires—the craze for sex, the ambition to buy everything that appeals to you, and the pride that comes from wealth and importance—these are not from God. . . . This world is fading away, and these evil, forbidden things will go with it, but whoever keeps doing the will of God will live forever. (TLB)

When we look for the culprits that have led to the kinds of damaging sexuality-related behaviors described in this chapter, we must look behind the pornographers, the actors, the TV moguls, the advertisers, and the MTV producers. Behind all of these, we find ourselves, who have allowed the world to press us into its mold. We are in need of transformation, declares Paul in Romans 12:2. Nonconformity is a concept that must be reaffirmed in our generation and in a more relevant and urgent form than ever before. As God's children, we can experience the goodness of the gift of sexuality as we were meant to do.

Discussion Questions

1. Is the development of a sexual counterculture possible? Where might individuals and congregations begin this development?
2. How might Christian people reinstate a religious and moral voice in discussions of sexual values and mores in our society?
3. How are individuals' private sexual behaviors impacting your community—toward or away from health?
4. If you are reading these questions in a group setting, determine if the members of the group have different or similar ideas about what constitutes sexual harassment.
5. How might congregations respond to the issues of pornography and sexual addiction?

6. Now that consciousness has been raised in various sources about the prevalence of sexual abuse in "Christian" homes, how should Christians respond?

7. What steps might individuals, families, and congregations take in trying to prevent the occurrence of adolescent pregnancy and sexually transmitted infections in the community?

16

The Gift Restored

Delores Histand Friesen

There are no easy ways to describe how restoration, healing, therapy, and forgiveness take place. Previous chapters have detailed some of the many ways the gifts of sexuality, integrity, and intimacy are misused, ignored, or destroyed.

The healing process cannot be reduced to techniques or advice or scriptural guidelines. Recovery is a process: it takes time to experience restoration and healing. It comes as God's power and the love and safety of the community help to cleanse and restore the identity and integrity of the person. Because our sexuality is relational, it requires human connection, communication, and dialogue.

Instead of giving general guidelines for persons who have experienced disappointment, victimization, or harassment, this chapter is directed toward the church. More specifically, it promotes a biblical and life-affirming view of the gift of sexuality. Such a view will help to provide a healing climate and resources for healing and restoration. This chapter deals with the congregation's role in restoring the gift of sexuality. Yet individuals and families who are seeking healing will also find ways to take steps toward healing.

After describing how important attention to sexuality is in our lives and ministries, practical suggestions will be given regarding climate, community, caregiving, and confrontation. Then goals and principles that every congregation would do well to implement will be presented.

Persons facing problems, concerns, and hurts in the area of sexuality are encouraged in this chapter to reach out to others who can be trusted. They may share their stories with those in their circle of friends and their congregation who are best able to understand, listen, and walk with them through the process of healing. Inviting others to a "meeting for clearness" or sharing the healing power of liturgical dance and the expressive arts, for example, can bring restoration to both the individuals and the congregation.

Climate

A climate of safety and acceptance is one of the first things that makes it possible for persons to share their experiences, hurts, and needs. Listening needs to come from both the heart and the head. Parker J. Palmer names some qualities that are helpful in establishing a healing climate, where persons can risk exposing their hurts, failures, and desires. These include respect; structure or intentionality; accountability; the ability to listen carefully, not only to what is said, but also to what is left unsaid; and a willingness to take risks (69, 74).

Palmer describes six paradoxical tensions that create a hospitable space where learning and growth can take place:

- The space should be bounded and open.
- The space should be hospitable and "charged."
- The space should invite the voice of the individual and the voice of the group.
- The space should honor the "little" stories of the individuals and the "big" stories of the disciplines and tradition.
- The space should support solitude and surround it with the resources of community.
- The space should welcome both silence and speech.

Some years ago on a rainy night, a woman was driving around, wrestling over whether to abort her pregnancy. She saw a sign to a Mennonite church and determined that night to go there and talk to someone before she made the final decision. Today she is a member of that church, and her children have grown up in a place where their voices were and are heard.

Congregations that want to restore persons to wholeness need to consider the climate, openness, and safety of both their physical and their spiritual space.

Centrality of Sexuality

A second way for the church to work at restoring the gift of sexuality is to recognize that our sexuality is central to who we are as human beings. Therefore, every congregation and denomination should give attention to sexual issues and education as part of an ongoing process rather than only as a response to crisis or situations of church discipline for sexual sins.

> Legend has it that Carl Jung once remarked that when people brought sexual questions to him, they invariably turned out to be religious questions, and when they brought religious questions, they always turned out to be sexual ones. . . . Inquiry about sexuality almost always has an inevitable religious dimension, . . . not only teachings about sexual morality; [religion] also bears great themes of sexual relevance: . . . creation and God's purpose in creating us as sexual beings, what we believe about human nature and destiny, sin and salvation, love and justice, and community—all these and many other basic beliefs will condition and shape our sexual self-understandings. (Nelson: 14)

To restore the gift of sexuality, the church needs to help its people take responsibility for sexual feelings, acts, behaviors, and attitudes. This is best achieved by teaching and preaching forthrightly and clearly about the beauty, joy, and sanctity of sexual expressions both within and outside the conjugal bond. If God created male and female in his image and expected them to relate in intimate, procreative, and relational ways, then this *very good* creation needs to be celebrated and cared for responsibly and joyfully.

In my classes at Mennonite Brethren Biblical Seminary, when students are asked to prepare a sermon on some aspect of sexuality, there are still too many who look at me incredulously, unable to imagine themselves or their church doing such overt teaching and preaching. Furthermore, some think there is hardly enough biblical material to provide useful texts, except for wedding sermons.

What, I ask them, is the grace of the gospel for those who do not marry? And *when* is such teaching needed? And *how many* wedding services have you attended where any open teaching was given on the sexual aspects of married life?

A survey of Scripture texts found in *Human Sexuality in the Christian Life* shows that the topic appears in more than half the books in the Bible. If we add the stories of the Bible to the teachings, letters, prophecies, and poetry, there are plenty of significant materials for teaching and preaching.

At least once a year, every congregation should emphasize right relationships and interrelationships between men and women, boys and girls. Many have made a good start by taking one month each year, perhaps February or May, to focus on friendships, fellowship, home, and family concerns. However, often single persons, comprising 30 to 40 percent of most average congregations, are woefully neglected in this programming. In addition to preaching and adult education, congregations should implement a planned age-graded program of sex education. Thereby everyone, from preschoolers to those past eighty, is included in the discussion, dialogue, training, and caregiving. Many denominations have produced material for such programs. *Body and Soul: Healthy Sexuality and the People of God*, produced by Faith & Life Press, is one current example.

If this kind of program is carefully followed year after year, it will help to develop healthy attitudes and knowledge of how to talk to one another about sexual matters in appropriate ways. It will create networks of accountability and pastoral care that provide the basis for the healing and processing of the more painful and abusive experiences. The media and the advertising commercialism of our hedonistic age tend to define social standards. In addition to congregational teaching, preaching, and education, our society needs the church's prophetic ministry.

Advocacy is also sorely needed, not only for victims, but also for the young, the old, the disenfranchised, the disabled, and those newly bereaved. We need some central theological constructs that include justice-making, process, and healing. The process of restoring the gift of sexuality can be long and difficult, but it can deepen and enrich the ministry of the church to its members and to the larger world.

Community

Human sexuality is best understood as God's way of enriching and creating community, not just between male and female, but also in the family and wider social structures. There is a danger that sexuality may become an end in itself instead of opening into the infinitely greater experience of connection and intimacy. Then it becomes a narrowing and limiting factor that undermines community and relationships. Instead, sexuality should be creating bonds of love and unity that build friendship, family, and community.

Some other world religions have tended to swing between the two extremes of orgiastic pleasure or denial, excess or celibacy. The Bible and our Christian faith support both celibacy and monogamy, with the commitment to become one flesh in a lifelong union. Churches and individuals need to keep talking and struggling together to offer truly faithful responses to human sexuality.

We need to hear about how women and men are relating well in liberating, life-giving ways. "Faithful responses to human sexuality . . . provide food for the journey in our lives of ministry and in our search for and participation in Christian community" (Eugene: 2). Our human sexuality is a wonderful and liberating resource.

We are called to work, not only for social justice, but also for sexual justice. "Sexual injustice, in many forms and on the basis of various customs and mores, is a global sore festering in fear, cruelty, and violence. . . . Patterns of sexual and gender injustice are linked inextricably to those of racial, economic, and other structures of wrong relation" (Eugene: 3).

Sometimes the congregation gives so much emphasis to the devastation of sexual abuse that it ignores those who experience miscarriage, infertility, postpartum depression, impotence, or other sexual difficulties. A young father wrote a thesis about how the church might acknowledge the pain and minister to families who experience miscarriage. He was deeply hurt by the callous way others dealt with the prenatal losses in his own family.

In his work as a minister, he has determined to reach out to men and women with unspoken and unnoticed griefs and longings. This, however, demands and assumes that there is a sense of community and a willingness to open up and share our hurts, questions, fears, and failures with each other. Restoring the gift may mean that we need to consciously consider who is relating to whom in our congregations. We can work at breaking through the walls of isolation and individualism so easily set up by our modern life. I think, for example, of a young mother of three, isolated on a cold prairie farm. She spent days alone with the children, wondering if she could get through another day without harming one of the children or herself.

When she and her anxious husband poured out their story to me (a safe visitor from outside their community), they were surprised to learn how common postpartum depression is. They were willing to take some steps to seek help and break her isolation and desperation. But it took great courage and a willingness to let others in the congregation know and share their fearful secret.

Others often overlooked include seniors. Many are living alone. Some formerly married are now single. Some may struggle with feelings of inadequacy. Others are disabled or have a chronic illness. Many cannot remember the last time they were hugged. All of us long for the blessing of human touch and compassion. The church has a significant ministry in reaching out to those who are older and those who live alone.

In another beautiful example of community, a teenaged birth mother handed her child in the baptismal font to a Mennonite pastor couple for adoption. As one mother passed the baby through the water to the other mother, words of commitment, release, and joy were shared; tears of sorrow, grief, and connection were shed. This was not a private ceremony. Family members and friends of the teenager were present, as well as church members and friends of the pastor couple. The individual pain and commitment became corporate as they wept with those who wept and rejoiced with those who rejoiced.

It was not easy for the adoptive family and the birth mother to establish a relationship. It will take much wisdom and work for them to maintain appropriate connection and distance. Yet here was a gathered community of God's grace that recognized pain and bonding. They blessed it with a service of release and acceptance, of letting go and holding on. This ceremony of blessing would not have had the same strengthening effect if it had been done in private. Here we see a godly response to circumstances of sexuality. It is also an example of God building community and of working together for good, even through our brokenness and pain.

The previous chapter on broken commitments described consumerism, individualism, secularism, dualism, idolatry, exclusive language, sexual harassment, pornography, sexual addiction, sexual coercion, and instant sexual gratification—all of which destroy community. Restored sexuality and community begins by first demonstrating the power of loving relationships and then teaching the same. Through our words and actions, we can develop relationships where love, honesty, intimacy, forgiveness, and grace are central and pure.

Caregiving and Confronting

In caregiving and confronting, we work out strategic, practical, and theological responses to a variety of sexuality challenges and issues. We also allow for personal issues to surface and to be dealt with. According to Toinette Eugene,

> The vast majority of religious statements on sexuality in the past have assumed essentially a one-way question, a question posed from a dominant, normative perspective: "What does Christian theology, or the Bible, or the church's tradition say about human sexuality?" . . . [We must also ask,] "What does our experience as sexual human beings say about the ways in which we experience God, interpret our religious tradition, and attempt to live the life of faith?" (2)

A congregation with skilled caregivers has eagerness and enthusiasm to address sexuality issues openly and move toward health, justice, and wholeness. Caregivers act with compassion to prevent deficits and promote assets. The pastoral issues grow out of ministry experience and involve education within churches, pastoral counseling, and social advocacy. Caregivers provide general attention to sexuality and specific attention to sexual violence and abuse, boundary violations, and sexual deviations and aberrations. They give reasons, not just rules.

The church needs to recognize and acknowledge that increased sexual involvement is occurring at earlier ages. In addition, more Christians are tending to accept such activity as moral. According to Charles Shelton, "More and more adolescents view such activity as morally acceptable. . . . Attitudes about sexual morality are currently guided less by rules and regulations and more by the personal commitment and affection that two people are experiencing" (235).

Responding to sexual issues is much more complex than saying a simple black-and-white yes and no. Many factors must be considered: spiritual, physiological, psychological, cultural, and experiential. A discerning church needs to ask, "What are the issues at stake in your life?" Then the church must walk closely enough with the person to help discern that and work toward healing covenant and commitment. Caregivers also need to affirm victims-survivors for breaking the silence, affirm that they were not responsible for the offenses, and affirm the survivors' own healing processes.

The community benefits from those who have experience in guiding discourse and deliberation that overcome ignorance and fear. Leaders need to be comfortable, knowledgeable, and effective in biblical work and be prepared for the challenges of sexuality concerns and issues. Then it is possible for a congregation to hold personal experience in creative tension with religious vision and to affirm the importance of sexuality without giving it undue emphasis.

Minimally, a congregation could have an advocacy team or couple in addition to the care-and-share committee, deacons, or pastoral care listening team. Such advocates need good skills and a willingness to educate themselves about the needs of those who have been harassed, abused, victimized. They also need to learn about the needs of persons who are perpetrators.

Those who provide these training-healing opportunities need to be comfortable with their own sexuality, have a healthy view of and mutual respect for the sexuality of others, be able to discuss without judgment, be lighthearted and humorous, and show appropriate openness.

Carolyn Holderread Heggen's recently revised book, *Sexual Abuse in Christian Homes and Churches*, is a great resource for advocates, deacons, and elders. In addition to the basics, it has helpful chapters on perpetrators, education, liturgies of healing, and many illustrative examples. In *Sexual Offending and Restoration*, Mark Yantzi explains new ways to provide hope to those who have been abused, to the abusers, and to their families.

Jesus ministered to the woman taken in adultery (John 8); the woman at the well, who had a series of partners (John 4); and the demon-possessed man, crazy from mental anguish (Luke 8). His encounters are biblical examples of how the church might confront and restore with compassion and grace.

In the first encounter, Jesus recognized that all of us have sinned, not only those caught in flagrant affairs. When the others recognized their own lack of perfection, Jesus looked at the woman and asked where her accusers were. Then he offered freedom from condemnation: "Go now and leave your life of sin" (John 8:11). When the church recognizes its own failures, it is able to meet people where they are and help them find the way to restore a life where sexuality is honored and healed.

When people have long histories of irresponsibility, confusion, and pain, it may take hours and months of earnest conversation and confrontation. Yet the church and the gospel always hold out hope. Holiness and honor are fruits of right relationships with God and each other; they do not come from impossible standards or rules.

We can ask those whose mixed-up sexualities have driven them and others crazy, "What is your name?" With God's power, believers can still cast out the legion of demons (Luke 8:26-39). Fear, mistrust, loss of identity, and emotional and mental illness respond best to solid compassion and safe boundaries.

Clearness

The Quaker tradition has a custom that could help greatly in learning how to restore each other in a spirit of gentleness. Whoever has a question, decision, or problem to sort out may call a "meeting for clearness." The troubled person selects several people, preferably from a wide range to maximize creativity and response. Then the individual presents a written account of the dilemma or issue that needs healing or discernment.

When the group meets, they first listen to the one who asked for the meeting for clearness. That person describes in some detail what has happened, what the situation is, and the questions over which struggle continues. All participants then may respond only by asking questions for clarification; they may not give advice or counsel.

The way ahead becomes clear as the group continues to ask and the person responds. It is amazing how often a clear consensus is reached. If it is not, the group adjourns and meets again. They follow the same procedure. The group works with a new written account of the directions and struggles clarified the last time. This is a wonderful discipline for pastors, parents, and counselors to only ask—not to tell, explain, or give insight.

Compassion and Holistic Healing

The healing and compassionate ministries of the church need to be grounded in the teachings and life of Jesus. Ministry is also enriched by the psalms of lament, the many stories of God's redeeming and creative acts in history, and the thundering messages of the prophets.

Robert Rencken has used a snow-covered volcano as a metaphor to describe some of the results of sexual abuse. The casual observer may think things look normal or even better than normal. Yet the secretive nature of much sexual abuse covers both the behavior and the damage, sometimes for many years. However, the dormant volcano is there, even though snow may be hiding treacherous rocks and holes.

When the volcano does erupt, there is anger and rage, love and hate, fear and guilt, power and weakness, scars, and perhaps a new face on the mountain. Other family members, friends, and communities who are indirect victims may also be buried in lava and snow, anger and distance. The anger, rage, and pain may be seen for years after abuse has ceased. The potential for further eruption continues, unpredictable in time, intensity, and cause (2).

One way to look at a more holistic ministry style is to recognize that these paradoxes of feelings and behaviors are part of the normal course of healing. There is often a tension in the church between focusing on the pain and loss, and focusing on the strength and resiliency that many victims exhibit. There are other tensions as well: We can individualize and polarize—or organize and communalize. We can move toward forgiveness and reconciliation—or move toward accountability and justice making. We can be concerned about moral responsibility—or be concerned about legal liability. We can emphasize present experience, stress historical accomplishments, or work toward fulfilling future dreams.

Many of these tensions can be resolved by agreeing to face and work through them rather than choosing to deny or avoid the tensions. To confront and support all parties takes individual courage, a commitment to study and understand their experiences, and a resolve to help others learn from them.

As part of the process, it often is necessary to refer people to therapists, groups, and agencies outside the congregation. However, referral to others does not lessen the congregation's responsibility and importance of the role the congregation can play. It also does not excuse laypersons from educating and enlarging their minds and hearts so they can be better caregivers and friends. While church members are receiving counseling or therapy, they still need pastoral care and support, perhaps even more than they did before. As a therapist, I find it quite helpful to have a pastor or a friend of the client who can provide times and places of nurture, prayer, and safety. This gives the client and therapist the courage and ability to go deeper in the cleansing and restoration process. It often is also encouraging if the congregation establishes a fund for counseling to help restore victims.

When the offender and/or victim are part of the congregation, the tensions or paradoxes are even more pronounced. In addition to the distrust, pain, and loss, there is a tendency for the congregation to polarize into two groups: those who see the need for forgiveness and reconciliation at odds with those who call for accountability and justice-making. Others will argue over moral responsibility versus legal liability. Some may try to silence the victim rather than expose the perpetrator.

Abuse must be confronted and reported to the proper authorities as required by law. The community must take action to ensure safety for all involved, including potential future victims. If the offender is a pastor, mentor, counselor, or spiritual leader, there must be consequences beyond reprimand or transfer. These consequences have to be tailored to each situation.

(See the references for more resources on sexual abuse by church leaders and others, including "Pastoral Sexual Abuse," *MCC Conciliation Quarterly*, Fall 1991, and materials from the Center for Prevention of Sexual and Domestic Violence in Seattle.)

Conscience and Covenant

Why then does the church experience so much difficulty in providing a healthy view of sexuality and a compassionate and effective healing ministry in the areas of sexual abuse? When people are frustrated and facing difficulties, this is an opportune time to work toward healing that is holistic, redemptive, and creative. Making covenant with God and each other is central to this process.

Part of maturing in sexuality is coming to understand one's sexual values, attitudes, feelings, and interests as distinct (and perhaps different) from others. We also come to assume responsibility for our own sexual self and behaviors (Shelton: 234).

Youth are not the only ones who construct a personal fable with the assumption that they are personally immune from the consequences of irresponsible or unthinking sexual behavior. Many persons believe that the consequences of sexual behavior can happen to others but not to them. We can see recent extensions of this kind of thinking when people do not take precautions to avoid AIDS and HIV-related illness; excuse politicians and other leaders for illicit and extramarital relationships; and use abortion as a birth-control measure.

Congregations need to name the problems they see, hold each other accountable, and help individuals know that sex is an act of self-disclosure, intimacy, affection, love, interdependence, maintenance, and exchange. Used responsibly and lovingly, it is very good. Used irresponsibly, it can kill, maim, and destroy.

Individuals and congregations need to determine to take some action and work at preventive strategies. They should learn to recognize the signs, symptoms, and results of abusive behavior. They must insist on appropriate consequences.

For this to happen, the church must see that pastors and other trustworthy members are educated to lead in this area. Individual Christians and congregations need to covenant to take both a proactive and a preventive stance. They can develop programs, policies, and liturgies that are truly responsive and led by the Spirit. Sin and injustice need to be dealt with honestly and compassionately. Churches must foster maturity and responsibility in managing our sexuality.

Change Process

Restoring healthy sexuality is a process requiring significant change and growth. However, change is often resisted because it is painful or scary. The world hunger movement has been helpful in describing the *change process* as a four-step model:

- Heighten awareness.
- Mobilize resources.
- Develop models.
- Reorder structures.

This process helps us enlarge the focus of change to include prevention and social action. For example, if there are incidents of pastoral sexual abuse, the congregation may benefit greatly from inviting consultants to study and to help the group work through their trauma and rebuild leadership and family structure. Those who are determined to survive and overcome need support and advocacy.

A congregation needs to follow due-process procedures and conference policies for responding to similar allegations and situations in other churches. The congregation will also need to wrestle with how it relates accountability to forgiveness. It needs to make sure that adequate mechanisms exist for regulating communication and information.

Often there is a premature desire to move on or to suppress painful, unwanted feelings and issues. There might be a tendency to blame the victims for not healing faster, for "holding on too long." A congregation needs to work at all four levels, not just heightening awareness or reordering structure. Then lasting changes can result.

Writing, journaling, and storytelling are good resources for heightening awareness. Somehow, opening the problem, uncovering it, and putting into words what has been secret or feared for so long—these things release and empower the victim. The victim's story can be told and heard. If the victim can access resources and see models or hear stories of how others have changed or healed, those experiences release powerful healing mechanisms of hope and courage.

Corporate action and worship can help to define events as part of who we are, not something to get over. An annual workshop that focuses on confession, remorse, and hope does much to stop the hidden power of secret, cut-off feelings and thoughts. Hannah Ward and Jennifer Wild's *Human Rites* is a resource with liturgies and celebrations for small groups and family settings as well as public worship. As the congregation mobilizes resources and develops models for healing and remembrance, the gift of sexuality can be restored.

Celebration

If sexuality is a gift that is *very good*, then it deserves to be celebrated and enjoyed. While we consider sexuality as celebration, we do not worship it as an ultimate concern or make sexuality so holy and extraordinary that it threatens us or dominates our lives. However, neither should one debase this gift by viewing sex, sexuality, and sensuousness as aspects of life that are essentially evil.

The miracle of birth, committed relationships, and beautiful bodies are celebrated by individuals, couples, and families. The church community also has many events and ways to celebrate the gift of sexuality. In addition to the use of drama, liturgy, liturgical and healing dance, intimacy, friendship, and spiritual direction, there are celebrative events and moments to treasure. They restore us and give us hope.

Three key resources for the healing process are often neglected: liturgy, drama, and sacred dance. Some years ago, a young seminarian told me the moving story of how her participation in sacred dance helped her to heal from multiple experiences of physical and sexual abuse.

Her body had been violated by violence, blows, and unwanted sexual contact. Hence, she found it empowering and healing to be able later to use her body as a vehicle for God's grace and love. To flow with abandon in front of a congregation; to lead others in worship; to feel her body expressing the Spirit, the creative acts and love of God, and the compassion of Jesus—these experiences healed her at a far-deeper level and in a more lasting way than years of therapy, confession, prayer, and confrontation.

In personal and corporate worship, many people find the use of movement to be a powerful symbol of growth, joy, peace, and love. In *Embodied Prayer*, the author suggests selecting a familiar hymn, such as "Have Thine Own Way, Lord." Experience it in silence with a friend, one person acting as potter, the other as clay, and then reverse the roles as the song continues to play (Schroeder: 194–95).

Since the sexual act is so dramatic and the consequences of its misuse are so great, drama can also deeply touch the soul. Years ago, Mennonite Central Committee sponsored a training event on sexual abuse where an original drama was performed. The silence, the chilling recognition of truth, the helplessness of the characters, the despicableness of the act—all these have remained with me long after the testimonies, speeches, and workshops have faded.

In another conference in British Columbia, the smashing of a crystal vase that held a long-stemmed rose made it abundantly clear that something precious is lost when a person is violated. Such worship effectively includes grieving and hoping.

In *A Winter's Song*, a liturgy of lament and forgiveness, Jane Keen allows participants to select the level of forgiveness with which they feel most comfortable. She encourages victims to acknowledge and choose the gifts of forgiveness and restoration in the ways and times and places they are able to celebrate.

Hope and Vision

Achieving wholeness and restoration involves the work of God's Spirit, but it often takes the conscience and commitment of God's people to stay with the process. How am I or how are we hindering or helping this movement of God in our midst?

The congregation models, teaches, and upholds the vision of forgiveness, restoration, purity, holiness, joy, celebration, unity as one flesh—and the enjoyment of the erotic and the body as in the Song of Songs. We count the creation of male and female as very good (Gen 1:26-31). The church continues the creative and redemptive work of God. It offers the love, forgiveness, and compassion of Jesus and the discernment, blessing, and empowerment of the Holy Spirit. These actions build community and break down dividing walls.

I close this chapter with two visions and a request that your congregation's families, agencies, and institutions hold a meeting for clearness. Set some vision and direction for how you might go about the work of God in restoring those who have been hurt and that which has been destroyed. The questions at the end of the chapter may be helpful in this process.

First let us look at two visions of redemption and restoration. Join in the creative and redemptive work of God; the love, compassion, and forgiveness of Jesus; and the discernment and blessing of the Holy Spirit's empowerment.

Walter and Ingrid Trobisch were a German-American couple who worked as missionaries in Cameroon, West Africa. After hundreds of letters and a series of booklets on questions of love and marriage, they found themselves in demand as speakers and workshop leaders.

One day they were ministering in a West African city and met a confirmed bachelor named Maurice, thirty-eight and still a virgin. He had lived with his mother and valued his privacy and the sanctity and purity of his life. They also met Fatma, a prostitute who had experienced almost every possible sexual and physical aberration, including abuse, abortion, rape, and attempted suicide. How Maurice and Fatma came together is a miracle story worth reading in *I Married You*.

Fatma declares, "I am an adulteress and a murderess. I killed my baby." She asks, "How can I ever make that good again?" Ingrid puts her arm around her and says, "Fatma, there are things we can never make right again. We can only place them under the cross."

When Maurice remonstrates that this is not the kind of woman he expected or planned to marry, Trobisch replies, "But she is a virgin. . . . She's cleansed—as the bride of Christ. Without spot. Without wrinkle. Without blemish" (Trobisch: 131–35).

The other vision is a visual one that utilizes several senses, including touch and smell. It is a communion box created by a gay man who lives with his partner but still wishes to hold membership in the congregation for which he created this work of art. It is a small box, perhaps eighteen inches square and three inches deep, made of wood, but covered with lamb's wool on the outside. It is lined with red velvet on the inside lid, and has mirrors on the inside walls and bottom of the box.

When the lid of the box is lifted, one is conscious of the sacrifice of the Lamb of God and the shed blood of Jesus, as one experiences the scent of aged wine from the rows of communion glasses carefully placed in the box. The mirrors reflect the red of the velvet. Even more striking is the fact that one's vision is drawn beyond the box and beyond the cups one can touch to the unending rows and lines of communion cups that reach into eternity and infinity.

May the cross of Jesus and the communion of the saints cleanse, equip, and empower each of us for the work of restoration and healing.

Discussion Questions

1. How is the covenantal aspect of sexuality communicated in our congregation, in my home, and in my life?
2. What do I need to communicate to others regarding sexuality?
3. How do my actions or inactions contribute to the building of community or the breakdown of community?
4. What is the climate of my church, family, and neighborhood communities?
5. Where and how might I show compassion? Where do I need healing and restoration?
6. How and when have I (we) celebrated the gift of sexuality? How could I release my gifts and those of others for celebration? (Examples are journaling, writing, singing, dancing, drama, liturgy, prayer.)
7. Should I call or participate in a meeting for clearness?

17

The Gift: Further Study

Delores Histand Friesen and Anne Krabill Hershberger

Each topic included in this book can be studied in much greater depth than is possible here. In this chapter, we will list some of the many resources for further study, in the hope that readers will be inspired to continue increasing their insights and understandings of sexuality from many different perspectives. Particular effort has been made to include resources that represent Christian and Anabaptist perspectives as well as some secular and scientific resources.

Each resource is listed only once, in a category where it mostly fits; however, some of the resources could be listed in many of the categories, due to the wide scope of their contents. Most of the resources are from the past two decades, although some excellent materials from earlier times have also been listed.

Many of the resources also contain their own lists of resources. Use them! One of the most profound biblical concepts regarding the sexual relationship is expressed in the term *knowing*. It is a deep and spiritual experience truly to know oneself and the other person. When we read, study, and experience other viewpoints, stories, and questions, we learn to *know* both ourselves and others.

It is hard to read a story like Geneva E. Bell's *My Rose: An African-American Mother's Story of AIDS* and still ignore the AIDS issue and the need for care and compassion of persons with AIDS. Watching videos where survivors of sexual abuse tell their stories increases compassion and understanding as well as the urgency to work toward prevention and a safer society. Wrestling with various questions and studies of biblical interpretation stimulates dialogue, understanding, and growth.

Conflicts and disagreements press us to do more study. Like the apostle Paul, Christians need to ask for the parchments and give attention to reading. If you are a congregational leader or teacher, you may wish to plan a yearly study or sermon series on human sexuality, taking one topic at a time. If you are working through family or personal issues or questions, choose areas of study and resources that speak to your needs. Above all, do not be afraid to ask questions and search the Scriptures as you study and read. Take time to reflect, pray, and study with other Christian believers.

It is a good discipline to come to resources such as these with an open mind and a teachable spirit. The "meeting for clearness" can take place as you study. Respond by continuing to ask questions as you think rather than arguing or trying to promote your own ideas. Build convictions and engage in actions based on Scripture, community, and dialogue. Using resources such as these is one way to take seriously both the community of faith and the worlds of science, art, and knowledge.

May God's gift of sexuality continue to be a good gift that is treasured, honored, and understood. This is our prayer:

> God, you have created us and called us to a life of holiness, joy, and union. May we accept and treasure the goodness and grace of sexuality. Help us to grow in our acceptance of ourselves and each other despite differences in orientation, conviction, and interpretation. Send your Holy Spirit to guide and teach us how to love and be loved. Through Jesus Christ our Lord. Amen.

Adolescent Sexuality and Pregnancy

Albanesi, Heather Powers. *Gender and Sexual Agency: How Young People Make Choices About Sex*. Lanham, Md.: Lexington Books, 2010.

Bender, David, and Bruno Leone, series eds., Karin L. Swisher, book ed. *Teenage Sexuality: Opposing Viewpoints*. San Diego: Greenhaven Press, 1994.

Card, Josefina J., and Tabitha A. Benner, eds. *Model Programs for Adolescent Sexual Health*. New York: Springer Publishing, 2008.

Carrera, Michael A. *Lessons for Lifeguards: Working with Teens When the Topic Is Hope*. New York: Donkey Press, 1996.

Cocca, Carolyn. *Adolescent Sexuality: A Historical Handbook and Guide*. Westport, Conn.: Praeger Publishers, 2006.

Crouter, Ann C., and Alan Booth., eds. *Romance and Sex in Adolescence and Emerging Adulthood*. Mahwa, N.J.: Lawrence Erlbaum Associates, 2006.

Doak, Melissa J. *Growing-Up: Issues Affecting America's Youth*. Detroit: Cengage Learning, 2009.

Kaethler, Andy Brubacher. "Becoming Adult, Being Sexual: Sexuality on the Long Road to Adulthood." *Vision*, Fall 2008: 41–50.

Millsaps, Cyneatha. "Let's Talk About Sex: What the Church Owes Our Youth." *Vision*, Fall 2008: 51–57.

Perito, John E. *Adolescent Sexuality, Too Much, Too Soon: Spiritual and Sexual Guidance for Parents*. Salt Lake City, Utah: Millennial Mind Publishing, 2008.

Pipher, Mary. *Reviving Ophelia: Saving the Selves of Adolescent Girls*. New York: Ballantine, 1994.

Westman, Jack C. *Breaking the Adolescent Parent Cycle: Valuing Fatherhood and Motherhood*. Lanham, Md.: University Press of America, 2009.

Aging and Sexuality

Bancroft, John H. "Sex and Aging." *The New England Journal of Medicine* 357, no. 8 (2007): 820–22.

Butler, Robert N., and Myrna I. Lewis. *Love and Sex After 60*. Rev. ed. New York: Harper and Row, 1988.

Camacho, Maria E., and Carlos Reyes-Ortiz. "Sexual Dysfunction in the Elderly: Age or Disease?" *International Journal of Impotence Research* 17 Suppl. (2005): S52–S56.

Davidson, Kate, and Graham Fennel, eds. *Intimacy in Later Life*. New Brunswick: Transaction Publishers, 2004.

Genazzani, Andrea R., Marco Gambacciani, and Tommaso Simoncini. "Menopause and Aging, Quality of Life and Sexuality." *Climacteric: The Journal of the International Menopause Society* 10, no. 2 (2007): 88–96.

Hartzell, Rose. "Senior Sex: Exploring the Sex Lives of Older Adults." *Journal of Sex Research* 43, no. 3 (2006): 292–93.

"Sexuality and Aging Revisited." *SIECUS Report* 30, no. 2 (December 2001/January 2002).

"Sexuality and Seniority." *Harvard Men's Health Watch* 13, no. 10 (2009): 1–4.

Walz, Thomas H., and Nancee S. Blum. *Sexual Health in Later Life*. Lexington, Mass.: Lexington Books, 1987.

Acquired Immunodeficiency Syndrome (AIDS)

Bell, Geneva E. *My Rose: An African-American Mother's Story of AIDS*. Cleveland: Pilgrim Press, 1997.

Bender, David L., and Bruno Leone, eds. *AIDS: Opposing Viewpoints*. San Diego: Greenhaven Press, 1992.

Bourke, Dale Hanson. *The Skeptic's Guide to the Global AIDS Crisis*. Rev. ed. Atlanta: Authentic Media, 2006.

Coming to Say Goodbye: Stories of AIDS in Africa. DVD. 30 minutes. Maryknoll Productions, 2004. P.O. Box 308, Maryknoll, N.Y. 10545-0308; www.maryknollmall.org.

Dortzbach, Deborah, and W. Meredith Long. *The AIDS Crisis:*

What We Can Do. Downers Grove, Ill.: InterVarsity Press, 2006.

Friesen, Delores. "Islands of Hope in a Time of Despair." In *Out of the Strange Silence*. Winnipeg and Hillsboro: Kindred Productions, 2005: 201–18.

Greaser, Frances Bontrager. *And a Time to Die*. Scottdale, Pa.: Herald Press, 1995.

Hall, J., et. al., eds. *A Guide to Action on AIDS: Understanding the Global AIDS Pandemic and Responding through Faith and Action*. World Vision, 2006.

Messer, D. E. *Breaking the Conspiracy of Silence: Christian Churches and the Global AIDS Crisis*. Minneapolis: Augsburg/Fortress, 2004.

PBS *Frontline. The Age of AIDS*. (www.pbs.org/wgbh/pages/frontline/aids/), May 30, 2006.

Taking Action: Peer Educators Work to End HIV and AIDS. DVD. Thirty-five minutes. Four-part series. Mennonite Central Committee, 2009. 21 S. 12th St., P.O. Box 500, Akron, PA 17501-0500; 717-859-1151; 888-563-4676. In Canada: MCC Canada, 134 Plaza Drive, Winnipeg, MB R3T 5K9; 888-622-6337; www.mcc.org.

Yesterday. DVD. Videovision Entertainment, 2004. Academy Award nominee, Best Foreign Language Film.

Cross-Gender Friendship

Bustanoby, Andre. *Can Men and Women Just Be Friends?* Rev. ed. Grand Rapids, Mich.: Zondervan, 1993.

Joyce, Mary Rosera. *How Can a Man and Woman Be Friends?* Collegeville, Minn.: Liturgical Press, 1977.

Harvey, John H., Amy Wenzel, and Susan Sprecher, eds. *The Handbook of Sexuality in Close Relationships*. Mahwah, N.J.: Lawrence Erlbaum Associates, 2004.

Heggen, Carolyn Holderread, Gayle Gerber Koontz, and Ted Koontz. "Can Women and Men Be Friends?" *Gospel Herald* 6, no. 21 (1994): 1–3, 8.

McDougall, Patricia, and Shelley Hymel. "Same-Gender Versus Cross-Gender Friendship Conceptions: Similar or Different?" *Merrill-Palmer Quarterly: Journal of Developmental Psychology* 53, no. 3 (2007): 347–80.

Gender Roles

Abrahams, George, and Shiela Ahlbrand. *Boy v. Girl? How Gender Shapes Who We Are, What We Want, and How We Get Along*. Minneapolis: Free Spirit Publishing, 2002.

Enns, Elaine, and Ched Myers. "Peace, Gender and Conflict." In Carolyn Schrock Shenk and Laurence Ressler, eds. *Making Peace with Conflict: Practical Skills for Conflict Transformation*. Scottdale, Pa.: Herald Press, 1999.

Foley, Sallie, Sally A. Kope, and Dennis P. Sugrue. *Sex Matters for Women: A Complete Guide to Taking Care of Your Sexual Self*. New York: The Guilford Press, 2002.

Jantz, Gregg L., and Ann McMurray. *Too Close to the Flame*. West Monroe, La.: Howard Publishing, 1999.

Kanyoro, Musimbi. "Sitting Down Together." *The Other Side* 34, no. 3 (May/June, 1998): 36–39.

Kimmel, Michael S. *The Gender of Desire: Essays on Male Sexuality*. New York: State University of New York Press, 2005.

Penner, Carol, ed. *Women and Men: Gender in the Church*. Scottdale, Pa.: Herald Press, 1998.

Sax, Leonard. *Why Gender Matters: What Parents and Teachers Need to Know About the Emerging Science of Sex Differences*. New York: Broadway Books/Random House, 2005.

Shalot, Wendy. *A Return to Modesty: Discovering the Lost Virtue*. New York: Simon & Schuster, 2000.

Thatcher, Adrian, and Elizabeth Stuart, eds. *Christian Perspectives on Sexuality and Gender*. Grand Rapids, Mich.: Eerdmans, 1996.

Grief and Sexuality

Bedford, Victoria Hilkevitch, and Barbara Formaniak Turner. *Men In Relationships*. New York: Springer Publishing, 2006.

Carr, Deborah, Randolph M. Neese, and Camille B. Wortman, eds. *Spousal Bereavement in Late Life*. New York: Springer Publishing, 2005.

Hartzler, Rachel Nafziger. *Grief and Sexuality: Life After Losing a Spouse*. Scottdale, Pa.: Herald Press, 2006.

Moore, Alinde J., and Dorothy C. Stratton. *Resilient Widowers*. New York: Springer Publishing, 2001.

Wright, Norman H. *Reflections of a Grieving Spouse: The Unexpected Journey from Loss to Renewed Hope*. Eugene, Ore.: Harvest House, 2009.

Infertility

Calhoun, B. C. *When a Husband Is Infertile: Options for the Christian Couple*. Grand Rapids, Mich.: Baker, 1994.

Resolve: The National Infertility Association. 1760 Old Meadow Road, Suite 500, McLean, VA 22102; 703-556-7172; info@resolve.org.

Salzer, Linda P. *Surviving Infertility*. New York: Harper Perennial, 1991.

Shapiro, Constance Hoenk. *Infertility and Pregnancy Loss*. San Francisco: Jossey-Bass, 1988.

Simons, Harriet Fishman. *Wanting Another Child: Coping with Secondary Infertility*. Lexington, Mass.: Lexington Books, 1995.

Zoldbrod, Aline P. *Men, Women, and Infertility*. Lexington, Mass.: Lexington Books, 1993.

Intimacy

Abbott, F. *Men and Intimacy*. Freedom, Calif.: Crossing Press, 1990.

Dawn, Marva J. *Sexual Character: Beyond Technique to Intimacy.* Grand Rapids, Mich.: Eerdmans, 1993.

McMinn, Lisa Graham. *Sexuality and Holy Longing: Embracing Intimacy in a Broken World.* San Franscisco: Jossey-Bass, 2004.

Schnarch, David. *Intimacy and Desire: Awaken the Passion in Your Relationship.* New York: Beaufort Books, 2009.

Winner, Lauren F. *Real Sex: The Naked Truth About Chastity.* Grand Rapids, Mich.: Brazos Press, 2005.

Marriage

Amatenstein, Sherry. *The Complete Marriage Counselor.* Avon, Mass.: Adams Media, 2010.

Breazeale, Kathlyn A. *Mutual Empowerment: A Theology of Marriage, Intimacy, and Redemption.* Minneapolis: Fortress Press, 2008.

Davis, Michele Weiner. *The Sex-Starved Marriage: Boosting Your Marriage Libido, A Couple's Guide.* New York: Simon and Schuster, 2003.

Gottman, John M., and Nan Silver. *The Seven Principles for Making Marriage Work.* New York: Three Rivers Press, 1999.

Harley, Willard F. Jr. *His Needs, Her Needs.* Grand Rapids, Mich.: Revell/Baker Book House, 2001.

Hertlein, Katherine M., Gerald R. Weeks, and Shelley K. Sendak. *A Clinician's Guide to Systemic Sex Therapy.* New York: Routledge, Taylor & Francis Group, 2009.

Markman, Howard, Scott M. Stanley, and Susan L. Blumberg. *Fighting for Your Marriage: Positive Steps for Preventing Divorce and Preserving a Lasting Love.* San Francisco: Jossey-Bass, 1994.

McCarthy, Barry W., and Emily McCarthy. *Discovering Your Couple Sexual Style.* New York: Routledge, Taylor and Francis Group, 2009.

Penner, Clifford, and Joyce Penner. *Fifty-two Ways to Have Fun, Fantastic Sex: A Guidebook for Married Couples*. Nashville, Tenn.: Thomas Nelson, 1994.

Penner, Joyce, and Clifford Penner. *Restoring the Pleasure: Complete Step-by Step Programs to Help Couples Overcome the Most Common Sexual Barriers*. Nashville, Tenn.: Thomas Nelson, 2003.

Schnarch, David, and James Maddock. *Resurrecting Sex: Resolving Sexual Problems and Rejuvenating Your Relationship*. New York: Harper Collins, 2002.

Smith, Earl, and Rose Smith. *Sizzling Monogamy*. Albuquerque: William Havens, 1997.

Thatcher, Adrian. "Living Together Before Marriage: The Theological and Pastoral Opportunities." In *Celebrating Christian Marriage*. Edited by Adrian Thatcher. New York: T. & T. Clark, 2001, 55–70.

Online Resources

American Association of Sexuality Educators, Counselors, and Therapists: www.assect.org

Center for Disease Control: www.cdc.org

Mayo Clinic: www.mayoclinic.com

National Coalition to Support Sexuality Education: www.ncsse.org

Religious Institute, The: www.religiousinstitute.org

Sexual Health Network, The: www.sexualhealth.com

Sexuality Information and Education Council of the United States: www.siecus.org

World Health Organization: www.who.int

Same-Sex Orientation

Biesecker-Mast, Gerald J. "Mennonite Public Discourse and the Conflicts over Homosexuality." *Mennonite Quarterly Review* 72, no. 2 (April 1998): 275–300.

Childs, J. M. *Faithful Conversation: Christian Perspectives on Homosexuality*. Minneapolis: Fortress Press, 2003.

Farley, Margaret A. *Just Love: A Framework for Christian Sexual Ethics*. New York: The Continuum International Publishing Group, 2006.

Gomes, Peter J. "The Bible and Homosexuality: The Last Prejudice." In *The Good Book: Reading the Bible with Mind and Heart*. New York: Wm. Morrow, 1996, 144–72.

Grimsrud, Ted, and Mark Thiessen Nation. *Reasoning Together: A Conversation on Homosexuality*. Scottdale, Pa.: Herald Press, 2008.

King, Michael A. *Stumbling Toward a Genuine Conversation on Homosexuality*. Telford, Pa.: Cascadia Publishing House, 2007.

Kreider, Roberta Showalter. *The Cost of Truth: Faith Stories of Mennonites and Brethren Leaders and Those Who Might Have Been*. Sellersville, Pa.: Roberta Showalter Kreider, 2004.

Showalter, Ann. *Touched By Grace: From Secrecy to New Life*. Telford, Pa.: Dreamseeker Books, 2006.

Swartley, Willard M. *Homosexuality: Biblical Interpretation and Moral Discernment*. Scottdale, Pa.: Herald Press, 2003.

White, Mel. *Stranger at the Gate: To Be Gay and Christian in America*. New York: Plume, 1995.

Same-Sex Orientation, Video/DVD Resources

Fierstein, Harvey. *Torch Song Trilogy*. DVD. 120 minutes. New Line Home Video, 1988.

Forster, E. M. *Maurice*. DVD. 140 minutes. Criterion Collection, 1971.

Karslake, Daniel. *For the Bible Tells Me So*. DVD. 98 minutes. Atticus Group, 2007. www.firstrunfeatures.com or www.amazon.com.

Lucas, Craig. *Long Time Companion*. DVD. 96 minutes. Samuel Goldwyn, 1990.

Mennonite and Brethren Gay Caucus. *Body of Dissent: Lesbian*

and Gay Mennonites and Brethren Continue the Journey.
DVD. 39 minutes. Bridge Video, 1994.

Sexual Abuse

Ask Before You Hug: Sexual Harassment in the Church. DVD.
31 min. United Methodist Annual Conference Commissions
on the Status and Role of Women, General Commission on
the Status and Role of Women, and UMCom Productions.

Beyond the News: Sexual Abuse. DVD. 21 minutes. Mennonite
Media, 1993.

Center for the Prevention of Sexual and Domestic Violence.
1914 N. 34th St., Suite 105, Seattle, WA 98103-9058;
206-634-1903.

Cochrane, Linda. *The Path to Sexual Healing.* Grand Rapids,
Mich.: Baker Books, 2000.

Croll, Marie C. *Following Sexual Abuse: A Sociological
Interpretation of Identity Re/Formation in Reflexive Therapy.*
Toronto: University of Toronto Press, 2008.

Doyle, Louise, and Peta Hammersley. *Helping Your Sexually
Abused Child.* Vancouver: Society for Assistance in the
Community Today, 1986.

Earle, Sarah, and Keith Sharp. *Sex in Cyberspace: Men Who
Pay for Sex.* Burlington, Vt.: Ashgate Publishing, 2007.

Fortune, Marie M. *Sexual Violence: The Sin Revisited.* Cleveland:
Pilgrim Press, 2005.

Gargiulo, Maria. *Not in My Church.* Part of Keeping the Faith
program series. VHS. 45 minutes. Michi Picures, 1991.

Goering Reid, Kathryn, with Marie M. Fortune. *Preventing
Child Sexual Abuse, Ages 9–12.* New York: United Church
Press, 1989.

Goode, Sarah D. *Understanding and Addressing Adult
Sexual Attraction to Children: A Study of Paedophiles in
Contemporary Society.* London: Routledge, 2010.

Hear Their Cries: Religious Responses to Child Abuse. DVD.
48 min. FaithTrust Institute.

Heggen, Carolyn Holderread. *Sexual Abuse in Christian Homes and Churches*. Scottdale, Pa.: Herald Press, 2010.

Hertlein, Katherine M., Gerald R. Weeks, and Nancy Gambescia, eds. *Systemic Sex Therapy*. London: Routledge, 2008.

Hoffman, David. *Why, God—Why Me?* DVD. 35 minutes. Varied Directions, 2002.

Hunter, Mic. *Abused Boys: The Neglected Victims of Sexual Abuse*. New York: Fawcett, 1990.

Katz, Jackson. *Tough Guise: Violence, Media & the Crisis in Masculinity*. DVD. 82 minutes. Media Education Foundation, 1999.

Laaser, Debra. *Shattered Vows: Hope and Healing for Women Who Have Been Sexually Betrayed*. Grand Rapids, Mich.: Zondervan, 2008.

Little Bear. VHS. 19 minutes. Bridgework Theatre, 1986. Available at www.newist.org.

Marshall, W. L., et al., eds. *Sexual Offender Treatment: Controversial Issues*. Hoboken, N.J.: John Wiley and Sons, 2006.

Mennonite Central Committee (MCC). 21 S. 12th St., P.O. Box 500, Akron, PA 17501-0500 (717-859-1151; 888-563-4676; www.mcc.org):

> "Abuse: Response and Prevention." 2008.
>
> *After Sexual Abuse*. Two-part video on incest survivor's struggle. VHS. 52 min. 1992.
>
> Block, Heather. "Understanding Sexual Abuse by a Church Leader or Caregiver." 2003.
>
> *Conciliation Quarterly:* http://us.mcc.org/programs/peacebuilding/resources/print/conciliationquarterly.
>
> "Created Equal: Women and Men in the Image of God." 2009.
>
> "Making Your Sanctuary Safe." (Resources for developing congregational abuse prevention policies.)
>
> "Pornography: The Secret Sin." A packet of resources. 2005.

Websites including www.dovesnest.net and http://abuse.mcc.org/ (Wide range of resources on abuse response and prevention.)

No More Secrets. VHS. 24 minutes. Films For the Humanities & Sciences, P.O. Box 2053, Princeton, NJ 08543-2053. 1-800-257-5126.

Seto, Michael C. *Pedophilia and Sexual Offending Against Children: Theory, Assessment, and Intervention.* Washington, D.C.: American Psychological Association, 2008.

"Sexual Harassment." *SIECUS Report* 28, no.3 (February/March 2000).

Strength to Resist, The: The Media's Impact on Women and Girls. DVD. 35 minutes. Cambridge Documentary Films, 2000.

Traina, Christina L. H. "Captivating Illusions: Sexual Abuse and the Ordering of Love." *Journal of the Society of Christian Ethics* 28, no. 1 (2008): 183–208.

Wexler, David B. *When Good Men Behave Badly: Change your Behavior, Change Your Relationships.* Oakland, Calif.: New Harbinger Publications, 2004.

Weitzer, Ronald, ed. *Sex for Sale: Prostitution, Pornography, and the Sex Industry.* New York: Routledge, 2000.

Yoder, Carolyn, and Howard Zehr. *The Little Book of Trauma Healing.* Intercourse, Pa.: Good Books, 2005.

Sexual Addiction

Ben-Ze'ev, Aaron. *Love Online: Emotions on the Internet.* New York: Cambridge University Press, 2004.

Carnes, Patrick. *Don't Call It Love: Recovery from Sexual Addiction.* New York: Bantam Books, 1991.

Kasl, Charlotte Davis. *Women, Sex, and Addiction: A Search for Love and Power.* New York: Harper and Row, 1989.

Sbraga, Tamara Penix, and William T. O'Donohue. *The Sex Addiction Workbook: Proven Strategies to Help You Regain*

Control of Your Life. Oakland, Calif.: New Harbinger Publications, 2003.

"The Debate: Sexual Addiction and Compulsion." *SIECUS Report* 31, no. 5 (June/July 2003).

Willingham, Russell. *Breaking Free: Understanding Sexual Addiction and the Healing Power of Jesus.* Downers Grove, Ill.: InterVarsity Press, 1999.

Sexuality Education

Bartle, Nathalie, and Susan Lieberman. *Venus in Blue Jeans: Why Mothers and Daughters Need to Talk About Sex.* New York: Dell/Random House, 1998.

Body and Soul: Healthy Sexuality and the People of God. Newton, Kan.: Faith & Life Press, 2010.

Byer, Curtis O., Lewis W. Shainberg, and Grace Galliano. *Dimensions of Human Sexuality.* 9th ed. New York: McGraw-Hill College Div., 2009.

Haffner, Debra W. *Beyond the Big Talk: Every Parent's Guide to Raising Sexually Healthy Teens—From Middle School to High School and Beyond.* New York: New Market Press, 2002.

———. *From Diapers to Dating: A Parent's Guide to Raising Sexually Healthy Children—From Infancy to Middle School.* New York: New Market Press, 2004.

———. *What Every 21ˢᵗ Century Parent Needs to Know: Facing Today's Challenges with Wisdom and Heart.* New York: New Market Press, 2008.

Harris, E. "How to Talk to Your Children About Sexuality and Other Important Issues: A SIECUS Annotated Bibliography for Parents." *SIECUS Report* 22, no. 3 (1994): 18–20.

Madaras, Lynda. *On Your Mark, Get Set, Grow: A "What's Happening to My Body?" Book for Younger Boys.* New York: New Market Press, 2008.

———. *Ready, Set, Grow: A "What's Happening to My Body" Book for Younger Girls.* New York: New Market Press, 2003.

————. *The What's Happening to My Body Book for Boys: A Growing Up Guide for Parents and Sons*. New York: New Market Press, 2007.

————. *The What's Happening to My Body Book for Girls: A Growing Up Guide for Parents and Daughters*. New York: New Market Press, 2007.

Maksym, D. *Shared Feelings: A Parent Guide to Sexuality Education for Children, Adolescents, and Adults Who Have a Mental Handicap*. North York, Ont.: G. Allan Roeher Inst., 1990.

Richardson, Justin, and Mark A. Schuster. *Everything You Never Wanted Your Children to Know About Sex (But Were Afraid They'd Ask)*. New York: Three Rivers Press, 2003.

Ritchie, James H. Jr. *Created By God: Tweens, Faith, and Human Sexuality*. Nashville: Abingdon Press, 2009.

Rizzo Toner, P. *Relationships and Communication Activities*. (Includes 90 ready-to-use worksheets for grades 7–12.) West Nyack, N.Y.: Center for Applied Research in Education, 1993.

Unitarian Universalist Association and United Church of Christ Board for Homeland Ministries. *Our Whole Lives: A Lifespan Sexuality Education Series*. United Church of Christ Board for Homeland Ministries, 700 Prospect Ave., Cleveland, OH 44115; 216-736-3282. 1999.

Weston, Carol. *Girltalk: All the Stuff Your Sister Never Told You*. 3rd ed. New York: Harper Perennial, 1997.

Sexuality and Theology

Ellison, Marvin M., and Sylvia Thorson Smith, eds. *Body and Soul: Rethinking Sexuality As Justice-Love*. Cleveland: The Pilgrim Press, 2003.

Mennonite Church and General Conference Mennonite Church. *Human Sexuality in the Christian Life*. Newton, Kan.: Faith & Life Press, 1985.

Nelson, James B. *Embodiment: An Approach to Sexuality and Christian Theology*. Minneapolis: Augsburg, 1978.

Nelson, James B., and Sandra P. Longfellow, eds. *Sexuality and the Sacred: Sources for Theological Reflection*. Louisville: Westminster, 1994.

Rogers, E. F. *Theology and Sexuality: Classic and Contemporary Readings*. Malden, Mass.: Blackwell, 2002.

Timmerman, Joan H. *Sexuality and Spiritual Growth*. New York: Crossroad, 1993.

Weaver, Andrew, John D. Preston, and Charlene Hosenfeld. *Counseling on Sexual Issues: A Handbook for Pastors and Other Helping Professionals*. Cleveland: The Pilgrim Press, 2005.

Sexuality in Illness and Disability

Carroll, Janell L., and Paul Root Wolpe. "Sexuality in Illness and Disability." *Sexuality and Gender in Society*. 3rd ed. New York: HarperCollins College Pub., 1996: 473–91.

Kelly, Gary F. "Sex and Disability Groups." *Sexuality Today: The Human Perspective*. 8th ed. Boston: McGraw-Hill, 2006: 232–36.

"Sexuality Education for People with Disabilities." *SIECUS Report* 29, no. 3 (February/March 2001).

Schover, Leslie R., and Soren Buus Jensen. *Sexuality and Chronic Illness: A Comprehensive Approach*. New York: Guilford, 1988.

Sexual Misconduct by Clergy

Ferro, Jeffrey. *Sexual Misconduct and the Clergy*. New York: Facts on File, 2005.

Flynn, Kathryn A. *The Sexual Abuse of Women by Members of the Clergy*. Jefferson, N.C.: McFarland and Company, 2003.

"Pastoral Sexual Abuse." *MCC Conciliation Quarterly* 10, no. 2 (Fall 1991): a report.

Pellauer, Mary D., et al., eds. *Sexual Assault and Abuse: A Handbook for Clergy and Religious Professionals*. San Francisco: Harper, 1991.

McClintock, Karen A. *Preventing Sexual Abuse in the Congregation: A Resource for Leaders*. Herndon, Va.: Alban Institute, 2004.

Mennonite Central Committee U.S. Peace Section. "Pastoral Sexual Misconduct: The Church's Response." *Conciliation Quarterly Newsletter* 10, no. 2 (Spring 1991).

Wilson, Earl and Sandy, Paul and Virginia Friesen, Larry and Paul Paulson. *Restoring the Fallen: A Team Approach to Caring, Confronting, and Reconciling*. Downers Grove. Ill.: InterVarsity Press, 1997.

Singleness

Brubaker, Shirley Yoder. "One Is a Whole Number." *The Mennonite* 1, no. 14 (May 26, 1998): 8–10.

Colon, Christine A., and Bonnie E. Field. *Singled Out: Why Celibacy Must Be Reinvented in Today's Church*. Grand Rapids, Mich.: Brazos Press, 2009.

Hsu, Albert Y. *Singles at the Crossroads: A Fresh Perspective on Christian Singleness*. Downers Grove, Ill.: InterVarsity Press, 1997.

Martin, Mariann. "Ten Questions to Ask a Single Person Other Than . . ." *The Mennonite* 1, no. 14 (May 26, 1998): 11.

Rolheiser, Ronald. *The Holy Longing*. New York: Doubleday, 1999.

Rosenau, Douglas E., and Erica S. N. Tan. "Single and Sexual: The Church's Neglected Dilemma." *Journal of Psychology and Theology* 30, no. 3 (2002): 185.

Winner, Lauren F. *Real Sex: The Naked Truth About Chastity*. Grand Rapids, Mich.: Brazos, 2005.

References

Foreword

Johnson, James Weldon. *God's Trombones: Seven Negro Sermons in Verse*. New York: Viking Press, 1929, p. 10.

1. The Gift

Fairlie, Henry. 1977. "Lust or Luxuria." *New Republic* 177 (October 8): 18–21.

Goergen, Donald. 1974. *The Sexual Celibate*. New York: Seabury Press.

Graber Miller, Keith. 2009. "Sex Without Shame." *Sojourners* 38, no. 9 (September/October): 20–27.

Nelson, James B. 1978. *Embodiment: An Approach to Sexuality and Christian Theology*. Minneapolis: Augsburg.

Nelson, James B., and Sandra P. Longfellow, eds. 1994. *Sexuality and the Sacred: Sources for Theological Reflection*. Louisville: Westminster John Knox.

Warren, Neil Clark. 1992. On back cover of *Sex for Christians* by Lewis B. Smedes. Grand Rapids, Mich.: Eerdmans.

2. Guidelines from the Gift-Giver: Sexuality and Scripture

Cahill, Lisa Sowle. 1985. *Between the Sexes: Foundations for a Christian Ethics of Sexuality*. Philadelphia: Fortress Press.

———. 1996. *Sex, Gender and Christian Ethics*. Cambridge: Cambridge University Press.

Charles, Howard. 1984. "Sexuality in the New Testament." Unpublished paper.

Kazantzakis, Nikos. 1998. *The Last Temptation of Christ*. New York: Simon & Schuster Trade, Touchstone.

Mennonite Church and General Conference Mennonite Church. 1985. *Human Sexuality in the Christian Life*. Newton, Kan.: Faith & Life Press.

Nelson, James B., and Sandra P. Longfellow, eds. 1994. *Sexuality and the Sacred: Sources for Theological Reflection*. Louisville: Westminster John Knox.

Smedes, Lewis B. 1992. *Sex for Christians*. Grand Rapids, Mich.: Eerdmans.

Stoltzfus, Edward. "Biblical Perspectives on Sexuality." Unpublished and undated paper.

Yoder, Perry, and Elizabeth Yoder. 1977. *New Men—New Roles*. Newton, Kan.: Faith & Life Press.

3. The Gift and Intimacy

Bauman, Harold. Goshen College campus pastor, 1958–1974.

Cooper, Rod. 1995. "INTO-ME-SEE/Intimacy." *New Man*, March/April.

Gilligan, Carol. 1982. *In a Different Voice*. Cambridge: Harvard University Press.

Graber Miller, Keith. 2009. "Sex Without Shame." *Sojourners* 38, no. 9 (September/October): 20–27.

Landers, Ann. *Chicago Tribune*, January 24, 1985; November 1995.

Rubin, Lillian. 1983. *Intimate Strangers: Men and Women Together*. New York: Harper & Row.

4. The Gift and Its Youngest Recipients

Nelson, James B. 1978. *Embodiment: An Approach to Sexuality and Christian Theology*. Minneapolis: Augsburg.

5. The Gift and Nurturing Adolescents

Bem, Sandra L. 1974. "The Measure of Psychological Androgeny." *Journal of Consulting and Clinical Psychology* 42, no. 2: 155-62.

Hershberger, S. L. and A. R. D'Augelli. 2001. "The Impact of Victimization on the Mental Health and Suicidality of Lesbian, Gay, and Bisexual Youth." In Ryan and Futterman. *SIECUS Report* 29, no. 4 (April/May): 5–18.

Paul, Pamela. 2004. "Behavior: The Porn Factor." *Time*, January 19, 73–75.

Ryan, Caitlin, and Donna Futterman. 2001. "Social and Developmental Challenges for Lesbian, Gay, and Bisexual Youth." *SIECUS Report* 29, no. 4 (April/May): 5–18.

Savin-Williams, R. C., and R. E. Lenhart. 2001. "AIDS Prevention Among Gay and Lesbian Youth: Psychosocial Stress and Health Care Intervention Guidelines." In Ryan and Futterman. *SIECUS Report* 29, no. 4 (April/May): 5–18.

6. The Gift and Singleness

Claiborne, Shane. 2007. *The Irresistible Revolution: Living as an Ordinary Radical*. Grand Rapids, Mich.: Zondervan.

Ferder, Fran, and John Heagle. 2002. *Tender Fires: The Spiritual Promise of Sexuality*. New York: Crossroad Publishing.

Nouwen, Henri. 1975. *Reaching Out*. Garden City, N.Y.: Doubleday.

Rolheiser, Ronald. 2007. *Forgotten Among the Lilies*. New York: Random House.

Vanier, Jean. 1999. *Becoming Human*. London: Darton, Longman, and Todd.

7. The Gift and Marriage

Alan Guttmacher Institute. 2010. "Facts On American Teens' Sexual and Reproductive Health." *In Brief*, January, 1–2.

Axinn, W. G., and A. Thornton. 1992. "The Relationship Between Cohabitation and Divorce: Selectivity or Casual Influence?" *Demography* 29 (1992): 357–74.

Charles, Howard. 1984. "Sexuality in the New Testament." In section "Toward Some Basic New Testament Guidelines." Goshen, Ind. Unpublished paper.

Holmes, Steven A. 1996. "U.S. Reports Drop in Rate of Births to Unwed Women." *New York Times*, October 5.

Rathus, Spencer A., Jeffrey S. Nevid, and Lois Fischner-Rathus. 2008. *Human Sexuality in a World of Diversity*. 7th ed. Boston: Pearson Education.

Rosen, Rosanne. 1993. *The Living Together Trap*. Far Hills, N.J.: New Horizon Press.

Sider, Arbutus, and Ron Sider. 1995. "Wedded Witness." *Prism*, September/October, 38.

Smedes, Lewis B. 1992. *Sex for Christians*. Grand Rapids, Mich.: Eerdmans.

8. The Gift and Same-Sex Orientation

Augsburger, Myron. 1998. "Futurism and Anabaptist Mennonites." *Christian Living* 45, no. 4 (June): 2.

Bird, Lewis P. 1982. Address at Goshen College, March 4, during "Sexuality Week."

Gomes, Peter J. 1996. *The Good Book: Reading the Bible with Mind and Heart*. New York: Wm. Morrow.

Grenz, Stanley J. 1998. *Welcoming but Not Affirming: An Evangelical Response to Homosexuality*. Louisville: Westminster John Knox.

Hays, Richard B. "Homosexuality." 1996. In *The Moral Vision of the New Testament: A Contemporary Introduction to New Testament Ethics*. San Francisco: Harper.

Headings, Verle. 1980. "Etiology of Homosexuality." *Southern Medical Journal* 73, no. 8 (August): 1024–30.

Kinsey, A. C., et al. 1953. *Sexual Behavior in the Human Female*. Philadelphia: W. B. Saunders.

Mennonite Church and General Conference Mennonite Church. 1985. *Human Sexuality in the Christian Life*. Newton, Kan.: Faith & Life Press.

Rathus, Spencer A., Jeffrey S. Nevid, and Lois Fichner-Rathus, 7th ed. 2008. *Human Sexuality in a World of Diversity*. Boston: Pearson Education.

Smedes, Lewis B. 1992. *Sex for Christians*. Grand Rapids, Mich.: Eerdmans.

Taylor, Daniel. 1997. "Confessions of a Bible Translator." *Christianity Today* 41, no.12 (October 27): 76–77.

Yancey, Philip. 1998. "And the Word Was . . . Debatable." *Christianity Today* 42, no. 6 (May 18): 88.

9. The Gift and Cross-Gender Friendships

Joyce, Mary Rosera. 1977. *How Can a Man and Woman Be Friends?* Collegeville, Minn.: Liturgical Press.

Kennedy, Eugene C. 1982. *On Being a Friend*. New York: Continuum.

10. The Gift and Aging

Cohen, Donna, interview in Elizabeth Pope. 1999. "When Illness Takes Sex Out of a Relationship." *SIECUS Report* 27, no. 3 (February/March): 8–11.

Crowley, Chris, and Henry S. Lodge. 2007. *Younger Next Year*. New York: Workman Publishing.

Davey Smith, G., S. Frankel, and J. Yarnell. 1997. "Sex and Death: Are They Related?" *British Medical Journal* 315, no. 7123: 1641–44.

Elias, Marilyn. 2007. "Grandma's Got Her Groove On." *USA Today*, November 18, D7.

Feldman, Sally. 2005. "Coming Out On Top." *New Humanist* 120, no. 4. http://newhumanist.org.uk/902/coming-out-on-top.

Hock, Roger R. *Human Sexuality*. 2007. Upper Saddle River, N.J.: Pearson Education.

Kelly, Gary F. 2006. *Sexuality Today: The Human Perspective*. 8th ed. Boston: McGraw-Hill.

The Kinsey Institute New Report on Sex. 1990: 227. In Rathus, Spencer A., Jeffrey Nevid, and Lois Fichner-Rathus. 2008. *Human Sexuality in a World of Diversity*. 7th ed. Boston: Pearson Education.

Koch, Patricia Barthalow, and Phyllis Kernoff Mansfield. 2001–2002. "Women's Sexuality As They Age: The More Things Change, The More They Stay the Same." *SIECUS Report* 30, no. 2 (December/January): 5–9.

Lacy, Katherine K. 2001–2002. "Mature Sexuality: Patient Realities and Provider Challenges." *SIECUS Report* 30, no. 2 (December/January): 22–29.

Laumann, E. O., J. H. Gagnon, and R. T. Michael. 1994. "A Political History of the National Sex Survey of Adults." *Family Planning Perspectives* 26, no. 1 (January/February): 34–38.

Livingston, Gordon. 2009. *How to Love*. Cambridge, Mass.: DaCapo Press.

Pope, Elizabeth. 1999. "When Illness Takes Sex Out of a Relationship." *SIECUS Report* 27, no. 3 (February/March): 8–11.

Shrestha, Laura B. 2006. "The Changing Demographic Profile

of the United States." *Congressional Research Service Report for Congress* 5 (May): 13–16.

U.S. Census Bureau. Cited in U.S. Embassy online documents: http://denmark.usembassy.gov/introus/americansociety/demographics.htm
http://www.efmoody.comestate/lifeexpectancy.html
http://www.data360.org/dsg.aspx?data_set_group_Id+195

Weil, Andrew. 2005. *Healthy Aging: A Life-long Guide to Your Well-Being.* New York: Anchor Books.

11. The Gift After Losing a Spouse

Billman, Kathleen D., and Daniel L. Migliore. 1999. *Rachel's Cry: Prayer of Lament and Rebirth of Hope.* Cleveland: United Church Press.

Clark, Keith. *Being Sexual . . . and Celibate.* 1986. Notre Dame, Ind.: Ave Maria Press.

Dunne, John S. 1979. *The Reasons of the Heart: A Journey into Solitude and Back Again into the Human Circle.* Notre Dame, Ind.: University of Notre Dame Press.

Gorgen, Donald. 1975. *The Sexual Celibate.* Garden City, N.Y.: Seabury Press.

Joyce, Mary Rosera. 1977. *How Can a Man and Woman be Friends?* Collegeville, Minn.: The Liturgical Press.

Perito, John E. 2003. *Contemporary Catholic Sexuality: What is Taught and What is Practiced.* New York: Crossroad.

Rohr, Richard. *Gate of the Temple: Spirituality and Sexuality.* Kansas City, Mo.: National Catholic Reporter Publishing.

_____. "To Unveil Our Faces: Reflections on Marriage and Celibacy." 1979. *Sojourners* 8 (May 1979).

Rolheiser, Ronald. 1999. *The Holy Longing: The Search for a Christian Spirituality.* New York: Doubleday.

Shuchter, Stephen R., and Sidney Zisook. 1987. "The Therapeutic Tasks of Grief." In *Biopsychosocial Aspects of Bereavement.* Edited by Sidney Zisook. Washington D.C.: American Psychiatric Press.

U.S. Census Bureau. "America's Families and Living Arrangements: 2007."
http://www.unmarried.org/statistics.html and

http://www.census.gov/compendia/statab/cats/population/
marital_status_and_living_arrangements.html

12. The Gift and the Sensuous

SC Communications. *The Sexiest Animal.* 1990. 37-minute video. Wombat Film & Video, 93 Pitner Avenue, Evanston, IL 60202.

Smith, Earl, and Rose Smith. 1997. *Sizzling Monogamy.* Albuquerque: Wm. Havens Publishing.

13. The Gift Expressed in the Arts

Breslin, J. G. 1994. *Mark Rothko: A Biography.* Chicago: University of Chicago Press.

Croce, Benedetto. 1922. *The Essence of Aesthetics.* London: Heinemann.

Danto, Arthur. 1981. *Transfiguration of the Common Place: A Philosophy of Art.* Cambridge: Harvard University Press.

Francoeur, Robert T. 1982. *Becoming a Sexual Person.* New York: John Wiley and Sons.

Hugo, Victor. 1947. *The Hunchback of Notre Dame.* New York: Dodd, Mead, and Company.

Kant, Immanuel. 1951. *Critique of Judgment* (1790). Edited and translated by J. H. Bernard. New York: Hafner Press.

Kermode, Frank. 1988. *History and Value.* Oxford: Clarendon.

Langer, Susanne K. 1978. *Philosophy in a New Key.* Cambridge: Harvard University Press.

Nussbaum, Martha. 1994. *The Therapy of Desire.* Princeton: Princeton University Press.

Polanyi, Michael. 1966. *The Tacit Dimension.* New York: Peter Smith.

Smith, Anna Deavere. 1994. *Twilight: Los Angeles 1992.* New York: Anchor Books.

14. The Gift and Celibacy

Bishops' Committee for Pastoral Research & Practices. 1989. *Faithful to Each Other Forever: A Catholic Handbook of*

Pastoral Help for Marriage Preparation. Washington, D.C.: U.S. Catholic Conference.

Brown, Raymond Kay. 1986. "As a Single, Could I Find Help From the Bible?" In *Resources in Singleness.* A Cooperative Effort of the Episcopal Church, Association of Evangelical Lutheran Churches, American Lutheran Church, Lutheran Church in America, and the U.S. Roman Catholic Conference. New York: Education for Mission & Ministry: 118–37.

Cahill, Lisa Sowle. 1985. *Between the Sexes: Foundations for a Christian Ethic of Sexuality.* Philadelphia: Fortress Press.

Comsia, Daniel, and David J. Rolfe. 1986. "Marriage Preparation with Cohabiting Couples." In *Resources in Singleness.* New York: Education for Mission & Ministry: 58–64.

Graber, Keith Miller. 2009. "Sex Without Shame." *Sojourners.* 38, no. 9 (September/October): 21–27.

Hawthorne, M. Roger. 1986. "What Is Wrong with Singles Ministry?" In *Resources in Singleness.* New York: Education for Mission & Ministry: 114–17.

Heggen, Carolyn Holderread. 1993. *Sexual Abuse in Christian Homes and Churches.* Scottdale, Pa.: Herald Press.

Hershberger, Anne Krabill, ed. 1999. *Sexuality: God's Gift.* Scottdale, Pa.: Herald Press.

Jung, Patricia Beattie, with Joseph A. Coray, eds. 2001. *Sexual Diversity and Catholicism: Toward the Development of Moral Theology.* Collegeville, Minn.: Liturgical Press.

Nelson, James B. 1986. "Singleness and the Church." In *Resources in Singleness.* New York: Education for Mission & Ministry: 96–103.

———. 1994. "Sources for Body Theology: Homosexuality As a Test Case." In *Homosexuality in the Church: Both Sides of the Debate.* Edited by Jeffrey S. Siker. Louisville: Westminster John Knox Press.

Norris, Kathleen. 1996. "Celibate Passion: The Hidden Rewards of Quitting Sex." *Utne Reader,* September/October, 51–53.

Nouwen, Henri J. M. 1972. *The Wounded Healer.* New York: Doubleday.

Paulsell, Stephanie. 2002. *Honoring the Body: Meditations on a Christian Practice.* San Francisco: Jossey-Bass.

Rolheiser, Ronald. 1999. *The Holy Longing.* New York: Doubleday.

Rosenau, Douglas E. P. 1972. "Sexuality and the Single Person." *Christian Perspective on Sexuality and Gender.* Edited by Adrian Thatcher and Elizabeth Stuart. Grand Rapids, Mich.: Eerdmans.

Sammon, Sean D. 1993. *An Undivided Heart: Making Sense of Celibate Chastity.* New York: Alba House.

Sheridan, Jean. 2000. *The Unwilling Celibates: A Spirituality for Single Adults.* Mystic, Conn.: Twenty-Third/Bayard.

Sipe, A. W. Richard. 1996. *Celibacy: A Way of Loving, Living and Serving.* Liguori, Mo.: Triumph.

Vogels, Heinz-J. 1993. *Celibacy—Gift or Law?* Kansas City, Mo.: Sheed & Ward.

Winner, Lauren F. 2005. *Real Sex: The Naked Truth about Chastity.* Grand Rapids, Mich.: Brazos.

Yoder, John H. 1986. "Singleness in Ethical and Pastoral Perspective." In *Resources in Singleness.* New York: Education for Mission & Ministry: 72–95.

15. The Gift Misused

AACAP (American Academy of Child and Adolescent Psychiatry). Updated May 2008. Facts for Families. "Child Sexual Abuse." http://www.aacap.org/cs/root/facts_for_families/child_sexual_abuse

Alan Guttmacher Institute. January 2010. Facts in Brief. "Facts on American Teens' Sexual and Reproductive Health." http://www.guttmacher.org/pubs/FB-ATSRH.html

Carnes, Patrick. 2003. "Understanding Sexual Addiction." *SIECUS Report* 31, no. 5 (June/July): 5–7.

Clapp, Rodney. 1996. "Why the Devil Takes VISA." *Christianity Today*, October 7, 19–33.

Faith & Life Resources. 2007. "Close to Home: Dealing with Pornography."

Florida Center for Parent Involvement. "Sexual Abuse and Young Children," as cited in Prevent Child Abuse America's "Fact Sheet: Sexual Abuse of Children."

Gilkerson, Luke. "Internet Porn, Magic Rings, and the Secret of Obedience." http://www.purelifeministries.org/index.

cfm?pageid=163&articleid=452 (accessed February 12, 2010).

Gushee, David P. 1995. "Divorce: Learning from Farmer Gachet." *Prism*, September/October, 18–19.

Kelly, Gary F. 2006. *Sexuality Today: The Human Perspective.* 8th ed. Boston: McGraw-Hill.

Koop, C. Everett. 1992. Personal conversation when Koop gave a Yoder Public Affairs Lecture at Goshen College, October 12.

Lorde, Audre. 1994. "Uses of the Erotic: The Erotic as Power." In *Sexuality and the Sacred: Sources for Theological Reflection.* Edited by James B. Nelson and Sandra P. Longfellow. Louisville: Westminster John Knox.

Marano, Hara Estroff. 1997. "Rescuing Marriages Before They Begin." *New York Times*, May 28.

Marty, Martin E. 1994. "M.E.M.O.: Our Own Worst Enemies." *Christian Century*, September 21–28, 879.

Maynard, Rebecca A., ed. 1996. *Kids Having Kids: A Robin Hood Foundation Special Report on the Costs of Adolescent Childbearing.* New York: Robin Hood Foundation.

Merton, Thomas. 1979. "Love and Need: Is Love a Package or a Message?" In *Love and Living: Thomas Merton.* Edited by Naomi Burton Stone and Brother Patrick Hart. New York: Farrar, Straus, and Giroux.

National Child Abuse Statistics. 2009. "Child Abuse in America." http://www.childhelp.org/pages/statistics.

Nelson, James B. 1997. Lecture at Goshen College, November 4.

Pellauer, Mary D. 1994. "Pornography: An Agenda for the Churches." In *Sexuality and the Sacred: Sources for Theological Reflection.* Edited by James B. Nelson and Sandra P. Longfellow. Louisville: Westminster John Knox.

Pure Life Ministries. "Sexual Addiction." MedicineNet.com. http://www.medicinenet.com/sexualaddiction/article.htm (accessed February 12, 2010).

Rathus, Spencer A., Jeffrey S. Nevid, and Lois Fichner-Rathus. 2008. *Human Sexuality in a World of Diversity.* 7th ed. Boston: Pearson Education.

Sider, Arbutus, and Ron Sider. 1995. "Wedded Witness." *Prism*, September/October, 38.

Storkey, Elaine. 1996. *The Search for Intimacy*. Grand Rapids, Mich.: Eerdmans.

WebMD/Cleveland Clinic. 2007. "Sexual Addiction." www. webmd.com/sexual-conditions/guide/sexual-addiction. September 24)

16. The Gift Restored

Center for the Prevention of Sexual and Domestic Violence, 1914 N. 34th St., Suite 105, Seattle, WA 98103-9058; 206-634-1903.

Eugene, Toinette M. 1991. "Faithful Responses to Human Sexuality: Issues Facing the Church Today." *Chicago Theological Seminary Register*, Spring, 1–7.

Heggen, Carolyn Holderread. 1993. *Sexual Abuse in Christian Homes and Churches*. Scottdale, Pa: Herald Press.

Keene, Jane A. 1991. *A Winter's Song: A Liturgy for Women Seeking Healing from Sexual Abuse in Childhood*. Cleveland: Pilgrim Press.

Nelson, James B. 1978. *Embodiment: An Approach to Sexuality and Christian Theology*. Minneapolis: Augsburg.

Palmer, Parker J. 1998. *The Courage to Teach: Exploring the Inner Landscape of a Teacher's Life*. San Francisco: Jossey-Bass.

"Pastoral Sexual Abuse." 1991. *MCC Conciliation Quarterly* 10, no. 2 (Fall).

Rencken, Robert H. 1989. *Intervention Strategies for Sexual Abuse*. Alexandria, Va.: American Association for Counseling and Development.

Schroeder, Celeste S. 1995. *Embodied Prayer: Harmonizing Body and Soul*. Liguori, Mo.: Liguori Press.

Shelton, Charles M. 1989. *Adolescent Spirituality: Pastoral Ministry for High School and College Youth*. New York: Crossroads.

Snyder, Eleanor, ed. 2010. *Body and Soul: Healthy Sexuality and the People of God*. Newton, Kan: Faith & Life Press.

Trobisch, Walter. 1971. *I Married You*. New York: Harper & Row.

_____. *The Complete Works of Walter Trobisch*. 1987. Downers Grove, Ill.: InterVarsity Press.

Ward, Hannah, and Jennifer Wild. 1995. *Human Rites: Worship Resources for an Age of Change*. London: Mobray.

Yantzi, Mark. 1998. *Sexual Offending and Restoration*. Scottdale, Pa.: Herald Press.

Contributing Authors

Anne Krabill Hershberger, RN, MSN, Editor

Anne is associate professor of nursing emerita at Goshen (Ind.) College, where she taught maternity nursing, human sexuality, and healthcare ethics.

She earned a BS in nursing from Goshen College in 1958 and an MS in nursing from Wayne State University, Detroit, in 1963. Her post-master's study has been in the area of bioethics at the Kennedy Institute of Ethics, Georgetown University, Washington, D.C. (1981–82) and the University of California, San Francisco (1988–89).

During her 1996–97 sabbatical leave in New York City, Anne did further study in sexuality at New York University, helped to design and teach an expanded Expectant Parent Education Program for the Morris Heights Birthing Center in the Bronx, and served on the Sexuality Curriculum Committee for the NYC Covenant House.

While living in Washington, in addition to her bioethics studies, Anne served as health coordinator of the Cities-In-Schools Adolescent Pregnancy Prevention Program. For seven years she served as director and instructor of the Expectant Parent Education Program at Goshen General Hospital.

Anne edited the book *Ethics and the Educated Person: A Teaching-Learning Resource* (1993). She has written chapters in Roman Miller and Beryl Brubaker's *Bioethics and the Beginning of Life* (1990); John Rogers' *Medical Ethics, Human Choices: A Christian Perspective* (1988); and Jo Joyce Tackett-Anderson and Mabel Hunsberger's *Family-Centered Care of Children and Adolescents: Nursing Concepts in Child Health* (1981). She has published articles in *Nursing Outlook, Journal of Advanced Nursing, The Mennonite Encyclopedia* (vol. 5), and *Mennonite Medical Messenger*, as well as other articles and book reviews.

Anne's current professional and community memberships include American Nurses' Association, Sigma Theta Tau International Honor Society of Nursing, Mennonite Nurses Association, and the American Association of University Women. She serves on the steering committee of New Perspectives on Faith, an ecumenical group in Goshen, and on two committees at Goshen General Hospital: the Institutional Review Board and the Organizational and Medical Ethics Committee. She was awarded a Lilly Endowment Faculty Open Fellowship in 1981 for her Washington, D.C., sabbatical; and the Delta Kappa Gamma Harriet Biddle Scholarship in 1972 for study of healthcare in Haiti.

Anne and her husband Abner's family includes two daughters, their husbands, and two granddaughters. They are members of College Mennonite Church and live in Goshen, Indiana.

Willard S. Krabill, MD, MPH
Prior to his death in January 2009, Willard held the title of college physician and associate professor of health education emeritus at Goshen (Ind.) College. He received his BA from Goshen College in 1949, and his MD from Jefferson Medical College, Philadelphia, in 1953.

He practiced family medicine in North Liberty, Indiana. Willard was married to Grace Hershberger of Goshen, Indiana. From 1955 to 1958 they served with Mennonite Central Committee in Banmethuot, South Vietnam, at a leprosarium. Upon returning to the United States, he practiced family medicine in Goshen. Later, after doing a residency in obstetrical medicine, he limited his practice to that area.

Willard pioneered the development of expectant parent education and the opportunity for fathers to be present at the birth of their babies at Goshen General Hospital—firsts in the region. In 1972–73 he earned a master's degree in public health at the University of California, Berkeley. He took an intensive course in bioethics at the Kennedy Institute of Ethics, Georgetown University, Washington, D.C. In 1984 he was a scholar-in-residence at the Institute for Religion and Wholeness, School of Theology, at Claremont, California.

In 1967, Willard became Goshen College physician. During his twenty-four years in that position, he emphasized the importance of each person assuming personal responsibility for her or his own wellness and health education. Willard developed and taught a popular human sexuality course. This was done when such courses were rare, especially on Christian college campuses. In addition, he developed and taught other courses: "Health in a Changing Environment" and "The Use and Abuse of Chemicals."

Throughout his career and into retirement, Willard was an articulate author, spokesperson, and innovator in the areas of health, wellness, sexuality, substance use and abuse, and bioethics. He held numerous professional memberships. He served as president and executive secretary of the Mennonite Medical Association. He served on the Health and Welfare Committee of the Mennonite Board of Missions and on the Human Sexuality Study Committee of the General Board of the Mennonite Church. He was a medical and bioethics consultant to Mennonite Mutual Aid Association.

Willard's awards include membership in Alpha Omega Alpha

(Honorary Medical Society). In 1988 he received the Allen H. Erb Memorial Award from the Mennonite Health Association. He was named Doctor of the Year by the Mennonite Medical Association in 1990. In 1995 he was given the Anabaptist Healthcare Award by Mennonite Mutual Aid Association.

Willard S. Krabill and his wife, Grace, parented four children, each of whom gave them grandchildren. Willard was a member of College Mennonite Church and lived in Goshen, Indiana.

Sue L. Conrad, MDiv

Sue grew up in Perkasie, Pennsylvania. She received a BA in Bible and religion and communication from Goshen (Ind.) College; an MA in speech communication from Penn State University in State College, Pennsylvania; and an MDiv from Associated Mennonite Biblical Seminary in Elkhart, Indiana.

Sue has worked as an admissions counselor, tennis coach, waitress, bank teller, college professor, and professional gift wrapper during various stages of her life. She currently serves as an associate pastor at East Chestnut Street Mennonite Church in Lancaster, Pennsylvania.

Delores Histand Friesen, PhD

Delores is professor of pastoral counseling at Mennonite Brethren Biblical Seminary in Fresno, California, where she has taught for twenty-two years in the area of marriage, family, and child counseling. She is a graduate of Hesston College and earned a BA in elementary education from Goshen College. Her master's degree in international and comparative education is from Indiana University, and her PhD in counseling and human development is from the University of Iowa.

After teaching for three years at Parkside Elementary School in Goshen, Delores and her husband, J. Stanley Friesen, worked for thirteen years with Mennonite Board of Missions in theological education with African Independent Churches in West Africa. This is where she began teaching and ministering in the area of human sexuality. She wrote a book on the subject, *Let Love Be Your Greatest* (Editions Trobisch, Kehl, German, 1979), which was translated into several languages.

Her other publications include *All Are Witnesses* (Kindred Publications, 1996); editor of a collection of Mennonite Brethren women's sermons; *Living More with Less Study/ Action Guide* (Herald Press, 1981; revised edition, *Alternatives for Simple Living*, 1999); chapters in *The Voice of a Writer, Violence and Peace: Creating a Culture of Peace in the Contemporary Context of Violence; Anabaptist Perspectives on Pastoral Counseling; Out of the Strange Silence; Sexuality: God's Gift; Healing the Children of War; Growing Towards Peace; and A Kingdom of Priests*; teaching guides for Adult Bible Study, including "Wisdom as a Way of Life" and "Stories Jesus Told"; articles and poetry in *Builder, Christian Living, Direction, Christian Leader,* and *Mission Focus.*

Delores is a licensed marriage, family, and child counselor, and maintains a small psychotherapy practice. She has served on the Board of Mennonite Brethren Missions and Services International for twelve years.

Delores and her husband, Stan, are the parents of three children and grandparents to six grandchildren. They are members of College Community Mennonite Brethren Church, Clovis, California, and are associate members at First Mennonite Church, Iowa City, where Delores was ordained to the ministry in 1988.

Lauren Friesen, PhD

Lauren Friesen is the David M. French Distinguished Professor of Theatre at the University of Michigan-Flint. He is chair of the department of theatre and dance and director of the Horace Rackam Graduate Program in Arts Administration.

His recent publications include articles on Anna Deveare Smith, Friedrich Durrenmatt, and Hermann Sudermann. In 2005 the University Press of America published his translation of Sudermann's comedy *The Storm Komrade Sokrates*. He recently translated Carlo Ross's holocaust novel, *But Stones Can't Talk*, and publication is pending.

For fifteen years Lauren served as professor of drama and director of the theater program at Goshen (Ind.) College. He pastored Seattle Mennonite Church from 1974 to 1980. For the General Conference Mennonite Church, he served as chairman of the Worship and Arts Committee for five years and chairman of the Media Division for four years.

Lauren has published and directed numerous plays and has published poetry in many journals. His other professional appointments include serving as chairman of The Kennedy Center/American College Theater Festival Awards Selection Team and chairman of Region III; Association for Theater in Higher Education Playwriting Program judge and dramaturge and chair of the Religion and Theater Program; vice-president of the Indiana Theater Association; dramaturge for the New Harmony Media Project (Ind.) for NBC and Walt Disney Studios' writers; and numerous roles in consulting and adjudication.

Lauren's degrees include a BA in history and philosophy from Bethel College, Newton, Kansas, in 1967; an MDiv from

Associated Mennonite Biblical Seminary, Elkhart, Indiana, in 1970; an MA in religion and the arts from Pacific School of Religion, Berkeley, California, in 1981; and a PhD in religion and the arts "with distinction" from the Graduate Theological Union in cooperation with the University of California, Berkeley, in 1985.

Lauren and his wife, Janet, are the parents of two adult children and have one grandson. They live in Flint, Michigan.

Rachel Nafziger Hartzler, RN, MDiv

Rachel Nafziger Hartzler is an ordained minister in Mennonite Church USA and has served as pastor of three congregations: Florence Church of the Brethren-Mennonite in Constantine, Michigan; Pleasant Oaks Mennonite Church in Middlebury, Indiana; and Mennonite Fellowship of Asheville in Asheville, North Carolina. She graduated from Goshen College in 1970 with a BS in nursing and from Associated Mennonite Biblical Seminary in 2004 with an MA in Christian formation.

During Rachel's thirty-year nursing career, she worked primarily in obstetrics and pediatrics in hospitals (including one year at Hospital Menonita in Aibonito, Puerto Rico), in a doctor's office, and in education, first as a clinical instructor at Goshen College and then as a childbirth educator.

Rachel married Harold E. Hartzler in 1971. Together they raised four children (Joel, Aaron Jon, Carrie, and Dori) and served as youth sponsors and Sunday school teachers at College Mennonite Church in Goshen, Indiana. After Harold's death in 1999, Rachel enrolled in seminary.

For her master's thesis, she did an empirical study of 152 widowed people, which she summarized in *Loss as an Invitation to Transformation: Living Well Following the Death of a Spouse.* This study was the basis for *Grief and Sexuality: Life After Losing a Spouse,* published by Herald Press in 2006. Rachel has participated in numerous writing projects and has published articles in *Christian Living, The Mennonite, Vision,* and *Mission Focus.*

Rachel serves on the Oaklawn Council on Faith and Mental Health at Oaklawn Psychiatric Center in Goshen and the board of directors at Menno-Hof, Shipshewana, Indiana. In addition she works as a spiritual director, leads retreats, and speaks on issues related to grief, spirituality, and sexuality.

Sexuality education has long been one of Rachel's interests. In secular settings she taught childbirth preparation classes and spoke to high-school classes about sexuality and childbirth. Within church and church-school settings, she has participated in and led retreats on sexuality for children and youth, served on the sexuality task group at College Mennonite Church, and worked as an assistant in the human sexuality class at Goshen College.

Rachel has had a role in parenting ten children: the four children she and Harold raised, three stepchildren, and three international "daughters" from China, Puerto Rico, and Tanzania. She currently lives in Goshen and travels regularly to western North Carolina to visit her four grandchildren and their parents.

Barbara J. Meyer, MD

Barbara is a family physician in Goshen, Indiana, where she practices with her husband, Lane Reed, and several others in a small, single-specialty group practice. She received her BA from Goshen (Ind.) College in 1985 and her MD from Indiana University, Indianapolis, in 1990.

Between college and medical school, Barb spent a year in voluntary service in Washington, D.C., serving as a medical assistant in an inner-city health services clinic. She completed her residency training in family medicine in St. Paul, Minnesota, and then moved across the border into rural Wisconsin to practice for seven years, before moving back to northern Indiana with her husband and three children in 2001.

Barb and Lane are active members of Benton Mennonite Church, where they have served as youth sponsors for the past six years. She has been addressing groups of young people in various settings on issues relating to sexuality since 2003.

Keith Graber Miller, PhD

Keith is professor of Bible, religion, and philosophy at Goshen (Ind.) College, teaching in the areas of sexuality, Christian ethics and theology, religion and politics, religious history, and the sociology of religion. He also has been a visiting faculty member at Associated Mennonite Biblical Seminary, Elkhart, Indiana, where he received his master of divinity degree in 1988.

He earned his BA from Franklin (Ind.) College in 1981. He completed his PhD in religion at Emory University, Atlanta, in 1993.

Keith has published numerous articles in academic journals, written chapters for more than a dozen edited texts, and written or edited four books. His first book, *Wise As Serpents, Innocent As Doves: American Mennonites Engage Washington* (University of Tennessee Press, 1996), was based on his dissertation. Subsequent books addressed the themes of Mennonite higher education, young adults and scriptural authority, and the writings of Mennonite ethicist J. R. Burkholder. He is currently writing a fifth book, tentatively titled *Shameless Sexuality.*

Keith is married to Ann Graber Miller, and they have three children. Together the Graber Millers own Graber Designs Gallery, an international art gallery in downtown Goshen. They are members of Assembly Mennonite Church and live in Goshen, Indiana.

Julie Nash, BA

Julie Nash is a musician and teacher who grew up in the Rouge Valley Mennonite Church in Markham, Ontario. She earned a BA in music from Canadian Mennonite University in 2003, a BA in music education from Wilfrid Laurier University in 2008, and a BA in education from Nipissing University in 2009. Study and work opportunities have led her to Winnipeg, Manitoba and Kitchener-Waterloo and North Bay, Ontario. She is currently teaching elementary-aged children in London, England.

Julie is always happy when she is singing or playing the piano. She has been a regular accompanist and song leader in each church where she has made a home.

Her chapter on singleness is based on a sermon preached at Stirling Avenue Mennonite Church, Kitchener, Ontario, in May 2009, as part of a worship series on sexuality.

James H. Ritchie Jr., EdD, MDiv

Jim is a pastor in the Western Pennsylvania Annual Conference of the United Methodist Church. In addition to his pastoral work, he served for several years as a children's curriculum editor for his denomination and focused on multigenerational ministries as president of Ritchie Faith Span Ministries.

Jim earned his BA from Mount Union College in Alliance, Ohio; his MDiv from United Theological Seminary in Dayton, Ohio; and his EdD in religious education from Vanderbilt University in Nashville.

He developed the *Created by God* human sexuality education resources for fifth- and sixth-graders and their parents, published by Abingdon Press, and has led *Created by God* events across the country. Jim is also the author of *Always in Rehearsal: The Practice of Worship and the Presence of Children*, published by Discipleship Resources; and is a composer of music published in a variety of curriculum and worship resources.

Jim and his wife, Tracy, are the parents of three adult sons and the grandparents of a grandson and a granddaughter.